WILMINGTON
Port of North Carolina

Studies in Maritime History
William N. Still, Jr., Series Editor

Stoddert's War:
Naval Operations During the Quasi-War with France, 1798–1801
by Michael A. Palmer

The British Navy and the American Revolution
by John A. Tilley

Iron Afloat:
The Story of the Confederate Armorclads
by William N. Still, Jr.

A Maritime History of the United States:
The Role of America's Seas and Waterways
by K. Jack Bauer

Confederate Shipbuilding
by William N. Still, Jr.

Admiral Harold R. Stark:
Architect of Victory, 1939–1945
by B. Mitchell Simpson, III

Raid on America:
The Dutch Naval Campaign of 1672–1674
by Donald G. Shomette and Robert D. Haslach

Lifeline of the Confederacy:
Blockade Running During the Civil War
by Stephen R. Wise

History and the Sea:
Essays on Maritime Strategies
by Clark G. Reynolds

Predators and Prizes:
American Privateering and Imperial Warfare, 1739–1748
by Carl E. Swanson

Honolulu:
Crossroads of the Pacific
by Edward D. Beechert

Wilmington:
Port of North Carolina
by Alan D. Watson

WILMINGTON
Port of North Carolina

ALAN D. WATSON

University of South Carolina Press

Copyright © 1992 University of South Carolina

Published in Columbia, South Carolina, by the
University of South Carolina Press

Manufactured in the United States of America

Library of Congress Cataloging-in-Publication Data

Watson, Alan D., 1942–
    Wilmington : port of North Carolina / Alan D. Watson.
      p.   cm. — (Studies in maritime history)
    Includes bibliographical references (p.   ) and index.
    ISBN 0-87249-778-X (hard cover : acid-free)
    1. Harbors—North Carolina—Wilmington—History. 2. Shipping—
North Carolina—Wilmington—History. 3. Wilmington (N.C.)—
Commerce—History.   I. Title.   II. Series.
HE554.W5W38 1991
386'.8'097512—dc20   91-27168

Contents

Illustrations		vi
Tables		vii
Introduction		1
Chapter 1	Origins of a Colonial Port	3
Chapter 2	Revolution and Independence: A Burgeoning Commerce	24
Chapter 3	Antebellum Wilmington: North Carolina's Maritime Entrepôt	46
Chapter 4	The Civil War: Lifeline of the Confederacy	71
Chapter 5	The Postwar Transition: A Struggle for Recognition	104
Chapter 6	Revival and Modernization in the Twentieth Century	136
Notes		168
Bibliography		191
Index		202

Illustrations

Following page 86

Spencer Compton, Earl of Wilmington
A North Carolina Turpentine Camp
Prometheus, First Steamboat at Wilmington
Wilmington Waterfront, circa 1853
Union Blockading Fleet Off Wilmington
Map of the Port of Wilmington
City of Wilmington, 1776–1886, Lithograph
James Sprunt of the Wilmington Merchant House Alexander Sprunt & Son
Vessels Loading Cotton at Sprunt & Son's Champion Compress and Warehouse Company, late 1800s
Paddle Wheeler Loading Rosin at Wilmington, late 1800s
River Steamboat *Wilmington*, Owned by Captain John W. Harper
Floating Pen for Flatboats and Rafts

Tables

Table 1	Shipping, North Carolina Customs Districts, 1763	10
Table 2	Export Tonnage, Selected Ports, 1768–69	11
Table 3	Exports, Port Brunswick, 1767–68	13
Table 4	Exports, Port Brunswick, 1788	33
Table 5	Customs Duties Collected, North Carolina Ports, 1801–05	45
Table 6	Cape Fear River Commerce Subject to Tolls by the Cape Fear Navigation Company	60
Table 7	Tonnage Entering and Clearing North Carolina Ports, 1832–33	67
Table 8	Tonnage Entering and Clearing North Carolina Ports, 1849–50	67
Table 9	Tonnage Entered and Cleared at Major Atlantic Ports, 1832–33 and 1849–50	68
Table 10	Principal Post-Civil War Exports, Port of Wilmington	105
Table 11	Post-Civil War Naval Stores Exports, Port of Wilmington	107
Table 12	Naval Stores Exports, Wilmington, Charleston, and Savannah, 1882–83	108
Table 13	Post-Civil War Cotton Exports, Port of Wilmington	108
Table 14	Cotton Exports, Selected Ports, 1875–1900	111
Table 15	Wilmington Imports and Exports Via the Clyde Line, 1882	123

Table 16	Wilmington Shipping, 1900–1915	139
Table 17	Estimated Traffic, Wilmington and the Smaller Rivers of the Lower Cape Fear	141
Table 18	Wilmington Commerce, 1914–38	150
Table 19	Tonnage, State Docks and the Port of Wilmington, 1952–63	159
Table 20	Shipping, Wilmington State Docks, 1970s and 1980s	162

Wilmington
Port of North Carolina

Introduction

As Wilmington, North Carolina, in 1990 celebrated the 250th anniversary of its founding, appropriate recognition ought to be accorded the role of shipping in the town that quickly became the state's principal port, a distinction that it retains today. Although it is located on the Cape Fear River almost thirty miles from the Atlantic Ocean, direct water access to the Atlantic and the ability to tap the produce of an extensive hinterland gave Wilmington an advantage over other state ports. Based on the export of naval stores and other wood products, Wilmington developed a thriving coastal, West Indian, and transatlantic trade by the advent of the Revolution.

Although the Revolution disrupted trade, the volume of commerce recovered quickly after the war, both in Wilmington and throughout the state, to exceed pre-war levels by the time North Carolina joined the Union in 1789. The antebellum era witnessed developments in transportation—steamboats and railroads—that contributed greatly to the growth of the town and its trade. The Civil War with its attendant blockade running transformed Wilmington into a critical entrepôt for Confederate trade and heightened its reputation as a port of international consequence. From the end of the Civil War to the twentieth century, however, Wilmington struggled to compete with neighboring ports of Norfolk, Charleston, and Savannah. The naval stores and wood products industries, though still significant, began to founder, yet cotton compensated for their decline.

Wilmington's fortunes as a port began to wane in the twentieth century with the decline and virtual disappearance of cotton from the export rolls. For the first time imports, principally fertilizer materials and petroleum products, exceeded exports. By the beginning of World War II Wilmington had become essentially a local port, catering to a limited interior market. Competition offered by Norfolk, Charleston, and Savannah, an inability to handle general as opposed to bulk cargo, and the inordinate excess of imports over exports hampered the port's development. Following World War II the General Assembly of North Carolina brought to fruition an idea conceived in the 1920s—the State Ports Authority. The SPA, opening in Wilmington in 1952 as the State Docks, reversed Wilmington's commercial fortunes. By enhancing shipping facilities in the port and complementing private shipping, the SPA engendered an increasing flow of traffic through Wilmington. Although the port's progress in the last half of the twentieth century has been encouraging, problems remain for Wilmington, largely in the form of intense competition from proximate ports on the Atlantic coast.

This book attempts to survey the shipping activity of Wilmington and to point out some of the factors that shaped the development of the port's maritime commerce. Too little attention has been accorded the water trade, both interior and ocean commerce, that undergirded Wilmington's rise to prominence in North Carolina and contributed to its reputation as one of the country's principal Atlantic ports. Maritime activity transformed Wilmington into the most populous town in the state during the nineteenth century, creating fortunes for some, employment for many, and a multifarious culture reflecting the national and international flavor of the port's trade and immigrants. Although shipping became part of a broader economic base in the twentieth century, river and ocean traffic remain an integral part of the economy of Wilmington and the state of North Carolina.

Chapter One

ORIGINS OF A COLONIAL PORT

Heaving a sigh of relief at the sight of land in North Carolina after a treacherous ocean passage through Frying Pan Shoals off Cape Fear, the seafarer entered the Cape Fear River. Susan D. Nye, traveling from Amenia, New York, in 1815, found the river passage pleasant after enduring a week of listening to the boom tackle "beat over my aching head as if it must come through into my cabin." Four decades earlier Janet Schaw, a young Scotswoman visiting North Carolina in 1775, was less impressed. As she sailed up the Cape Fear River, "all seem[ed] dreary, savage and desert." The desolation at last was interrupted by the town of Wilmington, some thirty miles from the sea, which had developed into North Carolina's leading port by the time of the Revolution.[1]

The Cape Fear River, the most majestic of the state's rivers and the only one emptying directly into the Atlantic, dominates southeastern North Carolina. Of its dual provenance, the more important is the Northwest branch, or simply the Cape Fear River, which begins at the confluence of the Deep and Haw rivers in present Chatham County and travels southeast about 150 miles to join the Northeast branch of the Cape Fear. The Northeast branch originates in present Wayne County and meanders some 100 miles to its junction with the Northwest branch. At that point the river flows as a single stream to the ocean about thirty miles distant.[2]

The two branches of the Cape Fear River drain over a quarter of North Carolina's present one hundred counties. Several streams, large and small, feed the main arteries. From the junction of the Northwest and Northeast branches just above Wilmington, the Cape Fear flows to the east of Eagles

Island. A tributary of the Northwest branch, the Brunswick River, bounds Eagles Island on the west and joins the Cape Fear River about three miles below the confluence of the two branches. Although narrow and sometimes tortuous, the Cape Fear eventually broadens to a width of two miles and near its mouth expands to an estuary three miles in breadth.

Guarding the entrance of the Cape Fear River are sandbars called Frying Pan Shoals, which stretch off the cape for some eighteen miles. While ingress from the east is restricted to several sloughs of a maximum depth of five feet through Frying Pan Shoals, large vessels might approach from the south and west. Crossing the bar, as the entance is termed, is dangerous, particularly in the face of shifting and shoaling sands that leave the depth of the water uncertain. A second entrance to the Cape Fear River appeared in 1761 when a hurricane opened New Inlet across the peninsula almost ten miles above the point of the cape. Although New Inlet could accommodate light-draft vessels, larger craft necessarily continued to cross the main bar. However, the opening of New Inlet caused increased shoaling downstream at the bar, a process that threatened Wilmington's ocean-going commerce involving deepdraft vessels.[3]

The first European known to have sighted and explored the coast of the Lower Cape Fear was Giovanni da Verrazzano. Sailing for Francis I of France and seeking sources of New World wealth as well as the Northwest Passage to the Orient, Verrazzano came by way of the West Indies to the North American coast in 1524. By the navigator's reckoning he sighted land a few miles north of the entrance of the Cape Fear River in October. After sailing south and then returning to the Cape Fear, Verrazzano anchored offshore and sent a party to the mainland. Friendly aboriginals and a lush landscape impressed the navigator, who penned a laudatory description of the area.[4]

Verrazzano's visit was soon followed by Spanish exploration and possibly settlement. In 1525 Pedro de Quejo coasted the Outer Banks of present North Carolina. Quejo was employed by Lucas Vasquez de Ayllon, a judge on the appeals court (*Audiencia*) at Santo Domingo, today the capital of the Dominican Republic and then the administrative center for much of the Spanish Caribbean. In 1526 Ayllon fitted out an ambitious armada at Santo Domingo, consisting of six vessels, for a proposed settlement on the mainland. The Ayllon expedition may have landed and even attempted to establish a town along the Cape Fear River, but the effort proved an abysmal failure.[5]

The inability of the French to take advantage of Verrazzano's discovery and of the Spanish to colonize present-day North Carolina left the English a belated opportunity to fill the void. However, Walter Raleigh's Roanoke Island settlements proved abortive, and the area remained in limbo until granted by English King Charles I to Sir Robert Heath in 1629. No apparent colonization having been accomplished under the auspices of that grant, the Heath patent was superseded by Charles II in 1663 when he granted the area called Carolina to eight prominent Englishmen, who became the Lords Proprietors of Carolina.

The permanent settlement of North Carolina occurred in the Albemarle region in the late 1650s as a result of the extension of the southeastern frontier of Virginia. Meanwhile the Lower Cape Fear soon became the focus of interest of prospective New England and Barbadian colonizers. Representing Massachusetts Puritans, specifically a company known as the Adventurers about Cape Fayre, William Hilton explored the Cape Fear River for some three weeks in October 1662, seeking a possible site for settlement. He returned to the northern colony with a favorable report, after which a colonizing expedition set out early in 1663. The settlers remained in the Cape Fear area for only two months, abruptly leaving for unknown reasons.[6]

Subsequently residents of the English colony of Barbados evidenced interest in the Lower Cape Fear. Again Hilton led the way, reconnoitering the Cape Fear River in the fall of 1663 on behalf of the Barbadians. He explored both branches of the Cape Fear, and named several landmarks. Returning to Barbados early in 1664 with glowing accounts of the river, flora, and fauna, Hilton found sentiment divided between those who favored colonizing the Cape Fear site and those who preferred a more southerly location.

Ultimately John Vassal tipped the balance in favor of the Cape Fear and personally led the expedition that landed in May 1664. Settlement centered about the village of Charles Town, the first of that name in the Carolinas. Situated twenty miles upstream on the west bank of the Cape Fear at the junction of the river and Town Creek, Charles Town was meant to serve as a trade center for those who lived in homes scattered some sixty miles along the banks of the Cape Fear. The effort proved futile. Division among the whites, opposition by Indians, inadequate support by the Lords Proprietors of Carolina, and lack of supplies doomed the Cape Fear settlement, which was abandoned in 1667.

The permanent settlement of the Lower Cape Fear in the 1720s, like the earlier effort in the 1660s, witnessed the immediate appearance of a trade center—Brunswick Town. While a few settlers from North Carolina's Albemarle traveled to the Cape Fear, South Carolinians provided the main thrust of immigration. They sought to escape onerous taxes and political maladministration of government. At the same time they were encouraged by the opportunity to obtain large acreages of land. Eventually the Lower Cape Fear in North Carolina greatly resembled the coastal region of South Carolina, not only in its geography and topography but also in its demography and economy.[7]

Settlement progressed haphazardly. By the end of June 1726 Maurice Moore, the earliest known resident of the area, had laid out Brunswick Town on the Cape Fear River and had sold the first lot in town. As the population of the area increased, a ferry was established in 1727 between Brunswick Town and the opposite bank of the river. The following year the settlement was described as a "dispersed multitude of People residing up and down Cape Fear." There were sufficient inhabitants by 1729 to justify the creation of New Hanover County by the General Assembly.[8]

In founding Brunswick Town, Maurice Moore chose a site on a low bluff of the west bank of the river approximately twelve miles from the mouth of the Cape Fear. At that point the Cape Fear was about a mile wide, with its channel running close to the west bank. Although convenient for ocean shipping, the area was too exposed to provide a safe harbor for small craft. In addition it was subject to enemy incursions in times of war, as evidenced by a Spanish invasion of 1748. Still, as the only center of trade in 1729, Brunswick Town was denominated the seat of New Hanover County.[9]

Brunswick Town never attained significant size. A visitor in 1731 described it as a "poor, hungry, unprovided Place, consisting of not above 10 or 12 scattering mean Houses, hardly worth the name of a Village." He did admit, however, that it was "likely to be a Place of [substantial] Trade." Yet by the mid-1750s Brunswick Town contained only 20 families, or 150 inhabitants, and to Lord Adam Gordon in 1765 it did not "seem very thriving." Echoing that sentiment was Janet Schaw in 1775, who said that Brunswick Town "is very poor—a few scattered houses on the edge of the woods, without street or regularity." Among its residents were several merchants and customs officials.[10]

Challenging Brunswick Town for hegemony on the Cape Fear River was a little village inaugurated in the 1730s on the east bank of the river just below the confluence of the Northeast and Northwest branches. George Burrington, North Carolina's first royal governor after the Crown purchased the Carolinas from the Proprietors in 1729, initiated the settlement. After a survey by William Gray in April 1733, plans were drawn and lots were sold for a settlement variously called New Carthage, New Liverpool, and Newton.[11] Many of the early residents of the village—James

Smallwood, Rufus Marsden, Daniel Dunbibin, Robert Walker, and James Murray—were merchants. Smallwood came from Charleston, South Carolina; Marsden and Dunbibin, from England; Murray and Walker, from Scotland and Ireland respectively.[12]

The arrival in 1734 of Gabriel Johnston, Burrington's successor as governor, gave impetus to the burgeoning village. Johnston bought land adjoining the settlement, announced his intention of opening a land office at Newton, and ordered his council, court of exchequer, and court of oyer and terminer to convene in the town. The council in 1735 also approved the designation of Newton as a town pending the erection of six brick buildings during the ensuing two years. Moreover, quitrent legislation in 1735 required the payment of that land tax in Newton and Brunswick, and quitrent bills in 1736 and 1739 designated only Newton as a collection center.[13]

Although the Brunswick Town interests objected to the recognition of the upriver settlement, Johnston in early 1740 secured legislation from the General Assembly to rename the village Wilmington, honoring Johnston's patron in England, Spencer Compton, Earl of Wilmington. The General Assembly justified the incorporation of Wilmington by the residence of several merchants, tradesmen, artificers, and other persons "of good fortune" in the village, by its convenient location at the confluence of the two branches of the Cape Fear, and by its deep, safe, and accessible harbor, which rendered the site more appropriate for a town "than any other part of the . . . river."[14]

Later in 1740 a subsequent session of the General Assembly reaffirmed the previous law. The legislation also invested Wilmington with the privilege of sending a representative to the General Assembly. Borough representation, which emanated from English precedent, was intended to allow the special economic interests of towns—the mercantile trade—to be heard in the legislature in conjunction with predominant agrarian interests. In 1745 the General Assembly granted self-government to Wilmingtonians by allowing the townspeople to choose their town commissioners. Wilmington thus became the first town in the province to be accorded democratic municipal government.[15]

The incorporation of Wilmington marked the slow decline of Brunswick Town. Saving the latter from virtual extinction before the Revolution was its status as a port of entry, which was largely due to the Flats, sandbars at the mouth of Old Town Creek that were almost equidistant between Wilmington and Brunswick Town. Because the Flats impeded the progress of large vessels, many lightered at Brunswick Town before going upriver and then took on final cargo at Brunswick Town before departing the province. Additionally, in 1764 the General Assembly created Brunswick County from parts of Bladen and New Hanover counties and designated Brunswick Town as the seat of the new county.[16]

The Revolution sealed the fate of Brunswick Town, however. Exposed to British incursions, most residents deserted their town at the beginning of the war. During the British invasion of the Lower Cape Fear in 1776, enemy soldiers roamed the empty streets and looted homes and businesses. After the establishment of state government in 1776, Brunswick Town lost its legislative representative in the General Assembly. The final blow came in 1779 when the legislature moved the seat of Brunswick County to the relative safety of Lockwoods Folly.[17]

The rise of Wilmington paralleled the decline of Brunswick Town. A population of some four hundred in Wilmington at mid-century swelled to about twelve hundred a quarter century later, making the town one of the most populous in North Carolina, though small by comparison with others along the English North American coast. As an urban center in the wealthiest region in colonial North Carolina, the Lower Cape Fear, Wilmington became a "place of elegance" where merchants developed a "taste for living." On the eve of the Revolution visitors described Wilmington as "the most flourishing town" and the "principal Trading port" in the province.[18]

The town commissioners of Wilmington were keenly aware of their role in the commercial process and attempted to promote local water trade by constructing public wharves, erecting market houses, and enacting commercial regulatory ordinances. Wharves were built at the foot of Dock and Market streets in 1749 and 1752 respectively. Provincial legislation required all taxable males in the town to assist in making and maintaining such structures, and periodically the commissioners called upon the men of the town for that purpose. In 1772 the town contracted for the construction of a boat slip at the Market Street wharf.[19]

The commissioners often addressed the regulation of activity on the wharves. Periodically they found the docks "encumbered" or "cluttered" with lumber and naval stores and ordered the removal of such goods. To guard against fire the town fathers enjoined the practice of boiling naval stores products on the wharves. Later they prohibited fires on the docks altogether, a directive subsequently modified to ban such fires only at night. After 1756 the commissioners decided to reserve the public docks solely for local trafic, forbidding any "Sea Vessell" to use the facilities.[20]

Wilmington and Brunswick Town constituted the principal ports of the customs district of Port Brunswick in colonial North Carolina. Almost a half century after its first permanent settlement in America and coinciding with the settlement of North Carolina, the English government instituted a concerted policy to regulate the commerce of its burgeoning empire. That effort, beginning in the Cromwellian era but pursued more vigorously upon the restoration of the Stuarts in 1660, was embodied in a series of parliamentary statutes called Navigation Acts. Dominated by mercantilist conceptions that particularly emphasized the importance of trade for national prosperity and military superiority, the English sought by the legislation to direct colonial commerce so that it might best serve and sustain the empire, especially the mother country.[21]

In order to effect the desired policy the navigation legislation created customs districts with designated ports of entry in the various North American colonies whereby shipping might be properly regulated. During the first fifty years of the colony's existence, when settlement was confined principally to the Albemarle region, two customs districts sufficed for North Carolina. Port Currituck included the area of Currituck Sound; Port Roanoke, with Edenton as its port of entry, encompassed the Albemarle Sound. As the colony expanded southward, ports Bath, Beaufort, and Brunswick were established to accommodate the growing provincial trade.

As early as March 1731, probably originating with the appointment and arrival of George Burrington, North Carolina's first royal governor, Port Brunswick became the official port of entry for the Cape Fear. The port encompassed the watershed of the Cape Fear River—in effect, the southeastern region of North Carolina. Shipping through Port Brunswick steadily increased during the four decades before the Revolution. Forty-two vessels left the river in 1734. By 1754 as many as a hundred ships annually entered Port Brunswick according to Governor Arthur Dobbs, who once saw sixteen craft on the river at one time.[22]

During the decade preceding the Revolution, Port Brunswick's import and export trade in terms of tonnage easily exceeded that of any other North Carolina port district and constituted about 40 percent of the colony's total commerce, as may be seen in Table 1. Much of the trade of Port Brunswick moved through Wilmington, but all entrances and clearances were recorded with the customs officials seated in Brunswick Town. Complicating matters was the presence of the Flats, which prevented larger vessels from trading directly with the town of Wilmington.

Historian Lawrence Lee has attempted to calculate the approximate trade of Wilmington and Brunswick by assuming that vessels of less than one hundred tons proceeded to Wilmington while others used the facilities at Brunswick Town. Lee believes that during the year from April 5, 1767,

Table 1
Shipping, North Carolina Customs Districts, 1763

	Ships	Tonnage
Port Brunswick	90	4,830
Port Roanoke	97	3,052
Port Beaufort	73	2,740
Port Bath	30	1,163
Port Currituck	6	77
	296	11,862

Saunders, *Colonial Records of North Carolina*, 6:968.

to April 5, 1768, almost three times as many vessels cleared Wilmington as they did Brunswick Town. But the total tonnage of the Wilmington vessels was less because the Wilmington trade was aimed at colonial coastal ports and the West Indies, whereas 87 percent of the vessels leaving Brunswick Town went to Great Britain.[23]

For three decades after the establishment of Port Brunswick, the trade of the district was confined primarily to the North American coast and the West Indies. From the northern colonies came manufactures, mainly cloth, utensils, tools, gigs, sulkies, and considerable amounts of foodstuffs, among which rum, molasses, sugar, and salt were the most prominent. The islands also sent rum, molasses, brown sugar, and salt to the province. In addition smaller quantities of fruit, coffee, ginger, and mahogany as well as a few slaves cleared the West Indies for North Carolina. One hundred and twenty-five bondsmen entered Port Brunswick during the year ending April 24, 1775. Moderate amounts of manufactured goods—iron utensils, earthenwares, and linens among others—also came from the West Indies, though undoubtedly most originated in England.[24]

Overseas commerce involving Port Brunswick increased gradually. According to Governor Dobbs in 1763, one-third of the English goods consumed in North Carolina came directly from the mother country. Because Brunswick Town was the premier deep-water port in the colony, most of the English trade centered in the Cape Fear. During the five-year period ending January 5, 1773, 139 of 215, or 65 percent, of the ships that entered the province from England went to Port Brunswick. Of the remainder, 49 went to Port Roanoke, 22 to Port Beaufort, and 5 to Port Bath; none went to Port Currituck. From England and Scotland came mostly manufactured goods, particularly cloth. Wearing apparel, shoes, and hardware were also prominent imports.[25]

It is well to remember, however, that much of the tonnage entering North Carolina toward the approach of the Revolution, perhaps a fourth, came in ballast. For the year ending April 24, 1775, 2,588 of 8,386 tons, or 31 percent, of the tonnage entering Port Brunswick arrived in that fashion. And that figure understates the total, for many ships undoubtedly brought less than a full cargo to port. Because the northern colonies generated a greater demand for British goods than the southern colonies, British vessels might come to North Carolina by way of northern ports at least partly in ballast to seek a homeward bound cargo.[26]

By the outbreak of the Revolution, Port Brunswick's export trade in terms of tonnage also surpassed that of the other customs districts in North Carolina. Moreover, due to its deep harbor and the nature of its surrounding economy, Port Brunswick's trade was increasingly directed toward transatlantic commerce. By 1768, when one-third of North Carolina exports in terms of tonnage was destined for the British Isles, 60 percent of Port Brunswick's outward-bound trade moved in that direction. More than one-fourth of its shipping headed for the British West Indies. One-tenth cleared for the mainland North American colonies. Only an occasional vessel was bound for southern Europe or Africa.[27]

As shown by Table 2, export tonnage from Port Brunswick, while exceeding that of the other North Carolina ports, fell far short of the tonnage leaving Charleston, South Carolina, and the larger northern mercantile centers. In fact, however, Charleston and Virginia ports prob-

Table 2
Export Tonnage, Selected Ports, 1768–69

Port	Tonnage Cleared
Boston	33,698
New York	23,573
Philadelphia	37,424
James River (Norfolk)	26,383
Currituck	717
Roanoke	7,692
Bath	2,158
Beaufort	3,760
Brunswick	8,608
Total North Carolina Tonnage	22,935
Charleston	31,551

Logan, "An Historical Geographic Survey of North Carolina Ports," 61.

ably shipped much of North Carolina's produce. According to one estimate the value of North Carolina exports in 1770 leaving through the province's own ports was £100,000; another £75,000 was carried overland to Virginia for export; an additional £20,000 left via Charleston; and perhaps £5,000 more went to Pennsylvania and other northern colonies. Thus North Carolina ports handled about half of the colony's external trade. In similar fashion, perhaps 50 percent of the province's imports passed through its ports, a fourth came by land from South Carolina, and the remainder was brought from Virginia and more northerly colonies.[28]

Exports from Port Brunswick were diverse, but centered upon naval stores and wood products, as may be seen in Table 3. Among the eastern seaboard colonies North Carolina was England's largest supplier of naval stores on the eve of the Revolution and enjoyed the parliamentary bounty designed to encourage the exportation of such goods. In 1768 one North Carolinian lamented the colony's reliance upon naval stores while planters in South Carolina reached a "pitch of opulence" with their rice, indigo, and hemp, commodities that North Carolina was equally capable of producing. However, the extensive pine forests and North Carolina's comparatively small slave population rendered reliance upon naval stores more feasible.[29]

Naval stores, variously defined but basically consisting of tar, pitch, rosin, and turpentine, derived from the longleaf pine. Crude or common turpentine was the resin collected from boxed, living trees. When crude turpentine was distilled, it produced spirits, oil of turpentine, and a residue called rosin. Burning pine wood in kilns produced tar. Boiling tar in open pits or in iron cauldrons yielded pitch, thicker than tar, but whose consistency depended upon the length of the boiling process. Three barrels of tar produced two barrels of pitch. The seemingly endless tract of longleaf pines along the coast and superb water transportation made the pine derivatives a mainstay of the economy.[30]

Naval stores quickly became a major component of North Carolina exports. They went primarily to England. In 1772 only one-tenth of those products were shipped elsewhere, mostly to New York and Philadelphia, from whence they were probably transshipped to the mother country. England relied heavily upon the American provinces, importing only 11,403 barrels of naval stores in 1772 from other sources, mainly Russia and Sweden. Since North Carolina was the principal source of English naval stores and the Lower Cape Fear annually supplied half those products, southeastern North Carolina, Wilmington, and Port Brunswick occupied a unique and valuable position within the British Empire.[31]

Table 3
Exports, Port Brunswick, 1767–68

Product	Amount
Rice	126 bu.
Pitch	919 bbls.
Tar	52,708 bbls.
Turpentine	8,627 bbls.
Lumber	1,823,650 ft.
Shingles	1,411,500
Staves	134,900
Pork	3,167 bbls.
Flour	416 bbls.
Corn	1,958 bu.
Tobacco	6 hhds.
Hog lard	89 bbls.
Fish	15 bbls.
Cedar posts	241
Timber posts	50 tons
Beef	57 bbls.
Flax seed	17 casks; 32 tierces; 13 bbls.; 355 hhds.
Bacon	1,000 wt.
Handspikes	97 doz.
Iron	1 ton
Reeds	16,500
Fur	7 bundles
Tallow	36 bbls.
Hemp	1,750 bu.; 19 bundles; 300 wt.
Pease	5,350 bu.
Biscuits	12 kegs
House frames	3
Scythes	4 doz.
Sickles	2 doz.
Bread	27 bbl.
Rawhides	109
Beeswax	1 cask; 100 wt.
Mahogany	800 ft.
Limes	10 bbl.
Dry goods	1 bale
Indigo	2 casks
Live hogs	70
Lignum vitae	4 tons
Raccoon skins	110
Timber	142 tons
Deer skins (dressed)	100 wt.

Logan, "An Historical Geographic Survey of North Carolina Ports," 51–52.

North Carolina also produced a variety of wood products, including sawn lumber (boards, plank, scantling), shingles, staves, heading, hoops, hogsheads, posts, oars, masts, spars, yards, and even house frames. Most important were boards, shingles, and staves. Most of the boards, plank, and scantling were pine and were cut in the colony's numerous sawmills, which produced two and a half to three million board feet annually. Cypress shingles and oak staves were laboriously cut by hand. Via Port Brunswick went approximately 70 to 75 percent of the province's exported sawn lumber, 25 percent of its shingles, and 10 percent of its staves. More than 90 percent of the exported wood products went to the West Indies.[32]

In addition to naval stores and wood products, a number of less significant exports found their way through Port Brunswick. Some provisions were sent to the West Indies. However, most foodstuffs were retained in the province to feed the local populace. Another exportable crop of increasing importance at the end of the colonial era was tobacco. As its growth shifted from the Albemarle region to the south and southwest to become the chief crop of the "middle parts" of North Carolina, some found its way down the Cape Fear River through Port Brunswick. George Washington, on his southern tour in 1791, reported that 6,000 hogsheads annually were exported from Fayetteville, presumably via Port Brunswick.[33]

Though far less significant than in South Carolina and Georgia, the cultivation of rice and indigo provided additional agricultural exports for North Carolina. About 1730 a traveler observed rice swamps along the Northeast Cape Fear. During the 1740s planters began to experiment with indigo, though only a few ever produced enough to make the effort worth their while. In the province the production of rice and indigo was confined almost exclusively to the lower reaches of the Northeast and Northwest branches and the Cape Fear River below Wilmington. Thus over 95 percent of the rice and over 80 percent of the indigo exported from the colony cleared Port Brunswick.[34]

To bring their produce to market along the inland waterways the colonials used a variety of craft. Merchant James Murray's advice to a friend in London in 1741, "If you intend to do any business here, a Cooper and a Craft that will carry about 100 barrels will be absolutely necessary," was apropos three decades later. Loyalist Maurice Nowland at Fayetteville counted among his lost property during the Revolution "1 boat for transporting products to Wilmington." Canoes—varying in size, with some propelled by sail as well as oar—and perriaugers—larger than canoes, capable of carrying eighty to a hundred barrels of tar and sometimes taken on coasting voyages—were popular. Yawls, small sloops, and bayboats also sailed the rivers and streams. For commercial purposes, however, the flatboat and raft were most important.[35]

Turpentine and rosin were transported on flatboats that might carry fifty to a hundred casks or on rafts bearing several hundred barrels. The rafts consisted of a framework of large timbers divided by crossbeams. Small saplings subdivided the sections into spaces about the length of a rosin barrel. The barrels were secured to the saplings by means of pliable hickory withes. On top of the barrels were boards covered with dirt or clay, which formed a deck on which raftsmen lived and cooked while floating downstream to market.[36]

The flatboats and rafts depended upon the current for motive power. Heavy oars, or poles, twenty to thirty feet long and mounted on two-foot fulcrums at either end of the craft, were used to steer the boat. Floating with the current meant slow travel. Between tides the raftsmen had to lay to, "having no power to move but by the force of the stream." The trip from Hallsville, ninety-two miles from Wilmington along the Northeast Cape Fear, required a week for a flatboat and perhaps ten days for a raft. Yet to one observer it was the best mode of transport, and had been "adopted by all the people up the country."[37]

At Wilmington the cargoes were delivered to commission houses in return for goods and credit. Rafts were dismantled and their timbers sold "for a trifle." Flatboats were usually loaded and then taken upriver against the current by means of poles worked from both sides of the boats as well as from the ends. A swift current might occasion warping the craft by fastening ropes to trees on the banks. In any case the work was extremely difficult, sometimes impossible when the water level was low. At that point wagons might be dispatched to haul the cargo overland. Upstream travel might take two to three times as long as that going in the opposite direction.

The rivermen or watermen who took the rafts and flatboats up and down the rivers were held in low esteem. One observer referred to them as "the poorest set of people" whom he saw in the province. He felt that they generally were "drunkards, and can be of little use in any other way; yet these get half-a-crown a day, and 3 gallons of rum per week." Many of the watermen were slaves who were familiar with every twist and turn of the rivers and creeks. In his will of 1768 Wilmington merchant John DuBois directed his executors to purchase four slaves to work his boats. Some fifty years later bondsman Harvey Jarman was hired from his master for $300 per year and the usual allowance of food and clothing to work on the Northeast Cape Fear.[38]

Diversity also characterized the craft engaged in the Cape Fear import–export ocean trade. During the year ending July 3, 1775, 112 vessels entered Port Brunswick. They included brigs, sloops, schooners, ships, and snows. Outnumbering all types, constituting 37 percent of the vessels calling at the port, were the brigs, equipped with two masts, a fore mast with square sails and a main mast partly square and partly fore-and-aft rigged. Most of the brigs were small; two-thirds were less than 100 tons. The remainder ranged upward in size to the 200-ton *Kernington*, sailing from Hull, England.[39] Also appearing regularly at the port were sloops and schooners, which numbered 27 and 20 respectively during the year under consideration. The sloop was single-masted, fore-and-aft-rigged; the schooner, two-masted with main and fore sails suspended by gaffs. In the Cape Fear trade they ranged from 10 to 60 tons and were manned by crews numbering from two to six.

The largest vessels calling at Port Brunswick were the ships and snows. The ships, three-masted and square-rigged, accounted for one-sixth of the craft entering the port. They averaged 130 tons and included the largest merchant vessel to visit Port Brunswick on the eve of the Revolution, the 230-ton *Hector*, owned by Brunswick Town merchant John Quince. Making infrequent appearances at the port were the snows, carrying two masts, resembling the fore and main masts of the ships, and just behind the main mast a third mast bearing a trysail. During the year preceding the Revolution only three snows called at Port Brunswick. They ranged from 65 to 120 tons and carried from six to ten crew members.

Although shipbuilding was not one of colonial North Carolina's outstanding manufacturing industries, many vessels plying the Cape Fear trade were constructed in the province. As early as 1727 a ship was built in the Lower Cape Fear, and by 1737 Wilmington was the site, at least briefly, of a shipyard. Later, ships were built in Brunswick Town as well. According to the port records, during the year ending July 3, 1775, 9 of the 107 identifiable craft that entered Port Brunswick had been constructed in North Carolina—8 in Brunswick and one in Beaufort. Mostly sloops, the vessels were small, averaging approximately 35 tons.

Altogether, Montego Bay in Jamaica easily produced most of the ships that visited Port Brunswick. Forty-four, or 41 percent, of the vessels that entered the Cape Fear in the year ending July 3, 1775, had been built on that island. Distantly following were craft of "British" origin, twelve in number. Another nine had been constructed in Connecticut and seven in New Hampshire. Most of the remaining British North American colonies contributed ships as well, including six from New York, four from Virginia and Rhode Island, three from Pennsylvania, two each from Nova Scotia and South Carolina, and one each from New Jersey and Maryland. The vessels were relatively new. Over 90 percent had been built in the 1760s and 1770s. Eight, however, were over fifteen years old, having been constructed in the 1750s, and one, the *Royal Union,* a British ship sailing from Scarborough, had been on the water for forty years.

The colonial legislature belatedly attempted to provide a measure of protection for the exposed Cape Fear River during the course of the many wars that engaged England and the colonies. Reacting to the outbreak of the War of Jenkins' Ear in 1739, a conflict involving England and Spain which merged into King George's War, the General Assembly in 1745 directed the construction of Fort Johnston at a site that later became Smithville (present Southport). However, the fort was still under construction when the Spanish invaded Brunswick Town in 1748, an attack that was repulsed by local residents. Although completed by mid-century, Fort Johnston fortunately was not tested in the lengthy French and Indian War beginning in 1754, for the installation lacked sufficient ordnance and was deemed to be in a dilapidated condition. Cannon arrived in 1758, but necessary repairs to the fort were not made until 1764, a year after the conclusion of the war.[40]

Local and provincial authorities sought to enhance the commercial potential of Wilmington and the Lower Cape Fear. The improvement of the channels of the Northwest and Northeast branches of the Cape Fear plus their tributaries quickly became and remained a prime concern. James Murray observed that logs, of which there were "millions," and other debris often obstructed the Northeast and Northwest branches, though where the river was clear there was six feet of water and an "easy current." In any case the county court of New Hanover, as authorized by provincial legislation, periodically directed residents along the rivers and streams to clear the watercourses.[41]

In order to facilitate shipping into and along the Cape Fear River to Wilmington, the General Assembly in 1751 passed the first of many laws to establish a system of pilotage for the river. The statute appointed five prominent residents of the Lower Cape Fear to be self-perpetuating commissioners of pilotage. They would examine and license pilots (to a maximum of seven) and dismiss those deemed guilty of "misbehaviour" in office. The law also provided a table of fees for pilotage service based on the draft of the vessels being guided over the bar and along the river. In "thick weather," when captains of vessels fired guns to inform pilots of their arrival, the commander of Fort Johnston was empowered to return the signal, dispatch pilots, and collect fees from the ship captains for the expended powder.[42]

The pilotage legislation of 1751 also provided for quarantine regulations to protect the colony from sickness abroad. The commander of Fort Johnston was required to question each ship captain to ascertain possible contagions on board. If the commander was not satisfied, the vessel could not proceed farther until the commissioners of pilotage had been notified and had given directions for quarantining the vessel. Such precautions may have reduced the incidence of imported disease but failed to protect Wilmington altogether, for periodically reports of epidemic sickness, including smallpox, emanated from the town and New Hanover County.[43]

During the ensuing decade the "great Increase of the Trade of [the] Cape Fear River" moved the legislature to reconsider the pilotage system. In 1764 it defined more carefully the responsibilities of the pilots, raised their number at the bar to twelve, admonished them strongly to obey the law, and reiterated the quarantine procedure. The statute increased the number of pilots serving the river from the bar to Brunswick from seven to eight and allowed the commissioners to appoint a maximum of four pilots on the river between Brunswick and Wilmington. Because many pilots failed to guide vessels along the river, fines were prescribed for their neglect of duty. Fees for pilotage were raised in 1764 and again in 1766.[44]

To facilitate navigation at the mouth of the Cape Fear River, legislation in 1764 provided for the erection of beacons and buoys at that point, to be paid for by a tonnage fee collected from all non–North Carolina-owned vessels trading through Port Brunswick. Two years later the General Assembly responded to the malicious removal or destruction of the markers by making such actions subject to stiff fines. The same statute also proscribed the practice of tying rafts, perriaugers, and other craft to the beacons and buoys.[45]

The General Assembly also addressed the troublesome problems of masters of vessels who surreptitiously carried slaves and indentured servants from the port or who sailed without paying pilotage fees. The legislation in 1766 required ship captains to post bond for proper performance before their departure from port. Still the secretive transport of slaves continued to plague Wilmington long after the Revolution, as evidenced by legislation and newspaper advertisements calling attention to the practice.[46]

In addition to pilots and masters the General Assembly also took cognizance of the seamen, rough-and-ready men who were at once feared, disparaged, applauded, and pitied by the general populace. They seemed ever present among the numerous colonial mobs, including a riotous scene in

Wilmington in 1765. On the other hand British seamen extinguished a fire in the town while residents and their slaves looked on helplessly. Provincial legislation governing the town of Wilmington and regulating taverns in the province specifically addressed the seamen in statutes that forbade tavernkeepers to offer extensive credit to seamen without the approval of their captains and also proscribed the harboring or detaining of sailors in port.[47]

Among other attempts to protect and improve the commerce of the Lower Cape Fear (and that of North Carolina generally) were the establishment of an inspection system to ensure the quality of North Carolina exports, the promotion of a more balanced economy, and the creation of towns to serve as centers of trade. The General Assembly resorted to an inspection system, begun in the proprietary era and expanded and improved in later years, to relieve North Carolina of the reputation of producing and exporting inferior products. Legislation fixed inspection sites in every county. Among the numerous items specified for inclusion under the inspection law were naval stores, staves, shingles, lumber, deer skins, rice, indigo, and pork, potential exports whose improved quality would certainly have benefited the Cape Fear region, a prime producer of those commodities.[48]

Dependent upon pine derivatives, the economy of the Lower Cape Fear fluctuated with the price of naval stores in Great Britain. From producers to merchants and governor, residents of the province complained incessantly about the small returns from naval stores as well as the high cost of imported goods. In part the difficulties stemmed from the British navigation legislation which restricted colonial trade to channels most profitable to the mother country and the empire as a whole. On the other hand the colonials also bore some of the blame. Carolinians were notoriously careless in their preparation of naval stores, and in fact colonial products rarely approached the quality of Scandinavian and Russian naval stores purchased by England (at exorbitant prices). In their objection in 1770 to Carolina pitch and tar English importers recommended a proper observance of the strictures of the parliamentary bounty act and the local inspection system as the means to improve Carolina exports.[49]

Governors Johnston, Dobbs, and Tryon encouraged North Carolinians, especially those in the Cape Fear, to expand their economic base by considering the cultivation of silk, flax, indigo, and hemp. To further the concept of diversification the provincial legislature offered bounties on the production of hemp, flax, potash, and pearl ash. Cotton was early grown in the Lower Cape Fear. Some was exported, but most was used locally.

According to one observer, "under proper management" cotton "would be an article of great consequence." Still, on the eve of the Revolution the Carolinians depended primarily upon naval stores, timber products, livestock, and food for commercial export.[50]

A major deterrent to Wilmington's growth as a port was the inability of the Lower Cape Fear to attract the backcountry trade. North Carolina's frontier commerce gravitated to Petersburg, Virginia; Charleston, South Carolina; and to a small extent northward as far as Pennsylvania. The pattern of backcountry migration was an influential factor in channeling the area's trade, as was North Carolina's geography, which made travel connections with neighboring colonies easier than with the east coast. Aggressive marketing, particularly by prominent Charleston merchant Henry Laurens, captured much of the backcountry trade, for the Charlestonians offered higher prices and better credit facilities.[51]

Potentially the most important of the frontier settlers were the Moravians, or the Brethren of the Unitas Fratrum, who began to migrate from Pennsylvania to North Carolina in 1753. They purchased and settled a tract of land called Wachovia near present-day Winston-Salem. Needing an outlet for the produce of their "Oeconomie," or communal economic system, the Moravians considered Wilmington. The opportunity came at a critical juncture for the port. Had the Brethren been persuaded to open a channel of commerce with the Lower Cape Fear, others in the west may well have followed. Moreover the timing was significant, coming as it did when lines of trade and communication were in their formative stages. However, most of the backcountry business was siphoned off to adjoining colonies, inhibiting the development not only of Wilmington and the Lower Cape Fear but also of the entire province. The adverse patterns of trade continued to retard North Carolina's economic development long after the Revolution.[52]

Also detracting from Wilmington's trade were the poor roads in the eastern portion of the province, which were generally inferior to those in the west. The road from Wilmington to South Carolina was described as "nothing but a sandy bank" in 1734; forty years later it was termed "the most tedious and disagreeable of any on the Continent." North of Wilmington the Duplin Road was admirable for a brief distance, then deteriorated into swampy morasses. The highway along the coast to Snead's Ferry and New Bern was sandy, barren, and gloomy. Affording access to roads across the numerous watercourses in the region were bridges and ferries. Bridges, often in a state of disrepair or simply nonexistent after heavy rains and rising waters carried away the structures, impeded traffic. So did ferriages over the Cape Fear at Wilmington and over the Northeast Cape Fear at present Castle Hayne, at least until a drawbridge was erected about 1767 at the latter site.[53]

In order to lure backcountry trade to the east coast the General Assembly made several efforts to extend roads from the western settlements to the Cape Fear during the decade prior to the Revolution. The prospects of the Moravian trade, following the appeals of Governor William Tryon and the opening of the Moravian town of Salem, prompted the General Assembly in 1768 to authorize a public road from the "Frontiers of the Province through the counties of Mecklenburg, Rowan, Anson, and Bladen, to Wilmington and Brunswick." Upon the failure of the road to materialize the legislature in 1771 passed a similar statute which was designed for "the Advancement of Trade and Commerce." Additional legislation envisioned a road from the Dan River to Campbellton on the Cape Fear River to draw traffic from Guilford and Chatham counties. And a third road was authorized to connect Charlotte, a recently chartered town in Mecklenburg County, to Elizabethtown in Bladen County.[54]

Towns had long been envisioned as stimulants to trade, though urbanization materialized slowly. In the southeast, in addition to Brunswick Town and Wilmington, New Exeter, located on the Northeast Cape Fear some twenty-five miles above Wilmington, was incorporated in 1754 at the urging of inhabitants of New Hanover, Onslow, and Duplin counties who wanted to encourage trade along that section of the river. South Washington (now Watha), located on the same river a few miles above New Exeter, soon appeared. And in 1773 Elizabethtown in Bladen County, acclaimed "a healthy, pleasant Situation, well watered and Commodious for Commerce," was incorporated after many years of informal existence. It provided a river landing on the Northwest Cape Fear between Wilmington and Campbellton.[55]

The most important urban nexus between the Lower Cape Fear and the backcountry was Cross Creek in Cumberland County. Cross Creek, a village located near the Northwest Cape Fear, had arisen in the 1750s, and was the southeastern terminus of a road authorized in 1755 to connect Orange Court House (subsequently Hillsborough) with the river. In 1762 the General Assembly incorporated Campbellton, located about a mile east of Cross Creek at the junction of that creek and the Northwest Cape Fear. That town was designed to divert North Carolina's backcountry trade from South Carolina and Virginia to the east coast, primarily to Brunswick Town and Wilmington. Campbellton was renamed Fayetteville in 1783, and eventually subsumed Cross Creek.[56]

Campbellton and Cross Creek served Wilmington admirably as transshipment points from the interior. Roads from the backcountry converged on Cross Creek; produce came from as far as Salem, Hillsborough, Salisbury, and Charlotte. According to one doubtless exaggerated report, forty to fifty large wagons a day could be seen in Cross Creek, bringing beef, pork, flour, corn, hides, butter, tallow, and other goods. As a result, Wilmington merchants established stores or kept agents in Cross Creek to purchase the produce and send it by raft down the Cape Fear River.[57]

Despite the appearance of towns in the Lower Cape Fear, first Brunswick Town and then Wilmington, much commercial activity occurred at the plantation wharves along the Cape Fear River and its tributaries. In 1734 Captain Amice Gabourel, who owned a plantation on the Northwest branch, was described as a "great merchant there," and his dock a constant scene of shipping activity. Sometimes the wealthy conducted their affairs directly with correspondents in England. Most, however, dealt with merchants operating stores in towns or at strategic river locations.[58]

A distinctive feature of colonial Wilmington was the concentration of Scottish and Scots–Irish merchants in the town. Those merchants not only conducted much of Wilmington's trade but also contributed to the port's commercial success abroad. They brought European, particularly British, commercial contacts with them. The Scots also helped to extend Wilmington's influence into the hinterlands and vigorously pursued the North Carolina backcountry trade.[59]

Notable among the later Scottish merchants was Robert Hogg, who moved from Scotland to Wilmington in the 1750s. He soon helped to establish the firm of Hogg and (Samuel) Campbell. James Hogg, Robert's brother, arrived in 1774 and briefly worked at branch stores in Cross Creek and Hillsborough, two of several businesses established by Hogg and Campbell beyond Wilmington. At its dissolution in 1778 the partnership of Hogg and Campbell claimed assets amounting to £18,330 sterling.[60]

In the main, members of the mercantile community, including the Scots, appeared to be local operators, largely independent of Charleston and the overseas infuences that controlled the northern counties of North Carolina and tidewater Virginia. Credit therefore remained relatively at a premium, and the shortage of cash and currency in the province compounded the credit problem. From the Cape Fear in 1775 Alexander Schaw declared that "there is no specie in the province. . . . Nothing in the stile of a banker or money merchant was ever heard of." Governor Josiah Martin described the "majority from the southern region" of the province as a people "almost universally necessitous and in debt," a condition ascribed by many colonials to stringent British restrictions on the emission of currency.[61]

Indeed the genesis of the American Revolution appeared in the form of urban, often mercantile, protests against restrictive British commercial policies in conjunction with denunciations of perceived British transgressions of American liberties. Wilmington and the Lower Cape Fear assumed a leading role in the revolutionary struggle in North Carolina from the Stamp Act crisis of 1765 to the ultimate repudiation of the British Empire in 1776. Merchants, shippers, sailors, and others directly or indirectly dependent upon trade resented discriminatory and coercive parliamentary legislation that threatened to injure a local economy so thoroughly absorbed in commerce. For those individuals political independence meant economic freedom.

Chapter Two

Revolution and Independence:

A Burgeoning Commerce

The revolutionary impulse in North Carolina centered in its seaport towns of Edenton, New Bern, and Wilmington, reflecting the urban, mercantile opposition to Great Britain throughout the colonies in the 1760s and 1770s. Yet North Carolina contained as many loyalists as any of the British provinces in rebellion, and loyalist sentiment was especially noticeable in Wilmington. However, the commanding influence of Cornelius Harnett II, the "Samuel Adams of North Carolina," and the Sons of Liberty in Wilmington and New Hanover County proved dominant in the Lower Cape Fear. From 1774 to 1776 the Wilmington–New Hanover safety committee, chaired by Harnett, was probably the most active in North Carolina in its zealous promotion of the patriot cause. By means of the safety committees the colonials subverted British authority, cowed loyalists, and instituted provisional government in advance of an independent state.

Although the Revolution sprang from diverse sources, the colonial desire to pursue economic goals unfettered by the mother country cannot be overlooked. The Navigation Acts imposed an overall burden on the colonies of 1 to 3 percent of per capita gross national product, but the southern provinces suffered most. More important, the British effort after 1760 to enforce more stringently the commercial legislation, even to the point of simply inconveniencing shipping, was abrasive. And, of course, the invidious effort of the British to tax by means of navigation laws was anathema to many provincials. In fact, the Revenue Act of 1764 not only sought to tax the Americans but favored British West Indian trade at the expense of that of the mainland colonies.

Parliament in 1764 exacerbated a long-standing Carolina grievance by the passage of the Currency Act, which forbade the colonial issuance of legal tender paper currency. The British had long sought to restrict the use of paper in the province. A memorial directed against North Carolina, bearing the date 1759 and signed by several "Merchants in London who trade to North Carolina and of Gentlemen and Merchants in and from that Colony," protested the colony's currency as "a breach of Public Faith, so contrary to Justice and equity that it totally destroys the credit of that Province."[1] But North Carolina's rapidly expanding population and an increasingly complex economy necessitated an enlarged medium of exchange. Specie was too scarce, and commodity money, commodity notes, and simple credit were insufficient to bridge the gap. While other issues ebbed and flowed, the Currency Act with its attendant constitutional disputes engendered continuing resentment.

The Stamp Act of 1765 made taxation manifest and heightened the cost and inconvenience of entering and clearing shipping. Moreover, the tax was payable in scarce specie. On October 19, 1765, a crowd of some five hundred gathered in Wilmington to protest the legislation; twelve days later, on the eve of the effective date of the Stamp Act, a more ominous demonstration occurred in which "a great number of people" were involved. And in November, Stamp Receiver William Houston resigned his position at the demand of a massive gathering, thus preventing the implementation of the Stamp Act in the Lower Cape Fear.[2]

In explaining his resignation to the authorities in London, Houston declared that it served "to quiet the Minds of the inraged and furious Mobb of Sailors &c." Indeed sailors had a very real stake in the revolutionary movement. The British practice of impressment, so often utilized by the navy in the eighteenth century, threatened the liberty and very lives of merchant sailors. Press riots along the American coast early served to involve seamen in violent protest, a form of demonstration that blended nicely with the opposition to the Stamp Act and other commercial legislation that might interrupt trade and result in unemployment. The sailors were not "mindless and manipulated" rabble; they were rational, independent men whose freedom and jobs were at stake in the jumble of revolutionary activity.[3]

The inability of the British to distribute stamps halted commerce on the Cape Fear River, because stamps had to be affixed to ships' papers in order to legitimate trade. A Cross Creek merchant complained that he could neither sell nor ship goods to Wilmington. Are we "Free Men.or Slaves?" he asked. "Rouze" and "open your Port and Courts," he admonished

Wilmingtonians. When Captain Jacob Lobb of H. M. *Viper*, stationed on the river, seized three incoming ships which did not have properly stamped papers, adverse sentiment quickly was voiced. According to a report from Wilmington, "The trade of this river is at present entirely ruined!" Another seven ships had lately been discouraged from putting into port. Together the ten vessels could have carried off a vast quantity of tar and turpentine, "which, in a few weeks, will be running through our streets."[4]

Although Parliament repealed the Stamp Act in 1766, the colonies soon faced the tariff impositions of the Townshend taxes. Opposition was less immediate and strident than to the Stamp Act. A meeting of the Sons of Liberty of the Lower Cape Fear in September 1769 adopted a nonimportation agreement, followed in November by an informal gathering of most of the members of the General Assembly which applied the principle of nonimportation to the province as a whole. The nonimportation association attributed the current recession to the British revenue acts and other laws depriving the Americans of their just rights, called upon all in the colony to support nonimportation, agreed to treat nonsympathizers with "the utmost contempt," and urged thrift and economy among the colonials.[5]

As the colony's principal center of trade and the focus of the most active of North Carolina's Sons of Liberty, the Lower Cape Fear remained in the vanguard of the opposition to England. A meeting in Wilmington on June 2, 1770, of the Sons of Liberty from six counties, mostly planters, agreed to boycott and publicize those who imported goods contrary to the nonimportation agreement. They expressed the hope that the merchants' "own interest will convince them of the necessity of importing such articles, and such only, as the planters will purchase," and established committees of inspection to carry out their resolutions. The effort was less effective than an embargo that followed the Stamp Act. Governor William Tryon, in 1771, contended that the ports of North Carolina had been open ever since the repeal of the Stamp Act.[6]

After a quietus in imperial–colonial relations, events in 1773 seemed to lead inexorably toward revolution. The Boston Tea Party and the British retaliation in the form of the Intolerable Acts evoked sympathy among North Carolinians, including those of the Lower Cape Fear. Wilmingtonians in July 1774 called for an extralegal provincial congress to meet in New Bern in August to elect delegates to a Continental Congress in Philadelphia. That gathering was the first of five provincial congresses in North Carolina that in turn supported the actions of the Continental Congresses, produced a call for independence, and drafted a constitution for the state of North Carolina.

The first Continental Congress, meeting in Philadelphia in September 1774, adopted the Continental Association, a nonimporation–nonexportation agreement. According to its terms, beginning December 1 imports from the British Isles as well as certain designated items from other places would be prohibited, and if colonial grievances had not been satisfied by September 10, 1775, a ban would be imposed on all exports to the British Isles and the West Indies. Coincidentally local safety committees appeared to enforce the trade sanctions against Britain as well as to pave the way for the colonial separation from the British empire.

Parliament responded to the colonial challenge early in 1775 by passing the Restraining (or Fisheries) Acts, which severely curtailed provincial trade and fishing privileges. Exempted from the statutes were New York and North Carolina, presumably to avoid antagonizing the substantial numbers of loyalists within those provinces. The Wilmington–New Hanover safety committee angrily denounced the exemption and retaliated by prohibiting all exports from Wilmington and New Hanover that might benefit the British army and navy in northern ports, Newfoundland, and elsewhere.[7]

The safety committee enforced the Continental Association proposed by Congress. Goods imported after December 1, 1774, the effective date of the agreement, were sold at public auction or reshipped. In late December the committee offered a cargo imported from Glasgow by John Slingsby & Co. for public sale. Shortly thereafter the committee instructed Harold Blackmore and Arthur Mabson to reship several recently imported slaves. The committee also brought pressure upon local merchants who refused to abide by the association, declaring such individuals to be "unworthy of the rights of freemen & Inimical to the Liberties of their country," and recommended the proscription of all social and economic relations with them.[8]

Nonexportation followed nonimportation in 1775 as relations with England deteriorated. The committee allowed all vessels loaded or cleared by customs officials by September 10 to sail, but none thereafter could carry a cargo to the British Isles or the West Indies without express permission. Shipping was closely monitored. In November 1775 the committee warned a Captain Batchelor that if he persevered in loading his vessel, he would be treated as an "Enemy of American Liberty." In January 1776 captains Batchelor and Butterfield were allowed to clear port "in Ballast only."[9]

The local safety committee not only enforced the Continental Association but also undertook to regulate prices on behalf of the commonweal. It called for a meeting of merchants to establish charges "to prevent as far as possible any advantage from being taken of the present situation." In the interim the committee itself priced salt and dry goods. The committee allowed William Wilkinson to raise the price of rum made in his Wilmington distillery because his imported molasses cost more and his exported product brought less. But when Jonathan Dunbibin sold salt at a higher price than that set by the committee, he was forced to apologize and promise to return the difference to the buyer. The guiding principle in the committee's determination was that merchants ought not make a greater profit on the sale of any item than they had previously realized during more tranquil times.[10]

River pilots became a primary concern of the safety committee once the threat of armed British intervention arose. The pilots were indispensable to any naval operations on the Cape Fear River. Accordingly the safety committee directed Colonel James Moore of the local militia to take all the river pilots into his custody. Subsequently the committee supervised the activities of the sequestered pilots by dictating the terms of their employment and their places of residence.[11]

In its most rebellious and destructive act to date, the Wilmington–New Hanover committee in July 1775 agreed to destroy Fort Johnston. It was rumored that the fort, under the command of Captain John Collet, was scheduled to receive reinforcements, and might become a rallying point for loyalists and even slaves that Collet might incite to revolt. Collet, with a garrison of only three or four men, removed the small arms, ammunition, and part of the artillery to a British ship in the river. He rendered the remaining artillery useless and evacuated the fort. The colonials from New Hanover and Brunswick proceeded to burn the installation and Collet's nearby residence. The rather hasty action prevented not only the British but later the Americans from using the fortification.[12]

At the onset of the war with England privateering appealed to North Carolinians. As early as February 1776 a privateer was being fitted out in Wilmington, but merchants in New Bern and Edenton seemed to be more active in the attempted spoliation of British shipping. Still, numerous prizes were brought to the Cape Fear, including in 1780 two armed brigs, one from St. Kitts, the other from Greenock, worth £10,800 sterling and reportedly the most valuable cargo ever brought to the state. And in February 1783 a large Jamaican vessel loaded with rum and sugar was brought as a prize to the Lower Cape Fear.[13]

Although the theater of war centered in the northern states, British naval vessels and privateers periodically brought commerce to a standstill in the Lower Cape Fear. After the marauding expedition of Sir Henry Clinton and Lord Charles Cornwallis to the area in May 1776, warships remained to watch the river. In May 1777 two British men-of-war crossed the bar to destroy a number of vessels at anchor in the river. Privateers also sailed the coast, practically stifling trade during the summer of 1779. The interdiction of commerce led to skyrocketing prices in Wilmington, if goods could be had at all.[14]

North Carolina naval operations little deterred the enemy. Early in the conflict the General Assembly voted to purchase and arm three brigs, probably converted merchantmen, whose operations were to be supervised by local boards of commissioners. The inability of that force to defend against the British or protect American trade eventually convinced the legislators either to send the brigs on trading and privateering ventures or to sell the craft. The three brigs included the *General Washington*, purchased at Port Brunswick in January 1776 and destined for service on the Cape Fear River. The *General Washington* apparently never fulfilled its mission. In December 1777 the state legislature approved the sale of the vessel, and in February 1778 the *General Washington* was scheduled to be auctioned in Wilmington.[15]

When the British shifted their attention from the northern and mid-Atlantic states to the South in 1778–79, Wilmington assumed strategic importance. After the subjugation of Georgia and the capture of Charleston, Lord Cornwallis, commander of the British troops, attempted to gain control of the South Carolina hinterland. When success eluded Cornwallis in South Carolina, he prepared to invade North Carolina. Hoping to use Wilmington as a supply base, Cornwallis ordered Lieutenant Colonel Nisbet Balfour at Charleston to send a force to Wilmington to occupy the port. Accordingly, a British squadron including three warships, three galleys, and an artillery transport sailed for Wilmington, reaching the Cape Fear on January 25, 1781, and anchoring in the river about nine miles south of Wilmington. At that point Major James H. Craig of the 82nd Regiment of Foot, commanding four to five hundred troops, marched overland while the naval squadron continued upriver. Craig took the town in the face of token Whig opposition. Wilmington remained occupied for almost a year. During this time Cornwallis brought his army of two thousand to the town for a respite in April before striking out for Virginia. The defeat of Cornwallis in Virginia in October prompted the evacuation of Wilmington. Craig and his men boarded transports and sailed away on November 14, 1781.[16]

Among the casualties of the Revolution was Brunswick Town. Deserted in 1776 after the British invaded the Lower Cape Fear, it never recovered. North Carolina's Fifth Provincial Congress in 1776 ordered the collector of Port Brunswick to keep his office in Wilmington, which became the unofficial port of entry for the shipping district. In 1783 a visitor described Brunswick Town as "completely ruined and demolished." Eight years later a few pilots had made their homes there, for it was convenient to New Inlet. However, at the end of the War of 1812 there were only two or three buildings left, one of which was a tavern. Subsequently the former town faded into memory, leaving only a few ruins as a reminder of its more prosperous days.[17]

Supplanting Brunswick Town on the lower reaches of the river was Smithville (later Southport), named for wealthy landowner and politician Benjamin Smith but instigated and promoted by Wilmingtonian Joshua Potts. The site contained a few houses of pilots who served the main bar. Smithville, incorporated in 1792 and designated the seat of Brunswick County in 1808, became a summer resort for Wilmingtonians as well as a small port. From a community of pilots Smithville grew slowly. In 1816 it boasted a permanent population of three hundred, supplemented by another two or three hundred during the summer and fall. Contact with Wilmington, mostly by water, was irregular in the early days. The sloop *Friendship* in 1804 and the schooner *Rising Sun* in 1806 briefly offered biweekly passenger and freight runs, but such services were shortlived.[18]

Fayetteville, incorporated in 1783, continued to grow, though much of North Carolina's backcountry trade still remained directed toward Virginia and South Carolina. Although Fayetteville in 1788 narrowly missed the opportunity to become the permanent capital of the state, the town contained 281 families in 1790 and 1,656 residents in 1800, making it the third most populous town in North Carolina. New roads and bridges in the vicinity improved land communications. A private company was formed to make Cross Creek navigable from the Cape Fear River to the upper part of the town. Many Wilmington merchants maintained branches in Fayetteville, and independent operators increasingly appeared. Still, backcountry communication to Fayetteville remained poor and river traffic was unreliable.[19]

Wilmington emerged from the Revolutionary War prepared to resume its position as a port of commanding consequence for North Carolina. Townspeople anticipated a renewal of trade with England. Backcountry contacts, including those with the Moravians, started to revive, and some former neutral or loyalist merchants such as John Burgwin began to return. Despite the setback of devastating fires in 1786 and 1798, Wilmington rebuilt quickly. By 1800 the port's population of 1,689 placed it just ahead of Fayetteville but distantly behind the state's most populous town, New Bern, which counted 2,469 inhabitants.[20]

During the 1780s Wilmington generally exhibited the prevalent urban, commercial antipathy toward the Articles of Confederation, the constitution adopted by the thirteen states in 1781 to create a new nation. The Articles of Confederation seemed unable to protect property at home or American honor abroad. It provided for a loose alliance of independent states which were free to determine tariff policy, emit currency, and pass stay laws. The fragmentation of the nation and uncertainty of the future militated against effective government and retarded economic development. Led by merchants and lawyers, Wilmington favored the more powerful central government proposed by the Philadelphia Convention in 1787 in the form of the Federal Constitution.

Most North Carolinians were far from enthusiastic in their support for a change in their national government. Although the state was represented in Philadelphia, its delegates were hardly typical of the great mass of relatively poor farmers who dominated North Carolina and were jealous of state rights, concerned about encroachments upon personal liberties, and suspicious of a distant, powerful, central authority. With its mercantile orientation Wilmington staunchly supported the new Constitution, which promised to stimulate commerce and protect contract rights, only to find that the Hillsborough Convention of 1788 failed to approve the document.[21] But the following year, to the elation of the town, a second convention in Fayetteville voted to ratify the Constitution. North Carolina joined the Union late in 1789.

Although the economic changes of the Revolution seemed relatively minor compared to independence and the formation of republican governments in the United States, the economic consequences of independence bordered on the disastrous. Per capita gross national product declined significantly, perhaps not reaching prewar levels until the 1790s or early 1800s. For North Carolina the wartime economic dislocations were reflected in severe inflation, the loss of the British West Indies market (at least directly and legally), and recession years during the mid-1780s. Exports declined along with per capita income. However, Frederick William Marshall overstated the case when he wrote, "The land itself, the people of property, commerce, public and private credit, the currency in circulation, all are laid waste and ruined." Actually economic recovery in the state, particularly in the commercial sector, was fairly rapid, and the 1780s should not be described as "critical," at least for North Carolina.[22]

In the late 1780s North Carolina's volume of shipping surpassed that of the late colonial period. Trade was sluggish in 1783, but during the following summer alone some 64 vessels, mostly British, were seen on the Cape Fear. During 1788–89 more vessels than ever before reached the Cape Fear, and the trade of the entire state had never been greater. The British still played a significant role in the Cape Fear commerce. Of the 218 vessels that cleared Port Brunswick in 1788, 60, or 28 percent, were British. Two Swedish and one Danish craft rounded out the foreign-owned ships.[23]

The prominence of the British vessels indicated Wilmington's dependence upon external shipping for carriage of much of the port's produce. As the *Wilmington Gazette* lamented in 1805, Wilmington had no shipping of its own, dependent as it was upon foreign and New England bottoms for transport. In 1800 the aggregate enrolled, registered, and licensed tonnage of Wilmington was less than that of New Bern, Washington, Edenton, and Camden. Not until 1814 did Wilmington's registered tonnage surpass that of every other shipping district in North Carolina.[24]

In terms of the tonnage of shipping, the state's exports in 1788 had doubled that of 1769. Wilmington led all ports, clearing 38 percent of the export tonnage. Destinations, however, changed. Half the tonnage was bound for the West Indies; two-fifths for other American states; little more than a tenth left for Great Britain. Though more important after the war, the West Indian trade was conducted on a different basis. Since the British closed their ports to American ships, North Carolinians traded with the French, Dutch, and Danish islands. Still, British vessels carried North Carolina goods to the British West Indies.[25]

Following the Revolution the flow of exports from Port Wilmington, as it became known in 1789 when it was officially changed from Port Brunswick, found Wilmington specializing in naval stores, wood products, provisions, and tobacco, as may be seen in Table 4. Still, the loss of the British bounty on naval stores depressed that industry; exports of tar, turpentine, and pitch declined in comparison with pre-revolutionary totals. The exportation of lumber and provisions surpassed prewar levels. North Carolina flour and rice were almost exclusively products of the Wilmington shipping district. The port also accounted for more than half of North Carolina's board and scantling exports. The West Indies remained the principal market for lumber products and provisions, though an increasing proportion of those goods went to the northern states.[26]

The most striking change in the export trade in North Carolina and the Lower Cape Fear was the increase in tobacco shipments. That commerce rose from 360,000 pounds in 1768 to 6,000,000 pounds in 1790. Before the Revolution tobacco was exported principally from Port Roanoke. After the war three-fifths of the state's tobacco shipped via water passed through Port (Brunswick) Wilmington, as the cultivation of tobacco had spread into the

Table 4
Exports, Port Brunswick, 1788

Product	Amount
Lumber	2,902,606 ft.
Shingles	4,934,670
Staves	560,257
Tobacco	1,406 hhds.
Tar	26,587 bbls.
Pitch	356 bbls.
Turpentine	6,540 bbls.
Pork	99 bbls.
Rice	522 tierces
Hides	783
Deer skins	13,477

State Gazette of North Carolina (Edenton), May 14, 1789.

central and southern regions of North Carolina. Fayetteville proved to be a major transshipment point from the interior of the state to the coast.[27]

The origin of imported goods also changed after the Revolution. The importance of Great Britain declined; that of the West Indies rose significantly. Although the percentage of total import tonnage arriving from the American states remained about the same as before the war, New England's prominence declined whereas trade with New York, Philadelphia, Baltimore, and Charleston expanded. The nature and variety of imports, however, changed little from the colonial era.

Shipping through Port Wilmington continued to increase between 1789 and the War of 1812. During that time Wilmington's import trade was conducted with the northern towns, mainly Boston, New York, and Philadelphia, and with Charleston, South Carolina. Exports left mainly for the West Indies (Martinique, St. Croix, Jamaica, Trinidad, Tobago, St. Thomas, St. Mary's, Barbados, Antigua, Cuba). Overseas traffic was unusual, though Liverpool, Cork, Cadiz, Cape François, Havre de Grace, Falmouth, Hull, and Greenock were mentioned in the shipping clearances.[28]

The following list of exports and imports, compiled from the *Wilmington Gazette* of December 15, 1807, shows that with few exceptions the products involved in the port's commerce changed little from the colonial and immediate postrevolutionary eras. Naval stores, lumber products, foodstuffs, and "cotton, upland," dominated exports. Bar iron from England (via the West Indies in many cases), coffee, molasses, rum, salt, and sugar comprised the bulk of the imports.

Exports		Imports
Bacon, assorted	Shingles, cypress, 22-inch	Coffee
Bacon hams	Staves, white oak rough	Bar iron
Butter	Staves, white oak dressed	Molasses
Beeswax	Red Oak hhd.	Rum, Jamaica, 4th proof
Corn	Red Oak dressed	Rum, Windward, 3d proof
Meal	Heading, white oak rough	Rum, American, 1st proof
Cotton, upland	Heading, white oak dressed	Salt, Turks-Isle
Flour	Lard	Salt, Liverpool
Flaxseed	Tar	Sugar, Muscovado
Lumber, pine	Turpentine	
Boards and scantling	Pork	
Timber	Peas	
	Rice	
	Tobacco	
	Tallow	

Regular packet runs from Wilmington were rare before the War of 1812. Usually exporters waited for advertisements for vessels preparing to sail or seeking a charter. Alexander Hattridge in 1812 offered his "remarkably fast sailing brig *Vigilant*," capable of carrying 900 barrels, to any port in the United States. Overseas sailings and returns were mainly to Liverpool, though C. & P. Pelham in 1803 were willing to send their 158-ton brig *Hope* to any port in Europe or the West Indies. Thomas Beatty, in need of transportation, may have sought the Pelhams' services; in 1803 he sought to charter two vessels, one for Europe and one for the West Indies.[29]

In order to implement commercial legislation and promote the shipping industry North Carolina retained essentially the same machinery that had been used in the colonial era. The Fifth Provincial Congress, which met in Halifax in December 1776, appointed "collectors," or naval officers, to enter and clear vessels at the ports of entry. Naval officers subsequently were named by joint ballot of the two houses of the state legislature and commissioned by the governor. Commissioners of navigation and pilotage for the various ports were appointed by law. The county courts continued to select inspectors of commodities. The General Assembly retained the five colonial ports of entry, though substituting Port Wilmington for Port

Brunswick in 1789 and designating Wilmington as the seat of the port. The legislature added a sixth port, Swansborough, in 1786. Special mercantile courts in the larger ports, including Wilmington, assumed former British admiralty jurisdiction.[30]

Pilotage for the Cape Fear River was briefly neglected upon the realization of independence, but in 1777 the General Assembly rectified that oversight by reestablishing a system similar to that of the colonial era. The legislation prescribed a schedule of pilotage fees, appointed six self-perpetuating commissioners of navigation and pilotage, and permitted the commissioners to license pilots. The pilots were bonded for proper performance. Ship captains were required to notify the commissioners of smallpox or other contagious diseases on their vessels in order that quarantine proceedings might be followed. The next year the legislature raised pilotage fees "to encourage such good men as are capable and willing to act as pilots" and to compensate those who risked such wartime dangers as capture by the enemy.[31]

At the end of the war, in 1783, the General Assembly again addressed the pilotage system because the "imposition, extortion, insufficiency and negligence" of the pilots had "greatly injured" the state's commerce. Legislation denominated new commissioners of navigation and pilotage for the Cape Fear who appointed pilots in the name of the governor (technically the governor made the appointments but actually he provided the commissioners with blank forms): four for the main bar, two for New Inlet, and four for the run from Brunswick to Wilmington. The legislature subsequently vacillated between a policy of assigning pilots to a specific bar—the main bar or New Inlet—or opening both bars to any pilot. Eventually it opted for the latter arrangement.[32]

Although the General Assembly in 1784 declared a harbor master essential for Wilmington, for reasons unknown it did not appoint one until 1789. In the meantime the legislature directed the commissioners of navigation and pilotage to assume the duties of harbor master. The inconveniences arising from the absence of a harbor master prompted the legislature in 1789 to appoint Robert Scott to that position. The commissioners of navigation and pilotage determined his fees and defined his duties. Legislation in 1802 made the commissioners thereafter responsible for appointing a harbor master for Wilmington.[33]

The prerevolutionary concern for improving transportation became manifest soon after the war. Individuals as well as the state acted on the premise that "navigation is the life and main spring of commerce." In 1788 Amaziah Jocelin of Wilmington, supported by residents of Wilmington,

Fayetteville, and Bladen County, offered to lead an effort to deepen the channel of the Cape Fear at the Flats. He sought private subscriptions for the project while promising to investigate machines used in the northern states to clear river channels.[34]

While Jocelyn's project foundered, the General Assembly sanctioned internal improvement projects, also initiated and underwritten privately, to facilitate trade. Legislation in 1805 incorporated the Long Creek Company to build a canal from Lockwoods Folly to Elizabeth River in Brunswick County; another statute in 1815 incorporated the Cape-Fear Canal Company to cut a canal from the sound to the Cape Fear River at Brunswick Town. Laws in 1812 tried to render navigable various portions of Long Creek in New Hanover County and Town Creek in Brunswick County.[35]

Wilmington also expected to benefit commercially from efforts to improve transportation on the Northwest Cape Fear. The General Assembly in 1792 created the Cape-Fear Company to "render safe and easy" the navigability of the Cape Fear River from Fayetteville to the junction of the Deep and Haw rivers, a distance of some ninety-eight miles. The lawmakers noted that the confluence of those rivers lay in close proximity to the permanent capital of the state, the state university, Hillsborough, and Pittsboro, an altogether promising location for trade to the interior of the state.[36]

Legislation in 1796 apparently superseded the previous statute by incorporating the Deep and Haw River Company to improve navigation from Averasboro on the Cape Fear in Harnett County to the confluence of the Deep and Haw rivers and up those rivers as far as possible by means of canals, locks, and sluices. The company was permitted to charge tolls, the rates of which were prescribed by the law, to offset the expense of cutting canals, erecting locks, and building dams. However, few positive results materialized before the War of 1812, and legislation in 1815 permitted the company to merge with the Cape-Fear Navigation Company.

The General Assembly had chartered the Cape-Fear Navigation Company in 1811 to open and improve the navigation of the Cape Fear River from the mouth of Cross Creek to Fayetteville to Wilmington. Incorporators named in the law represented Cumberland, Bladen, Brunswick, and New Hanover counties, and were allowed to raise money by lottery to finance their operations. After the company expended its funds, the courts of the counties bordering the river between Fayetteville and Wilmington were instructed to appoint overseers and workers to remove obstructions in the river.[38]

To facilitate shipping at the bar and on the lower Cape Fear River the General Assembly in 1784 imposed a tonnage fee, the proceeds of which were used by the commissioners of navigation and pilotage of the Cape Fear to erect beacons and buoys at the mouth of the Cape Fear to mark the channel of the river, and to build a lighthouse "at the extreme point of Bald-head or some other convenient place near the bar of the said river, in order that vessels may be enabled thereby to avoid the great shoal called Frying-Pan." Five years later legislation added four men to the board of commissioners, including Benjamin Smith, who owned Bald Head Island. Perhaps the addition of Smith recognized his gift of ten acres of land on the island for the erection of a lighthouse. In any event, the lighthouse was apparently under construction at the time of the legislative enactment.[39]

In various other ways the state government attempted to foster commerce. To assist import merchants legislation in 1802 directed the commissioners of navigation and pilotage to appoint three individuals to serve as port wardens. The port wardens were required upon request to inspect all damaged cargoes coming by sea to determine the extent, probable cause, and monetary value of the damage. If required, the port wardens also determined the seaworthiness of outward bound vessels. For merchants and others interested in the seagoing trade of Wilmington, a particularly helpful publication appeared in 1800, *The Cape-Fear Pilot, or Commerce & Navigation of Wilmington, North-Carolina*, which contained tide tables, pilotage, wharfage, storage, and lighterage fees, a description of the lighthouse, pilotage regulations, and names of the pilots.[40]

North Carolina, however, tardily embraced commercial banking, a stimulant to shipping and more generally to business. Legislation in 1804 chartered the Bank of New Bern and the Bank of the Cape Fear, the latter located in Wilmington but designed to serve both the port and Fayetteville. In legislative debates over the issue one member of the General Assembly contended that banks would help the state's "insignificant ports." Another lawmaker responded that sandbars accounted for the ports' plight and that banks could not erase nature's impediments to trade. Supplementing the first banks was the State Bank of North Carolina, chartered in 1810. The General Assembly established a central bank in Raleigh, the state capital, and branches in Wilmington and Fayetteville, among other towns.[41]

Wilmington, like all port towns, particularly feared the transmission of disease by ships sailing from infected areas. State officials reacted quickly to threatening contagions. Upon hearing of a "pestilential fever" in Philadelphia, Governor Richard Dobbs Spaight in September 1793 issued a gubernatorial proclamation directing the commissioners of navigation and pilotage of all ports and the commissioners of all port towns to provide strict quarantine measures for incoming vessels. Two years later the General Assembly created the position of health officer at the Port of Wilmington.[42]

Despite all precautions epidemic disease arrived. Yellow fever visited Wilmington in the mid-1790s, brought probably from the West Indies. Shortly thereafter a schooner from Dominica appeared in port with smallpox. Early in the nineteenth century the commissioners of navigation and pilotage openly warned the public of the dangers of smallpox, admitted that all vigilance could not protect the citizenry in the course of trade with other ports, and in a very farsighted proposal urged the residents of Wilmington to undergo kine-pox inoculation, the recent discovery of Edward Jenner.[43]

The North Carolina legislature in 1789 belatedly addressed the problem of ill and incapacitated sailors left in port upon the departure of their ships. Earlier the General Assembly had established a poor-relief fund to be administered by the individual counties. But parish taxes were insufficient, and the wardens of the poor in the respective counties were unable to cope with the additional burden of needy sailors. Thus the lawmakers required the captains and crew members of incoming ships to pay a fee to the port collector as "hospital money" for the benefit of ill sailors. Exempted from the imposition was anyone who had paid hospital money to the United States government within the previous month and masters and seamen residing in North Carolina who paid taxes to the state.[44]

Nonetheless, the wardens of the poor for New Hanover County continued to experience difficulty in dealing with dependent seamen, due largely to their inability to collect hospital moneys. Foreign sailors, discharged in Wilmington because of sickness or disability, became increasingly troublesome. Thus, contingent upon congressional approval, the General Assembly in 1804 compelled masters of foreign vessels to enter into bond for the proper support of all seamen left in the port of Wilmington. Two years later the legislature incorporated the New Hanover County wardens of the poor, in effect strengthening the authority of that body, and continued their responsibility for caring for sick and disabled seamen as well as for other indigents.[45]

The seafaring population continued to mount, much to the consternation of some Wilmingtonians, who complained to their town commissioners of assaults and property damage by disorderly sailors. Sailors' brawls punctuated Wilmington's waterfront life. In March 1789 a seaman from the brig *George* whose captain refused to pay his wages gathered some friends and hauled the ship's longboat into the streets of Wilmington. When the captain appealed to the town authorities for help, a general melee followed. After the boat had been returned through the efforts of the local magistrates and shipmasters in port, several sailors were imprisoned. Some of their comrades then threatened to set Wilmington on fire, which necessitated calling out a detachment of militia to protect the town. In this case the original issue of nonpayment of wages was obscured by the subsequent events; more commonly sailors brought suit in court to obtain moneys withheld from them.[46]

Once North Carolina joined the Union in 1789, the state shared control over commerce and shipping facilities with the federal government. Since Congress had approved a statute that invested the federal government with responsibility for lighthouses, beacons, buoys, and public piers throughout the country, the Bald Head lighthouse project fell within the purview of Alexander Hamilton's Treasury Department. State legislation in 1790 transferred the site and partially completed lighthouse to the national authority, but not until 1792 did Congress appropriate money to finish the project. Work proceeded slowly until George Hooper of Wilmington, merchant and one of the commissoners of navigation and pilotage, was appointed by President George Washington to expedite the construction. Despite delays caused by storms, on December 23, 1794, the lighthouse became operative.[47]

The imposition of a tariff by Congress, the principal source of income for the country until World War I, necessitated the appointment of collectors for the five federal customs districts of the state—Wilmington, New Bern, Washington, Edenton, and Camden. Wilmington immediately proved to be North Carolina's most remunerative port. Through 1791 almost $50,000 in duties and $10,000 in tonnage taxes were collected. New Bern and Edenton followed distantly with less than half those amounts. The figures for Washington were $7,573 and $1,100 respectively. Camden's receipts were much smaller.[48]

In recognition of Wilmington's trade as well as its ready exposure to invasion, by late 1792 Wilmington enjoyed the protection of the federal revenue cutter *Diligence*. Built in Washington, North Carolina, and first stationed in New Bern, the vessel was later transferred to Wilmington. The *Diligence* was one of ten such vessels envisioned by Secretary of the Treasury Hamilton to guard American trade and enforce commercial legislation passed by Congress. In effect, those revenue cutters constituted an incipient Coast Guard.[49]

Succeeding cutters served Wilmington and the Lower Cape Fear from their base at Fort Johnston. *Diligence II*, though apparently designed originally for ocean duty, was found too small. Thus it was stationed in the Cape Fear in April 1799 to replace the first *Diligence*, which had been auctioned to John Schuter, a Wilmington contractor and sailing master, in 1798. *Diligence II* was sold in 1802 for over $5,000, and replaced by *Diligence III*, which was lost in an 1806 hurricane. In turn *Diligence IV* appeared in 1807. The cutters not only fulfilled official government responsibilities but also participated in such civic functions as the observance of Washington's death in 1799 and the annual commemoration of the Fourth of July.[50]

United States shipping had barely recovered from the Revolution when European conflict in the 1790s again wrought havoc with commerce. As tensions mounted, President Washington attempted to preserve American neutrality by issuing a proclamation to that effect in April 1793. However, among the Jeffersonian Republicans throughout the country and in North Carolina there was widespread sympathy for France, which earlier had helped the United States win its freedom from England and which currently was undergoing an internal struggle to establish a republican government. Despite Anglophobic feelings he had fervently expressed while a delegate to the Continental Congress in the 1780s, Governor Richard Dobbs Spaight dutifully tried to enforce Washington's proclamation, but Francophilism produced violations of neutrality in Wilmington.[51]

While in Charleston, South Carolina, in the spring of 1793, the schooner *Hector* of Wilmington was turned over to the French and outfitted as a privateer, the *Bastille*, under the command of François Henri Hervieux. Secretary of War Henry Knox promptly wrote Spaight that the commissioning, equipping, and manning of privateers in American ports was intolerable, and instructed the governor to use the state's militia to prevent such actions in the future. To Spaight's dismay the *Bastille* sailed to the West Indies, captured an English sloop, the *Providence*, and brought the prize to Wilmington. Hervieux dismantled the *Bastille* and converted the more seaworthy *Providence* into a privateer renamed the *L'Aimee Marguerite*. He left Wilmington to capture a Spanish brig, the *St. Joseph*, which was brought to port in October. Upon the rumor that the privateer and its prize were to be seized, the pro-French Wilmingtonians rushed the *St. Joseph* from port so hurriedly that the prize left one of its anchors. The *L'Aimee Marguerite* anchored at the mouth of the Cape Fear river, beyond the reach of local authorities.

When Spaight called upon the New Hanover County militia to seize the French privateer, he received no cooperation from Colonel John Bloodworth, who resigned in the midst of the imbroglio, or from the militia rank and file. Enforcement of the governor's directive in the county devolved upon Major Thomas Wright (later elevated to colonel), who found only four men willing to accompany him to apprehend the *L'Aimee Marguerite*. The revenue cutter *Diligence* proved useless, being unarmed and its crew having been dismissed because they were "sick."

In his annual message to the General Assembly in December 1793, Spaight castigated the New Hanover County militia with the exception of Wright and professed himself "extremely hurt" by its conduct. The legislature responded by endorsing the neutrality proclamation and the governor's handling of the affair, but reminded Spaight that the people of the United States were "allied to the French by treaty and the still more sacred ties of principle and gratitude." The lawmakers hoped that American obligations to France would be "liberally construed." But by mid-1794 the privateer *L'Aimee Marguerite* was finally detained by Colonel Wright on the order of President Washington. The ship eventually was returned to its English owners.

The European war impressed the state and national governments with the defenseless condition of North Carolina's coast. As Governor Spaight told the state legislature, "The most trifling privateer might interrupt our commerce and insult our harbours." Although Spaight informed President Washington that a battery of four guns was needed near Brunswick Town to protect the river, federal legislation in 1794 called for the construction of an earthen battery on the site of the original Fort Johnston, to be manned by a small garrison. The North Carolina legislature ceded the necessary land to the federal government. A company of artillery briefly sojourned in Smithville but left in July 1795. The first of a regular series of garrisons did not arrive until 1801.[52]

While renewed European conflict, instigated by Napoleon in 1803, threatened American commerce on the high seas, the *Chesapeake* Affair in 1807 brought the war closer to home. The British attack on the American naval frigate, resulting in the deaths of four sailors and the impressment of four more, elicited an angry response. Wilmingtonians gathered in a town meeting to denounce the British action. They decided to interdict all trade with British warships and to request the commissioners of navigation and pilotage to refuse pilotage service to British warships and privateers. A committee was appointed to implement the proposals and to correspond with the governor of the state and President Thomas Jefferson on the subject of properly defending the port. Meanwhile, Wilmingtonians, expecting the worst, collected cannon for the defense of the town and with the assistance of a Philadelphia schooner conveyed the cannon to a site selected for a battery.[53]

For its part the Jeffersonian administration responded to the British attack in 1807 by imposing an embargo on all American trade but coastal shipping. It was hoped that a cessation of what was deemed a critical American commerce would force the British and the French to recognize United States neutral rights, which suffered at the hands of both belligerents. Not all abided by the embargo. The schooner *Hiram*, owned by Thomas Snead, left Wilmington reportedly bound for the West Indies with a cargo of rice and flour. Snead disclaimed any knowledge of the voyage and any responsibility for the captain's behavior. The identity of the "unprincipled wretch" who chartered the schooner remained undisclosed. Wilmingtonians happily noted the relaxation and modification of the embargo in 1809.[54]

When neither verbal protests nor trade restrictions produced a satisfactory recognition of American neutral rights, war ensued with the British. The War of 1812 found the country woefully unprepared for a military struggle, financially impoverished, and internally divided over the need for war. Opposition to the conflict, centered in New England, perhaps found its most fervent support outside that region in North Carolina. Beyond its ports, particularly Wilmington, agrarian North Carolina had little to gain economically from the war. Especially annoying was the unwillingness or inability of the federal government to protect the state's coast. Above all, much of North Carolina's "loyal opposition" simply felt that the administration of President James Madison did not have sufficient justification for involving the country in a war.

Practically speaking, the defense of the coast was an immediate concern. The *Chesapeake* crisis had found federal gunboat Number 7, commanded by Sailing Master Thomas N. Gautier, protecting Wilmington. Pleas from the citizenry secured the authorization to construct three additional gunboats at Wilmington, denominated 166, 167, and 168. Just prior to the advent of the War of 1812 gunboat Number 168 was reassigned to the federal flotilla at St. Marys, Florida. Gautier resented the loss, for he felt that Wilmington needed five gunboats and a heavy brig for proper protection. Otherwise an enemy might skirt Fort Johnston by using New Inlet, as had been done during the Revolution, and menace the river. Eventually Gautier received three more vessels and was given command of

Wilmington, Beaufort, and Ocracoke. However, orders in 1813 retired the gunboats and discharged their crews, actions to which Gautier reacted bitterly. But after the defeat of Napoleon the United States government expected a large-scale British attack and placed Gautier in command of a flotilla to protect Wilmington. The effort proved unnecessary, and fortunately so in light of Wilmington's meager defenses.[55]

At the onset of the War of 1812 Wilmingtonians appeared to support the military effort. Yet at a muster to seek volunteers or, if necessary, draftees to meet President Madison's call for seven thousand militia from North Carolina, no more than half the necessary number of men appeared, and those were without order or discipline. Wilmington merchants proved selfishly unpatriotic in taking advantage of military construction contracts to realize such great profits that they erected brick houses in town and drank the "best of wines." And during a crisis in 1813 one resident wrote that Wilmingtonians prepared "not to fight, but for flight, [for] safe creeks and swamps are diligently inquired after."[56]

Diverting attention from the local situation were occasional reports of a British presence along the coast. The British landing on the North Carolina coast at Ocracoke in July 1813 produced general alarm. Mildly threatening in June 1814 were two British ships and a brig that stood off the main bar of the Cape Fear River for several days. Three pilots were captured but released. The following month the *Peacock* approached Federal Point but espied militia that had been mobilized and quickly departed. Not so fortunate were the sailors sent ashore south of Wilmington by the *Lacedemonian* to seek cattle. Leaving their barge laxly guarded, the entire British party was captured by local militia.[57]

Fortunately the British never seriously threatened the Lower Cape Fear. Fort Johnston was woefully inadequate, "a mere apology" of a defense works. The battery was so near the water that high tides damaged it. The guns were so flimsy as to be virtually useless. Thirty feet behind the fort was a bluff of oyster shells that would scatter like schrapnel if hit. And homes of Smithville residents were too close to the fort, endangering citizens in case of attack. Moreover, light-draft vessels could come through New Inlet and bypass the fort altogether. Many agreed with Joshua Potts, longtime resident of Wilmington and the Lower Cape Fear, that Fort Johnston ought to be abandoned for new forts built at Oak Island and Federal Point which would more adequately guard the entrances to the river.[58]

Privateering was far more important than naval operations in the waters off North Carolina. It was also an immensely profitable undertaking. North Carolina ports outfitted four privateers: one each from Wilmington and Washington, and two from New Bern. Wilmington's *Lovely Lass* captured only one prize, a schooner carrying a cargo valued at $10,000. Subsequently the *Lovely Lass* was taken by the British vessel *Circe* off Montego Point in the West Indies in May 1813, after a nineteen-hour chase. Captain John Smith and his crew of sixteen were imprisoned at Nassau.[59]

Wilmington, however, received numerous privateers and their prizes. Three captured British ships arrived in 1812. Another five plus a tender to the British naval vessel *Admiral* appeared in 1813. During that year the privateer *Saratoga* disposed of the cargoes of four prizes and a large sum of specie in Wilmington. The peak year for prize condemnation and sale in Wilmington was 1814, during which fifteen prizes and the cargoes of several more came into town, where the goods and sometimes the vessels were sold at auction.[60]

Occasionally overzealous Americans illegally captured non-British vessels or those that claimed another country's flag. Owners resorted to the courts to regain their ships and cargoes. Several such cases originated in the Cape Fear district of the federal judicial system. One involved the *Fortuna*, captured by the *Roger* from Norfolk in April 1814 and brought to Wilmington. En route from Havana to Riga, the *Fortuna* carried 1,520 boxes of sugar. The owners claimed it to be a Russian vessel, but secret papers found on the ship indicated that the cargo was British. Appeals to the circuit court and then to the Supreme Court of the United States resulted in decisions that upheld the capture by the *Roger*.[61]

Despite the European wars of the 1790s and early 1800s North Carolina commerce expanded between the formation of the Federal Union and 1815. Registered tonnage in foreign trade increased 25 percent; domestic trade almost doubled. The value of foreign exports more than doubled. On the other hand, by comparison, the value of South Carolina's foreign export trade rose over 400 percent during that period.[62]

Since North Carolina was not a major exporter, it was not greatly affected by the British and French commercial restrictions or depredations visited upon American shipping during the Napoleonic wars. State exports averaged 1.67 percent of the national total annually from 1802 to 1812. North Carolina ranked between eighth and twelfth nationally in tonnage employed in foreign trade. The War of 1812 was a fillip for North Carolina shipping. After customs revenues at North Carolina ports remained almost unchanged between 1808 and 1812, a great increase occurred during the next three years. Apparently foreign shipping relied more heavily upon North Carolina ports due to the blockade of New England and New York ports during the War of 1812.[63]

Wilmington's preeminent position among North Carolina ports at the beginning of the nineteenth century was evident from the customs duties collected at the port, as seen in Table 5. During the four years ending March 31, 1805, revenue from Port Wilmington amounted to 42 percent of the state's total. New York, which led all ports in the collection of customs duties during that period, reported $12,862,020.

At the conclusion of the War of 1812 Wilmington had easily outdistanced rival ports in North Carolina. The port boasted superior market facilities, greater accessibility to the ocean, and better linkages to the interior. The value of Wilmington's exports was four times greater than the combined total of the other state ports. By contrast, however, the value of New York's exports was over eighteen times that of Wilmington.[64] Nonetheless, Wilmington and North Carolina looked to a roseate future following the "Second War for American Independence."

Table 5
Customs Duties Collected, North Carolina Ports, 1801–05

City	Amount	Rank in U.S.
Wilmington	$319,110.00	18
New Bern	146,429.00	23
Edenton	129,505.00	24
Washington	67,234.00	33
Plymouth	57,256.00	40
Camden	32,900.00	46
Beaufort	10,000.00	53

Logan, "An Historical Geographic Survey of North Carolina Ports," 69.

Chapter Three

ANTEBELLUM WILMINGTON:
North Carolina's Maritime Entrepôt

During the four decades preceding the Civil War, Wilmington solidified its position as North Carolina's leading port, though it achieved that distinction in the face of some adversity. In the aftermath of the War of 1812, North Carolina became known as the "Rip Van Winkle State" and the "Ireland of America." Its economy stagnated. One-party politics, dominated by the Jeffersonian Republicans with their strict construction of the Constitution, curtailed interest among the electorate and hampered economic growth. Towns were few and small in size. Educational and cultural opportunities were severely limited. As a result the more able and ambitious left the state in a migration that persisted throughout most of the antebellum era.

Though small relative to other Atlantic ports, Wilmington remained one of the larger towns in North Carolina, counting 2,633 residents in 1820. The advent of steam transportation on the Cape Fear and the consequent increase in trade swelled the population to 4,744 in 1840, enabling Wilmington to surpass New Bern as North Carolina's most populous urban area. That year the completion of the Wilmington and Raleigh (subsequently Weldon) Railroad greatly stimulated the port's growth, resulting in a doubling of its inhabitants to 9,552 by 1860.[1]

Beyond Wilmington on the Cape Fear was Fayetteville, which brokered the trade from the interior to Wilmington. Fayetteville continued to expand in conjunction with Wilmington, at least until 1840. Produce boated downriver from Fayetteville in the year ending September 30, 1816, included 2,337 hogsheads of tobacco, 8,292 bales of cotton, 11,813 bushels of wheat, 10,341 bushels of corn, 5,164 casks of flaxseed, 29,761 gallons of spirits of turpentine, 12,962 barrels of flour, and sundry tallow, wax, bacon, lard, furs, and feathers, all valued at $1,331,398.[2] Wilmington did not monopolize the upriver trade, however, vying as it did with Petersburg, Virginia, and Georgetown and Cheraw, South Carolina, as a supplier to Fayetteville.

Wilmington's growth in the antebellum era was not uniform. Periodic recessions, beginning with the panic of 1819, interrupted the advance of commerce. Wilmington hardly recovered from the panic of 1819 before slipping into another recession in 1827. Real estate values fell to their lowest since the Revolution. Yet six years later Wilmington and its environs boasted five steam sawmills, two steam rice mills, and one steam bark mill, in addition to other manufacturing operations. The impact of the panic of 1837 was countered by the completion of the Wilmington and Weldon Railroad in 1840. Still, the recessions of 1854 and 1857 arrested progress. A Wilmington paper in the latter year reported "upward of sixty vessels now lying in the port of Wilmington, owing to the difficulty of procuring Freight."[3]

Hampering Wilmington's development throughout the antebellum era were numerous conflagrations, inadequate hotel and banking facilities, and a reputation for unhealthfulness. Soon after President James Monroe's visit in 1819 fire destroyed some three hundred buildings in the town. Smaller blazes in 1827 and 1840 were followed by a major fire in 1843 that razed a goodly portion of the town, including the workshops of the Wilmington and Weldon Railroad. Yet another fire in 1845 interrupted the progress of rebuilding.[4]

A paucity of hotels and banks detracted from efforts to promote Wilmington's economy. Businessmen and visitors generally found accommodation "unworthy of the place." In the early 1850s the *Journal* editorialized about the lack of appropriate hotels; during the decade only one such establishment of consequence served the town. Banking facilities also failed to keep pace with the growth of the port. Throughout the antebellum era Wilmingtonians suffered for want of a sufficient medium of exchange to support the expansion of business and trade.[5]

The highly contagious diseases of yellow fever and smallpox occasionally threatened the town. Yellow fever appeared in 1796, 1819, and 1824; smallpox in 1816. Although a local paper declared in August 1838 that "no town in the Union has a worse reputation abroad for sickliness than Wilmington, and few deserve it so little," ironically the same issue carried a notice from the mayor and chairman of the local Board of Health warning the community of the current epidemic of "Stranger's Fever" that had taken four lives. Nonetheless, at the end of the antebellum era the mortality rate in Wilmington (among whites at least) was far lower than that in other Atlantic ports.[6]

Wilmington also contended with a mounting number of sailors arriving in port, approximately four thousand annually by mid-century, many of whom came in a diseased or debilitated condition that required medical attention. Such men were relegated to a "sailor's tavern," after which it was the duty of the collector of the port to provide a place for them. Yet according to a correspondent to the *People's Press*, such individuals were usually left "to the cold charity of the world, . . . and the probability that they will perish." Although the federal government required sailors to pay twenty cents per month for "hospital money," using the proceeds to build several marine hospitals along the east coast, Wilmington had been bypassed. Thus Wilmingtonians in the 1830s decided to construct a marine hospital. Humanitarianism was paramount, but a hospital benefited local commerce. Seamen and shipmasters alike preferred to sail to ports that provided charitable institutional assistance to the needy.[7]

By 1835 Wilmingtonians had brought the idea of a marine hospital to fruition. Legislation in that year incorporated the Wilmington Marine Hospital Association for the "relief of sick and disabled American seamen." Led by Edward B. Dudley, Robert W. Brown, Aaron Lazarus, and Platt F. Dickerson, among others, they had purchased land at Mt. Tizra, about three miles south of Wilmington, and erected suitable buildings. However, within five months after the hospital had been constructed, it apparently was being used as a "pest house" or quarantine station for those who had contracted smallpox.[8] Twenty years later the federal government erected a marine hospital at the site.

Wilmingtonians later sought to alleviate the poverty of the common sailor and to improve his uncouth character. Several prominent citizens in 1853 organized the Seamen's Friend Society of Wilmington, incorporated in the same year by the General Assembly. Designed to "improve the social, moral and religious condition of seamen," the society utilized a four-story structure on the corner of Dock and Front streets as its headquarters or "Home." Adjoining the Home was a church, or "Bethel," maintained by contributions from the American Seamen's Aid Society of New York City. The Seamen's Friend Society thus prepared to care without charge for destitute and shipwrecked sailors.[9]

An inadequate overland transportation system continued to militate against the expansion of the port. Wilmington's local trade suffered materially because farmers were unable to reach market with their produce or found high transport costs eroding profits. Roads were little improved during the nineteenth century. Particularly bothersome were the swamps or bogs, which were virtually impassable in wet weather. Causeways rapidly deteriorated. Bridges were neglected. The county magistrates, legally responsible for maintaining the roads and bridges, failed to punish road overseers for neglecting their duties. Unlike most other counties, New Hanover refused to levy a general tax whose proceeds could be used to build and repair bridges.[10]

Following the lead of Fayetteville, Wilmington briefly embraced the plank road movement in North Carolina. Failing to obtain a rail connection, Fayetteville responded eagerly to Governor Edward Graham's proposal to the state legislature in 1848 that North Carolina take advantage of plank roads to improve the state's highway system. Facilitating transportation would lower the cost of bringing goods to market, according to the governor, thus stimulating the economy as well as making travel easier. Fayetteville and Wilmington were the first and only towns in the legislative session of 1848–49 to obtain charters of incorporation for plank road companies. As the plank road craze swept the state during the next decade, Fayetteville became the hub of the movement. More plank road mileage converged upon that town than any other in the state.[11]

Although Wilmington helped to initiate the plank road movement in North Carolina, the port town did not realize the success of Fayetteville. The incorporation of the Wilmington and Masonboro Plank Road Company and the Wilmington and Walker's Ferry Plank Road Company in 1849 apparently produced few results. More successful was the Wilmington and Topsail Sound Plank Road Company, chartered in 1851. The twelve-mile road increased the flow of traffic from Onslow County and the northern part of New Hanover to Wilmington. Several overoptimistic members of the board of directors secured a charter in 1855 for an extension of the road to Snead's Ferry in Onslow County, but no record exists of the construction of the road.[12]

Jolting Wilmington from the economic doldrums following the panic of 1819 was that mode of transportation that most justified the term "transportation revolution" as applied to the antebellum era—the railroad. The General Assembly bypassed Wilmington in its abortive incorporation of railroads in the early 1830s, although the Fayetteville and Yadkin road, chartered in the 1830–31 legislative session, promised indirect benefits for the port. However, according to a correspondent to a Wilmington newspaper, the western counties refused to cooperate and Fayetteville citizens withdrew their support, a charge indignantly denied by the Cumberland town. Even in the consideration of coastal termini for possible east-west lines, Wilmington was ignored in favor of New Bern and Beaufort.[13]

Wilmingtonians, led by J. D. Jones, Edward B. Dudley, and William B. Meares, exerted their best efforts to secure support for railroad lines to the port in the state internal improvements conventions held in Raleigh in July and November 1833. The General Assembly responded in its session of 1833–34 by chartering ten railroad companies, including the Wilmington and Raleigh, capitalized at $800,000. In 1835 an amended charter for the Wilmington and Raleigh Railroad increased its capitalization, authorized construction from Wilmington to bypass Raleigh for a terminus on the Roanoke River which would connect with Virginia lines, and empowered the company to own and operate steamers.[14]

Even before its completion the railroad exerted a significant influence upon the Wilmington economy. Each section of track seemed to heighten Wilmington's status as a market. In October 1839 the first load of bacon ever shipped from Greene County to Wilmington arrived via rail. Later that month one train brought 83 passengers to town. Inland farmers announced their intention to ship their produce on a trial basis to Wilmington rather than to New Bern. The railroad met the most sanguine expectations before the last spike was driven in Edgecombe County in 1840 to finish the line.[15]

During the 1850s the Wilmington and Weldon Railroad shipped far more goods to Wilmington than to Weldon. Formerly much of that trade would have gone to Virginia. Apparently the railroad helped to achieve to some extent the long-standing desideratum of drawing North Carolina produce to state markets. The products carried by the Wilmington and Weldon fluctuated in the years before the Civil War. The railroad stimulated a trade in flour; shipments rose from 245 barrels in 1854 to over 10,000 barrels in 1860. Cotton also evinced a steady increase; shipments rose sixfold between 1854 and 1860. But the mainstay of the traffic was naval stores.

As the Wilmington and Weldon Railroad was making its impress upon Wilmington, the port city was alarmed by reports that citizens of Raleigh intended to link the state capital with the South Carolina Rail Road, thus bypassing Wilmington as a means of reaching Charleston. As the *Wilmington Journal* editorialized, it was surprising that a rail connection between Raleigh and Charleston had not already been erected, "which would render so much expence and inconvenience [from the steamers between Wilmington and Charleston] unnecessary." Quickly sentiment developed in Wilmington to construct a railroad from the port to the South Carolina Rail Road. For their part South Carolinians, meeting in Sumterville, greeted enthusiastically the Wilmington proposal to build a line to Fair Bluff (62 miles) near the South Carolina border, then to Sumterville (70 miles), and thence to Manchester on the Camden and Gadsden Railroad which was under contract.[16]

After the incorporation of the Wilmington and Manchester Railroad by the state legislature in 1847, Wilmingtonians eagerly contributed to the road's capitalization, subscribing to more than half of the $319,700 in stock that had been pledged by June of that year. Four years later, upon authorization by the General Assembly, the town of Wilmington subscribed to $100,000. At the time some Wilmingtonians also showed interest in supporting the Cheraw and Darlington Railroad in South Carolina, which might allow Wilmington to draw further on South Carolina produce.[17]

Work on the Wilmington and Manchester commenced in February 1849 in Brunswick County just west of the Brunswick River ferry. Twenty-five miles of track were in operation by 1852; sixty miles of track by 1853. The following year the line was finished, and by the Civil War the railroad had been extended over the Brunswick River to Eagles Island. A financial report for the fiscal year ending September 30, 1859, revealed a successful road which was paying dividends and reducing its bonded indebtedness. Receipts amounted to $427,000, of which 38 percent derived from freight transport, 11 percent from mail carriage, and most of the remainder from passenger traffic.[18]

As the Wilmington and Manchester neared completion. Wilmingtonians began to contemplate a rail line to tap the trade of the western counties, whose commerce naturally gravitated to South Carolina. Charlotteans took the initiative in the early 1850s. They found a ready response from a meeting of Wilmington citizenry in 1854, led by Alexander McRae, Dr. A. J. DeRosset, O. P. Meares, Henry Nutt, and R. H. Cowan, who agreed to send delegates to a Charlotte convention to push for an east-west railroad. As a result the General Assembly in its 1854–55 session incorporated the Wilmington, Charlotte and Rutherford Railroad Company to begin a road at Wilmington, Smithville, or some point on the Wilmington and Manchester, or some point on the Wilmington and Raleigh, which would run westward through Lumberton, Rockingham, Wadesboro, and Monroe.[19]

The commissioners of the railroad, led by McRae, held their first meeting in Wadesboro and agreed to seek subscriptions to underwrite construction. The town of Wilmington responded generously, buying $200,000 worth of stock in the company in 1857. Work progressed slowly. The first twenty-four miles of track from Walker's Ferry, the eastern terminus, were not finished until December 1859; laying track from the western terminus was not scheduled to begin until the spring of 1860. To alleviate the financial difficulties of the railroad, the General Assembly in its 1860–61 session agreed that the state could loan money to the company to complete its work.[20]

In conjunction with the railroad, the application of steam to water transport transformed the port of Wilmington. Although steam navigation on the Cape Fear became a reality in 1818, as early as 1812 the legislature responded favorably to the memorial of John Stevens of New Jersey, who desired a monopoly on steamer traffic in North Carolina. The following year petitions from Robert Fulton and Oliver Evans sought to invalidate Stevens's claim. John D. DeLacy, agent of Fulton, claimed in 1813 to have established several steamboat operations from Virginia to Georgia, including the Clarendon Company for the navigation of the Cape Fear River. But no record of the Clarendon Company's operation survives, and any effort on the part of DeLacy would have been illegal, for it violated Stevens's monopoly grant.[21]

After Stevens's five-year contract right lapsed, the legislature in 1818 approved James Seawell's petition for a seven-year monopoly of steam traffic between Wilmington and Fayetteville. Two steamers appeared on the Cape Fear River in 1818—the *Prometheus*, built in Swansboro by Otway Burns for Seawell, and the *Henrietta*, constructed in Fayetteville, the first of many to emerge from Fayetteville shipyards. Seawell and associates later formalized their arrangement by incorporating the Cape Fear Steam Boat Company in 1822. The Cape Fear Steam Boat Company expanded its operations in the 1820s, adding the steamer *North Carolina* and three steamboat flats in 1823 to the run of the *Henrietta*. By 1826, however, the Seawell monopoly of steamer traffic on the Cape Fear had expired.[22]

Once the river was opened competitively, the legislature in 1827 incorporated the Henrietta Steam Boat Company, based in Fayetteville but including Wilmington interests, and the Cotton Plant Steamboat Company. Both were allowed to buy land in Wilmington and Fayetteville for wharves and warehouses and to acquire one or more steamboats and towboats. During the 30s and 40s additional companies appeared: the Cape Fear and Western Steam Boat Company and the Merchants Steamboat Company of Fayetteville. The decade preceding the Civil War witnessed no decrease in shipping activity as the legislature chartered the Cape Fear and Deep River Steam Boat Company (changed to the Brothers' Steamboat Company), the Bladen Steamboat Company, the Wilmington and Smithville Steamboat Company, the Wilmington Steam Tug Company, and the Cape Fear and Ocean Steam Navigation Company.[23]

The Henrietta Company endured throughout the antebellum era; after a period of apparent desuetude in the early 1840s it was rechartered in 1847. The following year the company advertised the *Henrietta* and *Evergreen* as thoroughly repaired and ready to carry freight. Company steamers such as the *Southerner*, built in Fayetteville and drawing but twelve inches, also transported passengers. However, at mid-century Captain William T. Evans of that line had to defend himself against the charge of neglecting the traveling public when he passed by two persons waiting at Elizabethtown to be taken to Wilmington.[24]

The Henrietta Company was one of several lines linking Wilmington and Fayetteville. Seven steamers plied the river regularly between the towns in 1848. Doyle O'Hanlon, also a shipbuilder, was a prominent shipper in the 1830s and early 1840s. In 1845, after his death, his estate included the steamer *W. B. Meares* and three lighters. The *Fayetteville Observer* in 1854 listed five major steamboat operators: the Frank and Jerry Line, owned by Frank and Jerry Roberts, with steamers *Southern* and *North State*; the Cape Fear Line, with steamers *Flora McDonald* and *Chatham*; the Banks Line, with the steamer *Brothers*; the Lutterloh Line, with steamers *Fanny Lutterloh* and *Rowan*; the Express Line, with steamers *Evergreen* and *Eliza*.[25]

In his travels throughout the Atlantic and Gulf Coast states Frederick Law Olmsted left a vivid description of a steamer ride from Fayetteville to Wilmington. The vessel on which he booked passage, forty-five minutes late in its departure, was a stern-wheeler, with the boiler and (high pressure) engine placed at opposite ends in order to balance the weight. The bulk of the freight was turpentine, whose close proximity to the furnaces "suggested a danger fully equal to that from snags or grounding." "Wooding-up" along the river was a particularly interesting exercise to Olmsted. When they arrived at Amos Sikes's landing for that purpose, they found wood cut, split, and piled at the top of the bank with a chute that would convey it to the river. Everyone aboard, from master to passengers, with the exception of the engineer and chambermaid, hastily jumped out to help load the wood. On a tree near the top of the bank was nailed a box with a note asking those who took wood to leave payment at $1.75 per cord.[26]

Most of the early steamers were shallow-draft side-wheelers of approximately one hundred tons. Their flat bottoms, while reducing speed, enabled them to navigate the river except during periods of extremely low water. Stern-wheelers and iron-hulled steamers appeared in the 1850s. The steamers not only pulled towboats or lighters between Wilmington and Fayetteville but also towed vessels between Wilmington and the bar against adverse winds and currents. By the 1850s vessels such as the *Samuel Beery* were built expressly for towing as well as for salvaging.[27]

The feasibility of steam navigation on the Cape Fear spurred Wilmingtonians to boast of the advantages of their port. They contended that West Indies produce was cheaper in Wilmington than in any port on the eastern seaboard. And Wilmington could supply Fayetteville quickly and cheaply with groceries and dry goods. Goods sometimes reached Wilmington within seven days of their shipment from New York, and only two or three days were required to send the articles upriver. Prices approximated those in Wilmington with the exception, of course, of freight, which amounted to twenty cents per hundred pounds.[28]

Steamers not only stimulated the growth of Wilmington but also enhanced Fayetteville's position as an important center of upriver commerce. The vessels brought goods destined for Lexington, Pittsboro, Hillsborough, Salisbury, and New Salem as well as for merchants in Orange, Chatham, Montgomery, Davidson, and Guilford counties. As an example of river commerce, the *Henrietta* on one trip in 1824 took cargo to Fayetteville that was destined for sixteen merchants or mercantile firms. Among the cargo were dry goods, hardware, leather goods, cheese, loaf sugar, salt, and West Indian fruit, all of which was packed in boxes, trunks, hogsheads, kegs, boxes, and bundles.[29]

Steamer transport below Wilmington, while generally not as active as on the upper Cape Fear, found the *Calhoun* providing weekly passage to Smithville in 1848 and the *Spray* making four weekly trips to Smithville, stopping at Orton along the way, in 1854. The Wilmington and Weldon Railroad early supported a packet line of steamers from the port of Charleston, South Carolina. The Charleston connection not only encouraged passenger and light freight traffic but also enabled the railroad to procure a government mail contract. By 1839 the Wilmington and Weldon had a complement of four steamers on line, each of which made a weekly run to Charleston.[30]

The railroad steamers were the *North Carolina*, *Governor Dudley*, *C. Vanderbilt*, and *Wilmington*. The *North Carolina*, which appeared in December 1837, impressed Wilmingtonians by its speed—twenty-seven hours at sea for the round trip, including a two-and-a-half-hour stopover at Charleston. The *Governor Dudley* came to port in August 1838. The 487-ton vessel measured 175 by 24 feet, with a 10-foot hold, and drew 6 feet when loaded. The *Wilmington* was the last of the steamers to come on line, at a cost of $60,000. Its dimensions were similar to those of the *Governor Dudley*. The *Wilmington* offered accommodations for a hundred passengers; its 135-horsepower engine rendered the craft better able to cope with the currents and waves than its companion vessels.[31]

Unfortunately, passengers found their accommodations less than impressive on occasion. Arriving in Wilmington late one evening in the mid-1850s, Frederick Law Olmsted happened to see an advertisement of a railroad steamer for Charleston. Although the boat was scheduled to leave at ten o'clock, Olmsted felt sure that it would be late. He rushed to the docks, booked passage, and boarded the tardily leaving vessel. He found the cabin "small, dirty, crowded, close and smoky," so he located a warm spot on the deck over the furnace, "pillowed" himself on his baggage, and went to sleep. A bell awakened him at Charleston.[32]

At least Olmsted reached his destination without accident; not all passengers were so fortunate. The railroad steamers launched their runs inauspiciously. The *North Carolina* and *C. Vanderbilt* collided off Georgetown in January 1839. Both went to Charleston for repairs. The following year the *North Carolina* and *Governor Dudley* ran together in the early morning of July 26, about thirty miles northeast of Georgetown. The *North Carolina* sank, but all passengers were saved. Yet despite their early mishaps the railroad steamers had an enviable safety record. During the mid-1840s, after several years of travel without incident by the railroad steamers, the port wardens of Charleston in 1847 declared the *C. Vanderbilt* unsafe. Subsequently James Cassidey of Wilmington repaired the vessel on his marine railway, and Wilmington's port wardens pronounced the craft seaworthy and entitled to full public confidence.[33]

Rough seas certainly made the steamer passages from Charleston to Wilmington frightening at times. Often the passengers on the mail steamers expressed their appreciation to shipmasters who brought their vessels through stormy waters safely to port. Indeed, the vessels were not very powerful, and head winds considerably retarded their progress. Moreover, many passengers accustomed to large oceangoing steamers were naturally disappointed in the performance of the Wilmington and Weldon line. But the railroad operated the steamers at an economic loss and could not afford larger vessels even if the public was willing to pay higher fares.[34]

The Wilmington and Weldon steamers were discontinued upon the completion of the Wilmington and Manchester Railroad, which allowed passengers to travel by rail from Wilmington to Charleston. Subsequently regular water transport below Wilmington ceased. Captains Samuel Potter and Samuel Price sponsored several small sailing vessels on that route, but their service was unreliable. The Wilmington and Smithville Steamboat Company, incorporated in 1855, briefly operated the *Spray*, but that steamer burned at the end of its first season.[35]

Beyond the Wilmington–Charleston run other outbound steamer connections were contemplated. The 450-ton *Ontario* appeared in port in 1852, intended as a pioneer for a line of freight steamers between Wilmington and New York. The project apparently failed to materialize, for as late as 1860 some Wilmingtonians were proposing a steamship connection to New York. Actually bulky, low-value Wilmington exports, mainly naval stores, could not sustain the expense of steam transport. Moreover, federal safety legislation in 1852 virtually prohibited the carriage of spirits of turpentine on steam vessels. In the meantime the Wilmington Chamber of Commerce toyed with the idea of establishing a line to Havana, Cuba, and a resident of Onslow County suggested the possibility of a steamer line between that county and Wilmington to transport naval stores, corn, bacon, pork, chickens, eggs, and potatoes that normally took two to three weeks to reach the Wilmington market by sailing craft.[36]

Despite the appearance of the railroad and the utilization of steamboats, Wilmington remained dependent upon the vagaries of nature as reflected in the rise and fall of the Cape Fear River for the bulk of its "country goods." River traffic was sustained by small schooners, sloops, and a variety of other craft. From the tributaries of the Cape Fear above Wilmington came rafts and flats with naval stores, ton timber, choice timber for masts and spars for sailing ships, and other bulky items. Upon the advent of the railroad, cross ties were stacked and clamped to form rafts to float to Wilmington. On the steamer from Fayetteville to Wilmington, Olmsted passed many flatboats and rafts, blazing with great fires made upon a thick bed of clay and ringing with the songs of crews singing at their sweeps.[37]

Flats varied greatly in size. An advertiser in a Fayetteville newspaper sought the construction of four such craft, two measuring 48 by 10 feet and two measuring 30 by 6 feet, all to be made of heavy timber and banded together with strap iron. Alexander J. Swift, lieutenant of the Army Engineers, advertised in Wilmington for the construction of two open flats, 60 feet long, 16 feet in width, and 5 feet in depth. The larger flats carried 300 to 500 barrels of turpentine. The *J. L. Cassidey*, from Lyon's Landing on the lower Black River, arrived in Wilmington in April 1851 with 326 barrels of rosin, 64 barrels of tar, and 64 barrels of turpentine. Poled upriver, the flats could easily reach Whitehall, about 54 miles above Wilmington, which became a major center of trade. Those going beyond to Elizabethtown and Fayetteville were usually towed by steamboats.[38]

Water levels of the Cape Fear and its tributaries varied greatly, thereby affecting shipping. In Fayetteville the water in the spring was as much as eighteen feet above its lowest summer stages. However, during flooding, waters could quickly rise twenty-five feet or more, and one observer reported the difference between the extremes of low water and flooding to be as much as seventy feet. The flow of trade slackened during the summer when the river was low, perhaps only eighteen inches on the shoals, but heightened with the rising waters of the late winter and early spring.[39]

The Wilmington commercial market opened in November, was "brisk" in December, and increased in activity during the first three months of the new year. April witnessed decreasing volume, a trend that became more pronounced in May. June virtually concluded local trade, as the summer and fall seasons were "dull." The fall, moreover, was also the "sickly season," which further impeded trade. On the other hand, it was during the summer and fall that Wilmington and Fayetteville mercantile retailers stocked their stores with imports from New York and other northern cities. Wilmington merchants imported on long-term credit, making remittances in produce as it "suit[ed] their convenience."[40]

During the slow seasons commission merchants exercised special vigilance and care. According to one, John F. Burgwin, whose father had been a merchant in the Lower Cape Fear for many years, the business necessitated "sufficient Capital, ample Credit and respectable friends and correspondents." Merchants abroad seldom dispatched vessels to Wilmington without notifying their correspondents of the desired produce. Four to six weeks notice was deemed advisable in order that the agent might have the opportunity to procure a cargo at a reasonable price and have it ready by the time of the arrival of the ship. Otherwise, according to one Wilmingtonian, "great detention and disappointment often happen in consequence of voyages being abruptly commenced; as but seldom peculiar kinds of produce can be had on sudden notice."[41]

The commissioners of navigation and pilotage for the Cape Fear River continued to control local shipping in compliance with statutory mandates from the state legislature. The New Hanover county court annually selected five men to comprise the board. In its 1840–41 session the General Assembly decided to allow the Wilmington town commissioners to choose biennially five members and the citizens of Smithville to add a sixth man to the board. However, in its next session the legislature reversed its decision by reducing the board to five who were selected biennially by the New Hanover county court. Legislation in 1858 again added a sixth person to the commission of navigation and pilotage, requiring him to be a citizen of Brunswick County.[42]

The appointment of the commissioners of navigation and pilotage changed dramatically in 1847 when the state legislature politicized that body by making its members subject to popular election. The determination of board members became embedded in the party battles between the Democrats and Whigs (subsequently Know-Nothings). The Democrats early prevailed. By 1849 the Whigs successfully countered with their own slate of candidates, though the Democrats reclaimed control of the board in the early 50s as voter interest and participation heightened dramatically.[43]

Pilotage regulations changed little from the days of the early republic. The commissioners of navigation and pilotage determined the number of pilots, licensed pilots, set pilotage fees, fixed the number of decked pilot boats, established quarantine procedures, settled disputes between shipmasters and pilots, and decided where ballast might be deposited. Pilot applicants were required to present affidavits from at least three "nautical men" attesting to their ability to guide vessels and their knowledge of the river and the bars, to post bond for proper performance, and to keep at least one but not more than two apprentices.[44]

The commissioners of navigation and pilotage appointed a clerk, a harbor master for Wilmington, a port physician, three port wardens, fumigators to serve at Smithville and at Federal Point, and a shipping master. The harbor mastership was a lucrative position. In 1848 twenty-one written applications, in addition to many verbal requests, were submitted to the commissioners. Legislation in 1855 required the commissioners to appoint a shipping master whose duty was to oversee the employment of seamen in the foreign or coastal service of the port. The legislation directed the shipping master to maintain an office near the docks, where he could enroll sailors (for a fee of ten cents each) seeking jobs and assign them to captains needing hands.[45]

Also entrusted to the commissioners of navigation and pilotage was the duty to make all necessary regulations to prevent the escape of slaves in outgoing vessels. Many bondsmen stowed away. Others were befriended by captains and crews who opposed slavery and saw an opportunity to strike a blow for freedom. Wilmingtonians responded indignantly to the latter situation. Editorialized the *People's Press and Wilmington Advertiser*, "Our insulted commonwealth can find no salve in the presumption that those who are guilty are misled by unprincipled fanatics—that Garrison & Tappan, and other diabolical intriguers have perverted the understandings and excited a false sympathy in the breasts of those who come among us for commercial purposes."[46]

In addition to the efforts of the commissioners of navigation and pilotage to facilitate and promote traffic on the lower Cape Fear River, renewed attempts were made to improve the navigability of the river and its tributaries. When Archibald D. Murphey, state senator from Orange County, presented a series of reports to the legislature between 1815 and 1818 outlining an ambitious program designed to foster North Carolina's economic and social growth, he contended that the Cape Fear River "claims peculiar consideration, not so much on account of the fertility of its Lands, as of the facilities which exist of bringing to it for shipment the productions of nearly one-half of the Agricultural part of the State." He felt that the Cape Fear was navigable for steamers as far as Fayetteville and probably beyond to Haywood for small steam vessels. The rocks, shoals, and falls of the Haw and Deep rivers might be overcome to open navigation of those watercourses to Rockingham and Guilford counties respectively. Murphey even speculated on the possibility of uniting the Yadkin and Cape Fear rivers, thereby diverting produce to Wilmington that ordinarily went to Charleston.[47] In fact, the entire program was designed to break the economic dependence of North Carolina upon its neighboring states.

Anticipating Murphey was the Cape Fear Navigation Company, which was revived in 1815 and began work the following year to improve the navigability of the Cape Fear River between Wilmington and Fayetteville. However, the company maintained a precarious existence during the 1820s and 1830s. Legislative subscriptions to its capital in the early 20s gave the state a commanding voice in company affairs, even to the point that the legislature demanded that improvements to the river begin at Wilmington rather than at Fayetteville as originally proposed.[48]

During the 1830s the Cape Fear Navigation Company began collecting tolls on the river traffic between Wilmington and Fayetteville. Table 6 reveals the nature and extent of that commerce insofar as rated, enumerated goods were concerned. Nonenumerated products paid a flat 10 percent fee. Despite toll collections, the financial condition of the company remained tenuous, and complaints mounted about the difficulty of navigating the river. Wilmington shipper and shipbuilder Doyle O'Hanlon at first refused to pay the tolls, contending that it was unjust for the company to charge for improvements that had not yet been made. Loss of business forced O'Hanlon's compliance by February 1838, but he promised to continue his battle in the courts. The state also despaired. Legislation in 1835 and 1836 respectively directed the governor to sell the dredging machine belonging to the company and recommended a lawsuit to collect dividends due the state. By 1840 the Cape Fear Navigation Company was defunct.[49]

Table 6
Cape Fear Commerce Subject to Tolls by the Cape Fear Navigation Company

Downriver	11 Months ending May 1, 1835	12 Months ending May 1, 1839
Cotton bales	14,731	4,279
Flour (bbls.)	1,567	7,654
Tobacco (hhds.)	252	118
Spirits (bbls.)	16	2
Grain (bu.)	325	6,229
Flaxseed (casks)	1,714	1,639
Upriver		
Salt (bu.)	52,574	69,309
Merchandise (hhds. and pipes)	1,892	2,273
Merchandise (bbls.)	4,790	3,225
Merchandise (tierces)	338	441
Iron (tons)	316	356
Lime (casks)	1,838	1,856

People's Press and Wilmington Advertiser, June 10, 1835; *Wilmington Advertiser*, June 14, 1839.

A decade later a renewed effort to improve the Cape Fear beyond Fayetteville and the lower Deep River to Hancock's Mill in Sampson County was undertaken by the Cape Fear and Deep River Navigation Company. Chartered in 1849 with a state stock subscription of $40,000, the Cape Fear and Deep River Company sought to use a series of locks and dams as opposed to the abortive canals of the Cape Fear Navigation Company. The company began collecting tolls in late 1851. Among the thirty-three vessels using its facilities between December 30 and October 20, 1852, was the steamer *Brothers* from Wilmington. Most of the craft carried naval stores, lumber, corn, and iron.[50]

By the spring of 1853 the company had its own steamer, the *John H. Haughton*, which began regular runs between Haywood County and Wilmington two years later. In 1855 the *John H. Haughton* took a load of flour, cotton, and peas to Wilmington. In 1856 the steamer brought a load of coal from Chatham County to the port, probably the first of what was hoped to be a bonanza for Chatham County, Wilmington, and the state.

Most of the toll-paying traffic in the mid-50s, however, consisted of timber and lumber rafted to Wilmington and flatboats carrying naval stores. Generally those forest products came from Harnett County rather than counties along the Deep River.[51]

Although the General Assembly altered the charter of the company to permit increased funding, expenses always seemed to outstrip available moneys. Labor costs were underestimated, and the decision to hire a northern engineer to supervise the works divided the company. Wildly roseate predictions of the ease of constructing the improvements works and the consequent projections of increased trade failed to bear fruit. While the project was mostly completed by 1855, freshets continually damaged or destroyed the wood structures, eroded riverbanks, and washed building materials downstream even as far as Wilmington, resulting in constant and expensive repairs. "We are tired of alluding to this work, because unfortunately things keep on so much in their old tracks that . . . we have ceased to look for any thing from it but delay and disaster," editorialized the *Wilmington Journal*.[52]

The company remained optimistic despite an investigation by the state legislature in 1856 showing that eighteen of its nineteen dams and all twenty-two locks needed repairs. Two years later the company advertised two barges carrying merchandise and machinery as far as the Egypt coal mines in Chatham County. However, creditors forced the sale of the company in 1859, eventuating in the decision of the state to purchase the business, including the *John H. Haughton,* two flatboats, and a coal boat, in hopes of protecting its investment. Legislation in 1861 continued state support but forbade expenditures exceeding $30,000 annually. The state pinned its hopes on opening the river to the coal fields, but freshets and floods in the winters of 1859–60 and 1860–61 dashed such expectations. A government-initiated moratorium on the works in February 1861 proved to be permanent.[53]

When considering the improvement of the Cape Fear below Wilmington in 1819, Archibald Murphey noted that there was some sentiment for focusing on Smithville rather than Wilmington as the principal seaport of the region. Not only was Smithville more healthful, serving as a summer resort for Wilmingtonians, but the Flats continued to impede upriver transport, rendering lightering at Smithville necessary in the case of larger vessels. Moreover, Smithville's wide bay offered excellent anchorage. Objections to Smithville included the open river passage below Wilmington that was deemed dangerous for small craft, particularly the flatboats and rafts that brought naval stores and lumber from the interior. Additionally, as opposed to Smithville, Wilmington's fresh water provided a useful antidote to the ever-destructive shipworms. Murphey, however, felt that the advent of steamers obviated the first objection. The possibility of diverting and opening the Elizabeth River to Smithville, thus rushing a supply of fresh water to the Cape Fear, might overcome the second.[54]

Actually the Wilmington interests were too well entrenched to be dislodged by a Smithville challenge. Furthermore, the disadvantages of Smithville were not so easily removed as Murphey imagined. Wilmington eventually proved to be the direct beneficiary of Murphey's proposal to enhance the navigability of the river. The General Assembly established a Board of Internal Improvements to expend funds appropriated for the development of transportation. The board in turn hired an English civil engineer, Hamilton Fulton, to examine the state's waterways. Fulton proposed a comprehensive program for improvements, which bore only partial fruition. The panic of 1819 combined with an ever-stingy Republican legislature to prevent work on all but a few projects, among which was the lower Cape Fear River.

The funds for improving the navigability of the lower Cape Fear River came from the state and national governments. From 1823 to 1828 the General Assembly underwrote the project. Fulton commenced work in 1823 to improve the channel between New Inlet and Wilmington. His efforts to close minor channels, construct jetties, and dredge the shoals were unavailing, and Fulton was dismissed in 1825. Work continued under the direction of the Board of Internal Improvements until 1829 with few positive results. Concluding that state efforts were futile (as well as too expensive), North Carolina petitioned the federal government for assistance.[55]

Congress had appropriated funds in 1826 to conduct surveys of North Carolina coastal waters. Captain Hartman Bache of the Army Corps of Engineers made the required readings the following year and generally approved of Fulton's plan for enhancing the navigability of the Cape Fear. Between 1829 and 1838 Congress allotted $202,627 to improve the river channel from Wilmington to Campbell's Island, about nine miles below the town. The work consisted mostly of pile and plank jetties designed to concentrate currents. Combined with dredging, the operation significantly deepened the river channel—from ten to thirteen feet by the end of the decade, when the federal government ceased its funding. The channel was also broadened and straightened. Lightering, once essential, was "unused and unseen." Vessels arrived and departed Wilmington wharves without having to stop at Smithville.[56]

Shipping had been materially improved, as evidenced by the increasing number of vessels, particularly larger foreign ships, that called at Wilmington. The average tonnage of foreign and domestic vessels increased steadily from 1840 to 1850, reaching in the latter year 190 and 171 tons respectively. In 1853 a British barque and brig, drawing eleven and a half to twelve feet, passed over the main bar without touching. Two years later a Bremen barque, whose fourteen-foot, ten-inch draft was thought to have been the greatest in two decades, came to harbor.[57]

After a hiatus in governmental activity in the 1840s, occasioned by the panic of 1837 and the consequent dearth of federal revenues, the effort to improve the navigability of the Cape Fear was renewed shortly after midcentury. In order to generate interest in further river and bar improvements, Wilmingtonians held a meeting in March 1852 to encourage the state's congressional delegation to support such endeavors. R. W. Brown chaired the gathering but Duncan K. McRae was the driving force, eloquently noting how the South generally, and North Carolina in particular, had been neglected by the federal government. Ironically, the previous day New Hanover County Democrats, meeting in Wilmington, had denied the power of Congress "to commence and carry on a general system of internal improvements."[58]

Actually the improvement of the river and bar had bipartisan support. Politically, Wilmington was fairly divided between Whigs and Democrats, but the county was overwhelmingly Democratic. Although the county and the Democratic congressional representative of the Lower Cape Fear, William S. Ashe, ordinarily opposed government funding for internal improvements, they realized the impact of river trade upon the region and worked with the Whigs to secure government aid. Despite the best efforts of Ashe and North Carolina Whigs, Senator George Badger and Congressmen Abraham W. Venable, David Outlaw, and Thomas Clingman, a meager $20,000 was realized from the federal government in 1853.[59]

To maintain enthusiasm for river improvements in Wilmington, a Committee of Thirteen in the port town was created. In conjunction with local authorities the committee invited A. D. Bache, superintendent of the U.S. Coast Survey, to Wilmington. At a public gathering in 1853, chaired by John Dawson, magistrate of the police, Bache pictured a dismal prospect for Wilmington shipping if improvements were not quickly forthcoming. He noted that the main bar had widened from a half mile to three times that size in little more than a century. Both the main bar and New Inlet had shoaled considerably. Bache proposed immediate efforts to build jetties and to close small openings near New Inlet to reverse the shoaling process.[60]

Bache felt that eventually New Inlet should be closed in order to increase the depth of the main bar. That argument was not well received. Moreover, even if New Inlet were closed and the main bar deepened, Wilmington would not benefit until the river had been dredged, for by that time the Cape Fear could only carry ships of fourteen-foot draft to Wilmington. Also, most of the shipping to the port came from and departed to the northern states and would be more likely to use New Inlet. Additionally, the small coasters that came to market with corn and naval stores from the eastern part of the state would have to sail around Frying Pan Shoals to enter the river.[61]

In any event the shoaling of the bars had to be reversed. As Bache noted, Wilmington not only was the center of shipping in North Carolina but also was useful as a port of refuge for distressed ships and as a coaling station for steamers. The diminishing depth of the bars would eventuate in loss of trade, particularly European commerce. Exports, whose value had risen from $1,200,000 in 1840 to $6,000,000 in 1853, were sure to decline. The Bache-led meeting concluded with a resolution to collect $60,000 locally to supplement the $20,000 congressional appropriation. Within a month subscriptions to raise the $60,000 had been pledged.[62]

The movement to seek additional funding for deepening the bar received a stimulus from a river improvements convention in Wilmington in May 1854. Numerous county gatherings from as far as Guilford, Alamance, and Chatham and as near as Wayne, Bladen, Cumberland, and Sampson supported the effort and sent delegates to the Wilmington meeting. Governor David Reid chaired the convention, which memorialized Ashe and the rest of the North Carolina congressional delegation to continue to press for federal aid. Congress responded with an appropriation of $140,000 in 1854 to improve the entrance to the river by erecting jetties at Bald Head Point and by closing the beaches between Smith and Zeke islands.[63]

Work on the projects had commenced in 1853, based on the earlier appropriation of $20,000, and proceeded apace until 1857, when a three-day gale in September negated much of the jetty construction at New Inlet and, in fact, opened two new beaches south of the inlet. Government study commissions later in the year and in 1858 concluded that before the storm the works had been effective, that the jetties should be rebuilt, and that New Inlet should be closed in three years if the depth of the water on the main bar had not increased by that time. Although permanent improvement in the depth of the bars had not been realized, the government gained valuable experience that guided its efforts following the Civil War.[64]

Earlier Congress had also funded lighthouse construction and the marking of the Cape Fear channel to facilitate traffic on the river. After the War of 1812 the replacement of the first lighthouse on Bald Head Island was a prime concern of both mariners and Congress. The national legislature reappropriated $15,000 in 1816 to underwrite the project. The collector of revenue at Wilmington supervised the work. Whereas the old lighthouse had been located close to the Cape Fear River on the southwest point of the island, the new one was constructed on a high bluff several hundred feet from the river north of the original site. Contractor Daniel S. Way completed the structure in quick order; the 109-foot lighthouse was operational by 1817 or 1818.[65]

The Bald Head Island lighthouse was joined by a second lighthouse or beacon on Federal Point at New Inlet. An increasing number of vessels used that entrance to the Cape Fear River in order to avoid the shoals and bar at the mouth of the river. In 1814 Congress authorized the construction of a beacon at Federal Point on the north side of New Inlet. Two years later the 50-foot light was operational. Two decades later, in 1837, a lighthouse replaced the beacon at Federal Point.[66]

Federal funding in 1848 inaugurated the placement of a series of markers and lights from the main bar of the Cape Fear to Wilmington in a successful effort to outline the river channel. The program included buoys, lighthouses, beacons, and a lightship. All the lights were operational by 1850 with the exception of the lightship and the Upper Jettee beacon just below Wilmington. The lightship was anchored in 1851. With the illumination of the Upper Jettee lights in 1855, the Cape Fear River was finally marked properly.[67]

Improvements in the navigability of the Cape Fear River led to increased shipping at the port of Wilmington during the antebellum years. Immediately following the war with Great Britain the export sector of North Carolina's economy improved markedly with the reemergence of the free trade. For the year ending September 30, 1816, Wilmington accounted for virtually all of North Carolina's foreign trade and 80 percent of the value of the state's domestic exports by sea. New Bern, the next busiest port, shipped 6 percent of the state's domestic goods, followed in order of importance by Washington, Edenton, Camden, Plymouth, and Ocracoke.

Wilmington's export trade varied little from that of the turn of the nineteenth century. Overseas commerce involved the shipment of naval stores, timber, tobacco, flaxseed, rice, and cotton to Europe. Naval stores were the principal component of that commerce, and during the 1850s a fairly regular trade in those products obtained between Wilmington and Liverpool. The production of tobacco declined substantially after the beginning of the nineteenth century, amounting to less than half the quantity grown in former years. The primary reason for its decline was the popularity of cotton. The cultivation of cotton was deemed more dependable (in terms of market demand), required less labor, and initially appeared more profitable than tobacco.

The produce of the Upper and Lower Cape Fear remained particularly well suited to the West Indies. Wilmington-owned vessels as well as those of foreign countries and the northern states shipped lumber, flour, rice, pork, bacon, lard, butter, tobacco, shingles, tar, staves, naval stores, and livestock, scattering "in as many directions as there are Islands." Cattle and hogs were everywhere bred, but the former were too small and weak to endure the passage to the West Indies. Hogs raised on mast were sufficiently strong by November and December to make that voyage. Imports of West Indian sugar, rum, molasses, and coffee found a ready market in Wilmington.[68]

The coastal trade with northern ports likewise continued to form a crucial component of Wilmington's commerce. Few European goods were brought directly to Wilmington. Rather, "custom" had introduced the practice of supplying the Lower Cape Fear with dry goods, hardware, iron, and other items from ports along the northern coast of the United States. In addition to the usual assortment of dry goods, the main component of Wilmington's import trade, salt and crockery met with "tolerable sales."[69]

Imports were nominal, however, compared to Wilmington's export of naval stores, which comprised the port's most valuable articles of trade. Much of Wilmington's coastal trade involved New York and Philadelphia, and to a lesser extent Boston, Baltimore, and Charleston. Regular packets, including the schooners *Caleb Nichols* and *Caroline,* 163 and 200 tons respectively, sailed between New York and Wilmington following the War of 1812. By 1833 packets also connected Wilmington with Philadelphia, Boston, and Charleston. On September 20, 1839, the *Wilmington Advertiser* reported that six of the nine New York and Philadelphia packets were unloading at Wilmington's wharves. By 1857 the Philadelphia–Wilmington line of schooners included the *New Republic,* which could make five round trips in fifteen weeks.[70]

Table 7
Tonnage Entering and Clearing North Carolina Ports, Oct. 1, 1832–Sept. 30, 1833

	Domestic		Foreign	
	Entrances	Clearances	Entrances	Clearances
Wilmington	11,664	22,493	5,070	4,704
New Bern	2,555	2,653	39	39
Washington	1,311	2,832	94	94
Edenton	1,118	2,731		
Camden	1,961	3,045		
Plymouth	635	2,166		
Beaufort	451	316	88	88
Ocracoke	335	1,368		

The New American State Papers, 17:664.

Table 8
Tonnage Entering and Clearing North Carolina Ports, July 1, 1849–June 30, 1850

	Domestic		Foreign	
	Entrances	Clearances	Entrances	Clearances
Wilmington	11,555	19,718	9,115	11,380
New Bern	2,664	3,643		
Washington	2,118	1,372		
Edenton		131		
Camden	2,170	2,945		
Plymouth	1,205	2,175		113
Beaufort	473	755		

The New American State Papers, 32:693, 697.

During the antebellum era Wilmington not only remained the state's premier port but strengthened its position, as seen in Tables 7 and 8, mainly on the basis of naval stores exports. Wilmington accounted for 57 or 58 percent of the tonnage entering North Carolina ports and 61 to 64 percent of that which cleared. Compared to other South Atlantic ports, Wilmington's trade held its own vis-à-vis Virginia but suffered in comparison to South Carolina and Georgia, as seen in Table 9. By 1850 Wilmington's domestic export trade outdistanced that of Norfolk, and trailed only slightly that of Savannah. In foreign exports Wilmington's commerce

Table 9
Tonnage Entered and Cleared at Major Atlantic Ports
Oct. 1, 1832–Sept. 30, 1833

	Domestic		Foreign	
	Entrances	Clearances	Entrances	Clearances
Norfolk	8,341	23,144	13,314	17,199
Wilmington	11,664	22,493	5,070	4,704
Charleston	17,831	49,099	32,012	37,478
Savannah	10,780	39,662	20,780	22,592

July 1, 1849–June 20, 1850

	Domestic		Foreign	
	Entrances	Clearances	Entrances	Clearances
Norfolk	6,415	18,283	7,866	8,482
Wilmington	11,555	19,718	9,115	11,380
Charleston	52,414	68,537	44,205	52,830
Savannah	11,883	21,039	45,134	51,524

The New American State Papers, 17:664; 32:693–94, 697.

also exceeded that of a slumping Norfolk but remained far behind that of the ports to the south.

Wilmington became an increasingly busy port during the antebellum era. The wharves and river were crowded from late fall through the winter when the Wilmington market was at its height. Coastal and foreign shipping via Wilmington was conducted by relatively small craft due to the impediment of the bars. During the 1850s schooners comprised 75 percent of those calling at port, brigs 20 percent, and barques 5 percent. An occasional Dutch galliot appeared. In addition to the brigs, barques, and coastal schooners the most colorful vessels were the "corn-crackers," small North Carolina schooners that brought corn, provisions, and naval stores from neighboring counties such as Onslow. Most entered by way of New Inlet. Steamers and their towboats were also commonplace by mid-century, and all shared the river with the flatboats and rafts from the upper reaches of the Cape Fear.[71]

A few of the vessels in the port came from Wilmington shipyards. During the two decades prior to the Civil War the shipyards of James Cassidey in town and the Beery family on Eagles Island achieved some prominence. However, despite a prime location and the availability of excellent wood Wilmington was not a flourishing shipbuilding center. According to information gathered by historian William N. Still, Jr., twenty-seven vessels were constructed in Wilmington between 1815 and 1860. Half appeared during the decade prior to the Civil War. Of the total most were small: seventeen were under one hundred tons; only two exceeded two hundred tons. The majority were schooners. Seven steamers, three brigantines, and two sloops rounded out the total.[72]

Although Wilmington was the only North Carolina port to conduct a significant amount of foreign trade, the number of vessels engaged in that commerce annually calling at the port barely exceeded thirty until mid-century, when some sixty unloaded cargoes at Wilmington wharves. Significantly, the average tonnage of the foreign craft steadily increased, from 113 tons in 1834/35 to 190 tons in 1849/50, a reflection of the improvements made to the river and bar during the past two decades. The 1850s, however, witnessed a declining number of foreign-registered craft calling at the port. During the year ending May 6, 1854, 781 of 814 ships calling at the port were American; during the year ending May 1, 1858, 616 of 633. Non-American vessels were mostly British: 23 of 33 in 1853/54, and 13 of 17 in 1857/58. Occasional ships from Belgium, Holland, Norway, Sweden, Germanic countries (Bremen, Mecklenburg, Hanover), and Venezuela appeared in Wilmington.[73]

Wilmington shippers continued to rely upon outside shipping services, finding it cheaper to hire New England vessels than to procure their own. In 1840 only 2,911 of the 10,961 tons of foreign shipping registered in the port were "permanent." Permanently registered tonnage decreased to 1,407 tons ten years later but rose to 4,079 in 1860. Still, it amounted to less than a third of the registered tonnage in foreign trade. Tonnage for the coastal trade, all permanently enrolled, amounted to 7,270 tons in 1840, rising to 10,335 tons in 1860. Indeed, more tonnage was owned in Wilmington, 27 percent of North Carolina's total, than in any other state port.[74]

Wilmington's export commerce at the end of the antebellum era mainly depended upon the extractive forest industries of the region—naval stores and wood products. Crude and distilled turpentine, rosin, tar, pitch, timber, lumber, shingles, and staves, all bulky products that could be transported cheaply by water and rail, remained the staples of the export trade. Foodstuffs, except for rice and peanuts, figured less prominently in Wilmington's trade on the eve of the Civil War. Only 1,700 bushels of corn, one hogshead of bacon, and 29 barrels of beef were exported in 1860. Through the mid-50s, however, the export of rice and peanuts, the latter a relatively recent product, increased.[75]

As tobacco practically disappeared from the Wilmington market, cotton achieved eminence. The railroads were particularly instrumental in bringing cotton to Wilmington, though about 50 percent of the cotton carried by the Wilmington and Weldon went to Virginia. Still, Wilmington could attract cotton from as far north as Edgecombe County. Of 18,042 bales of cotton brought to Wilmington between October 1, 1859, and February 1, 1860, 11,595 arrived via the Wilmington and Weldon, 3,108 via the Wilmington and Manchester, and 3,339 via the river. Most coming from the Wilmington and Weldon was sold in Wilmington; that from other sources had been sold in Fayetteville and was merely being forwarded through Wilmington.[76]

The mid-century discovery of coal in Chatham, Moore, and Stokes counties, particularly at the Egypt mine in Chatham, portended a windfall for residents of the interior as well as those of Wilmington. The potential of the coal industry apparently depended greatly upon the ability of the Cape Fear and Deep River Navigation Company to improve the navigability of Deep River. The company enjoyed little success. Its steamer, the *John H. Haughton*, brought a load of coal to Wilmington in 1856, but few followed. Actually prospects for obtaining coal had been dim from the start. The coal deposits proved to be small and of marginal quality, and neither the company nor the state was able to improve materially the navigability of the Deep River.[77]

Nonetheless, at the end of the antebellum era Wilmington was a thriving port as well as a center of culture that boasted some of the amenities of progressive urban life—brick sidewalks and gaslights for its streets. A northern visitor in 1860 considered the town "finely situated for trade." Merchants representing some forty mercantile houses formed a Chamber of Commerce in 1853, an organization that succeeded the Board of Trade, started in 1839.[78] The continued impediments of the bars at the mouth of the river still restricted shipping to relatively small vessels, though the improvements in the navigability of the Cape Fear River and several railroad connections augered well for the future. Wilmington was the state's busiest port on the eve of the Civil War, and the only one that conducted more than a modicum of foreign trade.

Chapter Four

THE CIVIL WAR:
Lifeline of the Confederacy

Following decades of debate over the interpretation of the Constitution, the nature of the Union, and remedies for aggrieved states, the election of Abraham Lincoln sparked the secession movement of 1860–61. The specter of John C. Calhoun haunted the polls in November 1860, when the Democrats divided their forces, North and South, to allow the Republican Lincoln to win the presidency with little more than 40 percent of the popular vote. Believing that Southern Rights and the "peculiar institution" would be jeopardized by the advent of a "Black Republican" president, South Carolina departed the Union in December 1860. Six additional states left early the following year. Together the seven formed the Confederates States of America.

The news of Lincoln's election elicited a mixed reaction in Wilmington. The newspapers predictably divided: the Whiggish *Daily Herald* counseled moderation; the Democratic *Daily Journal* advocated secession. The secessionists enjoyed the momentum. They held one of the first secessionist meetings in the state when they convened on November 19 in the New Hanover County courthouse. In the meantime, reflecting the martial tenor of the times, the Cape Fear Minute Men organized. Not to be outdone, the Wilmington Light Infantry and the German Volunteers, the town's oldest militia units, paraded through the streets.[1]

The secessionists met with only partial success, for the unionists likewise organized and held meetings. And unionists counted on the support of prominent businessmen, lawyers, and politicians in Wilmington. As a correspondent to the *Daily Herald* noted, Wilmington was dependent upon

71

the New York trade. He did not believe that Wilmington merchants would be willing to risk that commerce for the "soap bubble humbug *honor.*" The letter concluded, "The practical result to come from such secessionist meetings . . . is utter stagnation of trade in your port, and bankruptcy of two thirds of the merchants of your town."[2] However, the position of the unionists visibly eroded. The *Daily Herald* began to waffle, declaring that it was not for union at any cost. Congressman Warren Winslow, representing the Lower Cape Fear, found the situation hopeless. Then news arrived of South Carolina's secession on December 20. In response the Minute Men fired a hundred-gun salute. Shipbuilder Benjamin W. Beery added another salvo, and the schooner *Marine*, anchored in the river, responded gun for gun to the salute.[3]

While Wilmington early favored secession, it remained for the bombardment of Fort Sumter on April 12, Lincoln's call for troops to suppress the rebellion, and Virginia's departure from the Union to convince North Carolina of the necessity of joining the Confederacy. The decision was formalized by a state convention on May 20, 1861. In the interim Governor John W. Ellis ordered the Wilmington militia to seize forts Johnston and Caswell and appointed Major William H. C. Whiting of the Confederate States Army to take charge of North Carolina's coastal defenses. Whiting, who had arrived in Wilmington by April 27, quickly sought to improve the dilapidated works. He also initiated the construction of Battery Boles, built and manned by the Wilmington Light Infantry, which became the nucleus of Fort Fisher.[4]

Wilmingtonians early felt the impact of the war. A Federal expedition in August 1861 took Fort Hatteras and gained control of the Outer Banks, leading to fears that the Cape Fear port was a potential target of a Union attack. A representative of the town asked President Jefferson Davis of the Confederate States to consider appropriate measures for protecting the coastal area of the state, mainly the Lower Cape Fear. The Confederate government had already placed Brigadier General Joseph R. Anderson in command of the District of the Cape Fear within the Department of North Carolina. Brigadier General Samuel R. French replaced Anderson in March 1862, and in turn was succeeded by Brigadier General William H. C. Whiting in November of that year.[5]

The Cape Fear River constituted the key to the region and to Wilmington. Despite his own initial work, when Whiting took command of the Cape Fear District, he contended that little effort had been made to fortify and defend the river with the exception of Fort Fisher. Colonel William Lamb, a brilliant engineer who was placed in charge of Federal (renamed Confederate) Point in October 1861, supervised the construction of the fort. Continuously improved and enlarged throughout the war, Fort Fisher remained unfinished in 1865. Nonetheless, Admiral David D. Porter, who commanded the Union naval force that captured the fort, reported that Fort Malakoff, the Russian stronghold, would not "compare either in size or strength to Fort Fisher."[6]

Of the remaining forts in the Lower Cape Fear, Fort Caswell was the most important, guarding the western entrance, or old bar, to the river. Work had begun on the structure in 1827, but plans envisioning a fortification to house five hundred men and ninety guns never materialized. A small garrison had been sent to the fort before its completion in 1839, but subsequently was withdrawn because the men were needed for the Seminole Indian War in Florida. During the two decades preceding the Civil War an ordnance sergeant maintained the fort, which contained only eighteen unmounted guns in 1860. The Confederates strengthened the works with sandbags, but Fort Caswell was not well armed and apparently not expected to withstand a heavy bombardment.[7]

Forts Johnston and Anderson also guarded the river. The garrison of the former had been withdrawn in 1838, after which the fort rapidly deteriorated and was described in 1841 as a "mere open battery at the mouth of the river." The Mexican War, reinforced by sectional tensions at midcentury, brought a reactivation of the fort, but following the crisis the troops were withdrawn and the fort was left to the care of an ordnance sergeant. At the beginning of the Civil War, Fort Johnston mainly offered a guarded anchorage for blockade runners. Fort Anderson, located about halfway between the entrance of the river and Wilmington, mounted a "formidable battery," and was meant to prevent enemy gunboats from ascending the river and attacking the town.[8]

Heavy earthworks encircled Wilmington, the strongest entrenchment seen during the war by a member of the Seventh New Hampshire Volunteers. Ponds and ditches surrounded the entrenchments into which water could be poured through a series of sluices and gates. A partially completed line of earthworks, constructed in anticipation of an attack in 1862, ran through the town. Batteries above and below Wilmington guarded the Cape Fear River. Downstream the Confederates erected four such works, each overlooking obstructions in the river designed to impede an enemy naval invasion. The obstacles in the water ranged from sawyers and spiles to cribs of stone and a floating chain and log boom.[9]

Whiting later reinforced the land defenses with mines, or "torpedoes" as they were called, in the river. The Confederates experimented with various explosive devices. Torpedo stations were established at Wilmington, Richmond, Charleston, Savannah, and Mobile, with substations at other ports. So effectively mined was the Cape Fear that ships at Fort Johnston and at Wilmington had to take on local pilots, licensed by the military, who could safely steer vessels along the river.[10]

To assist in the defense of their town Wilmingtonians organized a Committee of Safety, chaired by Mayor John Dawson, on April 16, 1861. The committee purchased supplies for the families of soldiers, helped to establish a wage schedule for work performed on local defense projects, and obtained loans amounting to $100,000 from the town's three banks to underwrite the construction of fortications. Although the protection of Wilmington and the Lower Cape Fear rested mainly upon the Confederate government after North Carolina's secession, the Committee of Safety remained a vital force in mobilizing public opinion, and a year later spearheaded an effort to build an ironclad vessel to secure the town.[11]

Wilmingtonians and General Whiting lived in constant expectation of a Union attack for three and a half years before the actual invasion in December 1864. Rumors compounded the tense atmosphere. In early June 1861 a report that "500 Lincolnites were landing on Wrightsville Sound" roused all able-bodied men, who shouldered their muskets and went to the local armory. Federal incursions into North Carolina—the occupation of Roanoke Island in August 1861 and the fall of New Bern in March 1862—aroused anxieties in Wilmington. Mrs. Armand J. DeRosset wrote in October 1861, "Our town is in a state of excitement expecting the Fleet to make an attack at any moment." Early in 1862 a soldier looked "for Old Mr. Burnside to give us a call some of these days."[12]

Another invasion scare in December 1862, extending into the early months of the following year, prompted General Whiting to request women and children to evacuate Wilmington. Commission merchant Alexander McRae among others complied, sending his family upriver to Fayetteville on a steamer amidst exceptionally crowded conditions. The decision had to be made quickly, however, for Whiting would need the transportation facilities for the movement of troops once the invasion began. Although the Federals had planned an assault on Wilmington, at the last moment they directed their effort toward Charleston.[13]

Whiting continually complained to his superiors that he lacked the necessary manpower to defend Fort Fisher against a determined invasion. The general argued for the importance of the port of Wilmington to the Confederate effort, claiming that from "here there is no retreat." Once taken by the enemy, Whiting claimed, the port "cannot be retaken by means belonging to the Confederacy."[14] Residents of Wilmington shared Whiting's trepidation. When they heard the news of a prospective Union invasion in the winter of 1862–63, they feared the worst. James Green wrote to his sister, "I wish we could say that we were *prepared* to meet [the enemy], but this is not the case."[15]

Despite the obvious importance of the port of Wilmington, Whiting's fears of a Federal invasion did not immediately materialize. The Union did not make a determined effort to capture the town until December 1864. A pressing need for naval resources in other theaters of the conflict may have delayed the attack. Obvious deterrents included the bar at the mouth of the river which rendered the entry of larger vessels extremely hazardous. Fort Fisher, though unfinished, appeared to be a formidable work. In fact, however, the Federal authorities probably overestimated the strength of the Confederate fortifications.

Certainly the Confederate navy stationed in the Lower Cape Fear failed to deter the enemy. Lacking an offensive naval force capable of competing with that of the United States, the Confederacy concentrated its efforts on protecting its rivers and harbors. Not all in the Lower Cape Fear were satisfied with the feeble precautions. "Civis," writing to the *Journal* in January 1862, suggested that measures be taken to improve the defense of the Cape Fear and Wilmington. Relying solely upon the batteries at the bars was dangerous.[16]

The fall of New Bern in 1862 impelled Wilmingtonians to action. In a town meeting on April 2, Wilmingtonians authorized their safety committee to take charge of the town's naval defense. That group in turn formed a gunboat committee, composed of prominent merchants William A. Wright, Oscar G. Parsley, and Armand J. DeRosset, to proceed as quickly as possible with the construction of an armored wooden vessel. The success of the C. S. S. *Virginia* at Hampton Roads in early 1862 sparked support in Wilmington and throughout the Confederacy for the construction of ironclads to defend the coast. Having previously opposed ironclad construction as a waste of money, the *Wilmington Daily Journal* apologized for its error and called for a committee to raise funds for building an ironclad for the protection of the port: "The feeling is abroad—the people are ready to act."[17]

Goaded into action by the Wilmingtonians, the Confederate government undertook the construction of two ironclads in the town in 1862. As the decision was made at approximately the time of the Wilmington town meeting, possibly the gathering spurred the government to action. In any event the *North Carolina*, a 150-foot-long vessel mounting four guns and carrying 150 men, emerged from Benjamin W. Beery's shipyard on Eagles Island. The vessel was patterned after the Richmond class of Confederate ironclads, the most numerous of the Southern armored craft, which in turn were improved versions of the C. S. S. *Virginia* prototype. The *North Carolina* was commissioned in 1863 or early 1864.[18]

Despite an appearance that was fearsome to some, the *North Carolina* failed to frighten or even harass Federal blockaders. Indeed, defective engines, in part salvaged from an old tug, seriously hampered her speed, forcing the Confederates to use the vessel as a floating battery anchored off Smithville to protect incoming and outward-bound blockade runners. Although the *North Carolina* occasionally sailed upriver to Wilmington, she failed to spend enough time in fresh water to kill the toredo worms. By July 1864 the *North Carolina* remained only twelve inches off the river bottom. In September the *North Carolina* sank at her moorings, the victim of a worm-riddled hull.[19]

The *Raleigh*, Wilmington's second ironclad, was constructed at James Cassidey's shipyard in town. Soon after the *Raleigh* was commissioned, at least by April 1864, she was sent into battle. On the afternoon of May 6, accompanied by two wooden steamers, the *Yadkin* and *Equator*, the *Raleigh* anchored just inside New Inlet to await high tide. Soldiers in the forts were unimpressed. Considering the navy "a tremendous humbug," William Calder doubted that the ironclad would attack the Union fleet.[20]

Although the *Raleigh* and its companions had been observed by the Union gunboat *Mount Vernon*, no alarm was raised until the Confederates slipped across the bar at 8:00 P.M. and attempted to engage the nearest blockader, the *Britannia*. After firing off alarm rockets and failing to stop the ram with its thirty-pound Parrot gun, the *Britannia* fled. Subsequently the ironclad blundered through the night, sighting and firing on the blockader *Nansemond*, which also escaped. Although aroused, other Federal blockaders assumed the noise and confusion meant the presence of blockade runners. Daybreak found the *Raleigh* several miles from the bar, facing the *Mount Vernon*, *Britannia*, *Nansemond*, and other Union warships. In the confrontation between the ironclad and the Union vessels, little damage was inflicted by either side. After approximately two hours of shelling the *Raleigh* disengaged and followed the *Yadkin* and *Equator* across the bar, receiving a salute from the guns of Fort Fisher.[21]

The exultation of the moment soon turned to despair. While steaming back to Smithville, the *Raleigh* grounded on a bar. At the ebbing of the tide the weight of the armor proved too great for her wooden construction. The vessel's hull cracked, giving her the appearance of a "monstrous turtle, stranded and forlorn." Guns and iron were salvaged, but the *Raleigh* was a total loss. A court of inquiry blamed faulty construction for the disaster and exonerated the ship's commander, though observing that he should not have attempted to cross the bar. In any event, Flag Officer William F. Lynch, senior naval officer in North Carolina, was understandably "very much down in the mouth about it."[22]

The navy undertook the construction of a third ironclad, the *Wilmington*, in 1864. The vessel reflected a new design unveiled by the Confederates, a double-ended ironclad with two octagonal casemates. Although the contractor hoped to build the *Wilmington* in three months, one sailor realistically remarked that "if they finish her in 9 months they will surprise me very much." Actually the *Wilmington* was still on the ways when Federal forces captured Wilmington in February 1865. The Confederates burned the vessel as they evacuated the town.[23]

In addition to the ironclads the Confederate navy at Wilmington included wooden vessels. The C. S. S. *Artic* was a converted lightship whose engines were removed for use in the ironclad *Richmond*. The vessel itself became a three-gun, iron-plated, floating battery stationed in the lower part of the Cape Fear River.[24] The tug *Uncle Ben*, stripped of its engines for use in the ironclad *North Carolina*, eventually was sold to a group of businessmen who outfitted the vessel as a privateer.[25] Among the remainder of the navy's complement of vessels in Wilmington were the *Equator*, *Yadkin*, and *Caswell*. The first was a side-wheeler tug; the *Yadkin*, a 300-ton propeller steamer. Both mounted one gun. The unarmed *Caswell* served the navy as a river taxi. All the wooden ships were destroyed by the Confederates upon the fall of Fort Fisher and Wilmington early in 1865.[26]

Supplementing the ironclads and wooden vessels at Wilmington were torpedo boats, at least one of which, the C. S. S. *Squib*, was constructed and commissioned in the port by the navy. Two other torpedo boats were destroyed by fire before they were finished. Reflective of the interservice rivalry, the army also built torpedo boats. One naval engineer observed late in 1863 that manning the torpedo boats would be dangerous, but "if they succeed in destroying any Yankee boats they will be covered All over in glory."[27]

Confederate sailors spent a life of relative ease along the Cape Fear River. When those on board the ironclad *North Carolina* were not picking up turkeys that flew off passing blockade runners, they enjoyed clamming, oystering, and crabbing. Perhaps the monotony as well as inflationary prices—"two months' pay hardly meets one month's washing bill"—contributed to the desire of some on the *North Carolina* to forsake the Confederacy. On the other hand idle time led to boisterous conduct. One Wilmington resident complained that "nearly every night a party of men, said to belong to the C. S. Navy, are *allowed* to roam the streets, committing sundry outrages to the annoyance of the men and to the terror of the women and children."[28]

Wilmingtonians generally viewed the navy with disdain. At the outset the navy was considered too elitist and too authoritarian, "a bad school for Southern patriots." In picketing New Inlet to prevent furtive Union raids, a soldier complained that the army performed "the duty of those drones stationed at Wilmington, commonly known as the C. S. Navy." In fact, at the time the "drones" were probably "sporting their gold lace and shoulder straps in houses of prostitution about Wilmington." The *Daily Journal* also wondered why the navy was not patrolling the coast rather than "eating idle bread, and plenty at that."[29]

Actually the mentality of the Confederate naval officers, accustomed "to big frigates, fancy war steamers, all of the paraphernalia of the U.S. service," according to the *Daily Journal,* did not well comport with the "class of vessels" that the Confederacy could command. The navy in Wilmington controlled ironclads and small steamers, the total firepower of which probably did not equal that of any one of the Union blockading craft after 1861. Still, the Wilmington squadron might have offered a respectable harbor defense, but the ironclads were lost and the remainder of the fleet proved useless.[30]

Serving in an essentially defensive capacity throughout the war, the Confederate navy took the war to the enemy with its famous (or infamous) privateers and cruisers. As an open port throughout most of the war, Wilmington originated many of those offensive strikes against United States commerce. Among the first of the Confederate privateers was the *Mariner*, a small screw steamer under the command of Captain Benjamin W. Beery, who apparently had been promised the opportunity to capture Federal merchantmen in return for the use of his shipyard. The *Mariner* sailed from Wilmington in July 1861, capturing her only prize, the schooner *Nathaniel Chase*, late in the month.[31]

Leaving from Wilmington the following year was the *Retribution*, originally the tug *Uncle Ben*. The navy sold the hull of the tug to a group of businessmen, mostly Louisianans and Texans, who obtained letters of marque from Richmond. After taking a cargo of turpentine and cotton through the blockade to St. Thomas, the *Retribution* was armed with a 20-pound rifle and two 12-pound smoothbores. She harassed United States shipping in the vicinity of the island, eventually taking three prizes in January and February 1863. As the *Journal* observed, "That a vessel of her class has been able to make herself such a terror to the enemy, speaks volumes for the boldness and enterprise of her officers and crew."[32]

After making several trips through the Wilmington blockade, the runner *Atalanta* was renamed the *Tallahassee* and commissioned as a Confederate man-of-war under the command of Captain John Taylor Wood. Mounting a 32-pound rifle, a lighter rifle, and a brass howitzer, she carried a crew of 110 in addition to officers. On August 6, 1864, the *Tallahassee* left Wilmington on a nineteen-day cruise along the north Atlantic coast of the United States. During the voyage she burned sixteen vessels, scuttled ten, bonded five, and released two before returning to Wilmington.[33]

The *Tallahassee* underwent a change of command and name—to the *Olustee*—and ran the blockade again in October. Off the coast of Delaware and New Jersey she captured seven merchantmen. After battling three Federal cruisers and a gunboat sixty miles from the Cape Fear bar, the *Olustee* returned safely to Wilmington. There her battery was removed. She was converted into the government-owned blockade runner *Chameleon* under the command of John Wilkinson.[34]

To accompany the *Tallahassee* (*Olustee*) in the fall of 1864 the Navy procured a small, twin-screw blockade runner named the *Edith*, which was commissioned as the *Chickamauga* under Captain Wilkinson. The *Chickamauga* took four barques within two days, burning three and bonding the fourth. After scuttling two schooners at the entrance of Long Island Sound and capturing a barque at sea, Captain Wilkinson put into St. George, Bermuda, ostensibly for repairs but actually to obtain coal. From there he took the *Chickamauga* back to Wilmington after a "hard cruise" of eight weeks, and there she remained for the duration of the war.[35]

The success of the *Tallahassee* in 1864 raised fears among Wilmingtonians, blockade runners, and military authorities that the Federals might attempt to reduce Fort Fisher or at least strengthen the blockade. A naval officer on board the *Tallahassee* believed that "the Yankees have watched the entrance to Wilmington with redoubled viligance." According to General Whiting, since the *Tallahassee*'s raid not only had the blockading squadron been doubled but the number of blockade runners lost had risen. Among those lost was the pride of the governor and state of North Carolina, the *Advance*. Whiting appealed to Governor Zebulon Vance to use his influence to stop the activities of the "privateers" (cruisers), even to the extent of having the ships turned over to the army to be used as troop transports.[36]

The Confederate cruisers also engendered ill will among the blockade runners by compelling them to supply the navy craft with hard coal. Forcing the blockade runners to use soft coal, which produced dense black smoke and more easily identified those vessels, resulted in the rapid loss of seven, according to Whiting. Governor Vance sympathized inasmuch as the *Tallahassee* had taken coal from the *Advance*. More broadly, the governor resented the Navy Department's general policy of giving priority to the commerce raiders, thus neglecting the needs of North Carolina and endangering Wilmington.[37]

The level of discussion proceeded to a higher plane, involving Secretary of War James A. Seddon, Secretary of the Navy Stephen R. Mallory, and President Jefferson Davis. The use of the cruisers ultimately found favor with the president, who possessed a greater appreciation for Confederate naval potential than for his army personnel and Governor Zebulon Vance. Davis argued that the cruisers, which had not been constructed as warships, would be ineffective against an attack, certainly one by land. If they remained in Wilmington, the North would be tempted to increase its efforts to blockade the port to prevent their departure. By going to sea, the *Tallahassee* and *Chickamauga*, might draw "off the fastest vessels of the [Federal] squadron in pursuit of them, at a time when valuable cargoes were expected to arrive, a result in which the expectation of the Government has not been disappointed."[38]

Moreover, Davis felt that destroying United States commerce could weaken the enemy. According to the president, "Our only hope of peace, beyond the achievement of our noble armies in the field, must lie in making the burden of war oppressive to the people of the North." If the Confederacy withheld the commerce raiders, "how is the [Northern] shipping interest to be made to feel those burdens? Or is it to be left in undisturbed security to wield all its wealth, power, and influence for our destruction?"[39] It was sound strategy. Only Confederate command of the open sea might possibly have broken the blockade.

President Davis also roundly criticized the army, particularly Whiting. According to Davis, "It is to be regretted . . . that General Whiting should so frequently have violated the courtesy due to the naval arm of the military service." In fact the *Tallahassee* and *Chickamauga* were not "privateers," and Whiting's reference to them as such should have precluded his correspondence from finding a place in the files of the War Department. Moreover, the general's reports on the activities of the *Tallahassee* demonstrated an ignorance of the events and a disregard for others about whose duties he had no right to report. Davis left the final disposition of the dispute to General Braxton Bragg, who had been dispatched to Wilmington in 1864 before the imbroglio.[40]

Bragg, however, refused to countenance further naval operations of the cruisers. Writing to President Davis, Bragg stated that "the naval expedition should not sail until the question of the attack here is decided. Its presence in the harbor may become of vital importance; its operations at sea can be but secondary at best." Robert E. Lee, to whom Whiting had written, agreed. He wrote, "If the naval boats and officers required for the defense of Wilmington can be sufficiently used for that purpose, I think they had better be so applied. The loss of Wilmington to us would weigh more than the destruction of the enemy's coasters." As a result the *Olustee* (formerly the *Tallahassee*) was converted to a blockade runner; the *Chickamauga* remained in port.[41]

As Whiting and Bragg had hoped, the navy assisted in the defense of the first assault on Fort Fisher in December 1864. Thirty-two men and officers of the *Chickamauga* were called to the fort to man two Brooke guns. To his credit Whiting commended the efforts of the men of the *Chickamauga* in his official report. Upon the second attack on Fort Fisher in January 1865, the army again sought the aid of the navy. However, the *Chickamauga* was deemed too shorthanded to comply. The vessel shelled the attackers from her position in the river, then returned to Wilmington. Subsequently the Confederates burned and sank her to obstruct the Union's progress upriver. After the war some "enterprising Yankee" raised the hull and converted the *Chickamauga* into an "inglorious West India fruiterer."[42]

The military protection—army and navy—accorded Wilmington derived from the port's strategic location as a shipping entrepôt. While the commercial importance of Wilmington was well understood by North Carolina residents before the Civil War, during the conflict the town's reputation as a port gradually spread across the country and abroad. Wilmington became the "lifeline of the Confederacy," achieving its principal eminence as a port in 1863 and 1864. As a center of Confederate blockade running, the town's docks, wharves, yards, warehouses, and foundries were taxed to their limits. Remaining open to blockade runners until January 1865, Wilmington helped to keep the Army of Northern Virginia in the field. "After the capital of the Confederacy there was not in the South a more important place," wrote a soldier stationed in the port.[43]

While shipping constituted Wilmington's principal contribution to the Confederate war effort, some manufacturing developed in the port. As he passed through Wilmington in November 1862, Confederate Vice-President Alexander Stephens visited the Wilmington Sword Factory. Clothing, civilian and military, and Confederate caps were also made in Wilmington. Henry Lowe & Company advertised in 1862 for one hundred women and girls to work in a stocking factory at the foot of Chestnut Street. Although prospective employees were so numerous that some had to be turned away the following year, by 1864 the business languished in the face of rising costs for food and lodging in Wilmington. Those women who ordinarily might have sought work in the stocking factory preferred "washing for the Nassau steamers," for which they could expect far greater remuneration.[44]

Manufacturing also included shipbuilding, which had become increasingly prominent in Wilmington on the eve of the war. The Beery Ship Yard on Eagles Island, called the Confederate Naval Yard during the war, was owned and operated by Benjamin W. Beery. The yard's first work for the Confederacy consisted of converting the steam tug *Mariner* into a privateer of which Beery was commissioned captain. The Beery yard also produced the ironclad *North Carolina*, the steamer *Yadkin*, a dispatch boat for Flag Officer Lynch, and several smaller launches. Across the river in Wilmington the Cassidey Ship Yard built the ironclad *Raleigh*.[45]

Rail and water connections tied Wilmington to the interior of the state and the remainder of the Confederacy. At the outset of the war slightly less than a tenth of the nine thousand miles of railroad track in the Confederacy lay in North Carolina. Deteriorating physical facilities, varied rates, uncoordinated schedules, different track gauges, and consequent delays militated against the effective use of railroads, which both Union and Confederate governments eventually realized would play a major role in the war. The Confederate Congress in May 1863 authorized the War Department to seize and manage the railroads, and eventually gave that agency complete control over all transportation and communication.[46]

Wilmington was the terminus of two of North Carolina's most important railroads, the Wilmington and Weldon and the Wilmington and Manchester. The former funneled supplies to Lee's army in northern Virginia; the latter, according to Confederate Major General J. F. Gilmer, formed "an essential link in the great line of Southern Rail roads; and there is no exaggeration in affirming that the safety of our people and the possibility of maintaining the present contest with success depend to a great degree, on the preservation of this Road in an efficient condition." By 1863, however, the Wilmington and Manchester, like all other railroads in the South, was "seriously impaired and worn by the constant call upon it for heavy transportation."[47]

The river trade between Wilmington and Fayetteville continued apace, and any decrease in civilian use of steamers was offset by military demand. As before the war, cotton, naval stores, and other agricultural products of the interior were boated or rafted downriver; mercantile goods traveled in the opposite direction. Passenger traffic remained important. The steamers

A. P. Hurt, Kate McLaurin, and *North Carolina* provided regular service between Wilmington and Fayetteville. The *Reindeer* and the *Enterprise* transported coal from the vicinity of Deep River to Wilmington.[48]

Blockade running, however, was the focus of the port's economy. It transformed Wilmington, according to Captain John Wilkinson, turning the staid old town "topsy-turvy." Formerly a center of culture and refinement, inhabited by many old families of hospitality, intelligence, and polish, Wilmington became a fortified entrepôt of Confederate trade and a cauldron of soldiers, speculators, and thieves. Most of the older citizens left, if not immediately then during the yellow fever epidemic of 1862 or the various invasion scares that punctuated the war. Those who remained led secluded lives, the ladies rarely being seen on the streets.[49]

Secession and the Union blockade marked the inauguration of an unsettled state of commercial affairs in Wilmington, followed by a rapid realignment of trade. Initially a flurry of activity resulted in the loading of vessels with all available naval stores. Later the turpentine distilleries ceased to operate. Business was depressed. As a Boston merchant wrote to his partner in Wilmington, "All the masters are panic-stricken & don't know what to do—fear to do anything." The northern trade soon concluded; the last vessel from a northern port entered Wilmington on May 18, 1861.[50]

Although Abraham Lincoln initiated the blockade of North Carolina's coast on April 27, not until July 21, 1861, did the *Daylight* take up its station off Cape Fear. At that juncture vessels trading to the port of Wilmington technically engaged in "blockade running," though the blockade remained minimally effective for some time thereafter. Still, the "corncrackers" quickly disappeared from port. Sailing schooners followed, and shipping eventually devolved upon blockade-running steamers.[51]

Blockade running was dominated by English and Scottish firms which had the ships and capital to venture in such a hazardous enterprise. Many, however, took "little pains to disguise their contempt and dislike for [the Confederates] even in our own ports," noted the weekly *Wilmington Journal.* The British mercantile houses were joined by somewhat less affluent American entrepreneurs. Mitchell and Gerney of Charleston and the Albion Trading Company of New Orleans maintained representatives in Wilmington to oversee their interests. A group in Petersburg, Virginia, operated the steamer *City of Petersburg.*[52]

Wilmingtonians played a relatively minor role in the trade. Perhaps it was just as well, for one major venture by local capital ended in failure. In the summer of 1863 a group of Wilmington businessmen purchased the

Merrimac, which they loaded with cotton and tobacco and sent to Nassau. After two days at sea the vessel was captured. The *Journal* rather uncharitably consoled the investors in Wilmington by observing that the sufferers at least were among those who most could afford the loss.[53]

Representatives of the blockading-running companies achieved prominence, if not respectability, in Wilmington. They lived sumptuously, paying a "king's ransom" in Confederate money for housing. Blockade running also well rewarded the captains of those vessels. They lived prodigally compared to most in Wilmington. On Sunday evenings, after a luxurious dinner attended by a dozen or more friends, one would order the cloth removed from the table and two gamecocks would be brought forward. A pile of twenty-dollar gold pieces at each end of the table evidenced the bets on a favorite bird. A servant with wooden rake would draw the gold coins to the winners. "Those were flush days in Wilmington," remembered one of the town's residents.[54]

On the other hand, most military personnel and civilians in Wilmington suffered from a shortage of provisions and high prices during the course of the war. Wrote one soldier to his father in January 1863, "It is very hard times here now. We do not get half enough to eat, and that is not fit to eat." The scarcity of food, he believed, was almost as severe as that during the recent yellow fever epidemic of 1862. The *Journal* feared that Wilmington "must soon be a starved out community." To make matters worse, soldiers plundered private gardens.[55]

After 1863, the dearth of food and rising prices were attributed to blockade running. Captain John Wilkinson observed that the agents and employees of the blockade-running companies virtually monopolized the "country market" in provisions. Not only did the agents eat well, but the blockade-running crews, sometimes numbering fifty, absorbed large quantities of the available beef and bread. A correspondent to the *Journal* contended that the blockade runners ought to bring in an amount of salted provisions commensurate with that taken from the port, and General Whiting eventually issued a proclamation to that effect.[56]

Scarcity and rising prices produced rampant speculation that heightened with the prolongation of the war. According to Mrs. Armand J. DeRosset, "Pocket handkerchiefs that we used to give $1.50 a doz. sold at . . . auction at $13.50." She had "never heard of such fabulous prices in fairy tales." Bona fide merchants could not compete "with the professional speculators and monopolists who have a game to play and will play it at any price," declared the *Journal*. Nonetheless, the very people who condemned speculation also embraced it, or at least took advantage of its opportunities on a limited scale. Mrs. DeRosset beseeched her daughter to send her a barrel of potatoes, for, she wrote, there were no vegetables in the Wilmington market at present and "I can dispose of them at a large profit."[57]

In any case the driving ambition of most in Wilmington was money, for some simply to meet basic living expenses, but for others to support a prodigal life style. Although some of the older Wilmingtonians were Scot descendants, "shrewd, canny, money-making, and not to be beaten at driving a bargain by any Yankee," they met their match in the no-holds-barred competition instigated by wartime trade. Remembered one Wilmington inhabitant, "Talk about Yankees worshipping the almighty dollar! You should have seen the adoration paid the Golden Calf at Wilmington during the days of blockade-running. Everybody was engaged in it save the private soldiers and a few poor line and staff officers, who were not within the 'ring,' and possessed no influence or position there by which they could grant favors."[58]

Indeed a number of Confederate officers speculated in groceries and dry goods. Rarely were men of high rank involved, however. Certainly General Whiting, who "left his family badly off," remained above suspicion. Most of the military speculators were small fry, men engaged in mercantile pursuits before the war, who could not abandon their "old store habits." Whatever the extent of such activity on the part of civilians or soldiers, it fueled the speculative fires, leading to harder times for those on fixed incomes and making the Confederate war effort more difficult to sustain.[59]

The arrival of a blockade runner in Wilmington marked the beginning of celebration and intense speculative trading. According to tradition, revelry started as a steamer passed the Dram Tree, a large cypress about two or three miles below Wilmington, where sailors customarily took a drink to symbolize the end of a voyage. Once in port festivities began. An Englishman wrote of "the congratulations we received, the champagne cocktails we imbibed, [and] the eagerness with which we gave and received news. All, . . . combined with the delightful feeling of security from capture and the glorious thought of a good night's sleep in a four poster bed, wound one up into an inexpressible state of jollity."[60]

After his first successful run of the blockade, from Nassau to Wilmington on the *Banshee*, supercargo Thomas Taylor held an open house on the vessel, treating the invited and uninvited alike. When the cabin filled, the overflow enjoyed food and drink on deck. Taylor enjoyed watching those "accustomed to live on corn-bread and bacon, and to drink nothing but water" savoring "our delicacies; our bottled beer, good brandy, and, on occasions, our champagne." The hospitality was worth the cost, for "if any special favour were asked," Taylor wrote, "it was always granted, if possible, to the *Banshee*."[61]

While congratulations upon a successful voyage were exchanged, the feverish disposition of the cargo began. Men, women, and children rushed to the wharves to see the steamer and to buy, beg, or steal something. Wrote one, "The beggars at the gangways . . . were as thick as those in Egypt crying 'bucksheesh.' " The first people aboard were the agents, and then came the officials and officers, friends, and "bummers," "hunting after drinks and dinners, and willing to accept any compliment, from a box of cigars or a bottle of brandy down to a bunch of bananas or a pocketful of oranges."[62] From the wharf the goods were sent to the consignment houses or, in many cases, to auction. Wrote one Wilmingtonian, not long after the arrival of a blockade runner, "The wharf is about deserted. Everyone [is] at the big Auction." Although local auctioneers knocked off the goods, most of the purchasers were not Wilmingtonians or even North Carolinians. Reported the *Journal* in August 1863, "The sale is a very large one, and the attendance exceeds anything that we have ever seen on a similar occasion. There are bidders from all directions, . . . and the continents, peninsulas, and 'Isles of the Sea,' have sent forth their children, so that we expect nothing less than very full prices to be the order of the day."[63]

In addition to valuable cargoes blockade runners may have brought yellow fever to Wilmington. The steamer *Kate* from Nassau apparently introduced the disease in July, though an epidemic did not occur until September. The *Daily Journal* carried the first public official reference to the presence of the disease on September 17, 1862, when Dr. James H. Dickinson informed the mayor of Wilmington of the presence of several cases of yellow fever in town. The fever raged until November, killing an estimated six hundred and fifty people and reducing the Wilmington population to four thousand as residents fled to the countryside or the interior of the state.[64]

The commissioners of navigation and pilotage responded to the epidemic by enacting stricter quarantine regulations. Military authorities, however, feared that a mandatory two-week quarantine imposed by the commission on suspect vessels might interrupt the flow of needed war matériel. Although the Confederate government refused to interfere with what it considered to be local commercial regulations, General Whiting reached a compromise with the port officials whereby vessels under quarantine could unload below Wilmington. The army would provide security

Spencer Compton, Earl of Wilmington, for whom the port was named.

(Courtesy of the North Carolina Division of Archives and History.)

A North Carolina turpentine camp, source of one of Wilmington's most important eighteenth- and nineteenth-century exports.

(Courtesy of the North Carolina Division of Archives and History.)

Prometheus, first steamboat at Wilmington, circa 1819.
(Courtesy of the North Carolina Division of Archives and History.)

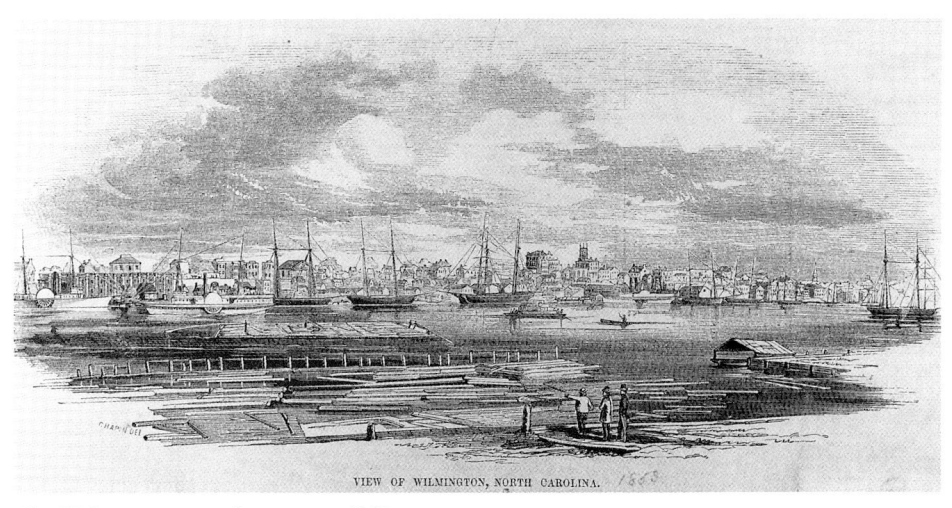

The Wilmington waterfront, circa 1853.
(Engraving published in *Gleason's Pictorial Drawing-Room Companion*, courtesy of New Hanover County Museum of the Lower Cape Fear.)

The Union blockading fleet off Main Bar (top) and New Inlet. (Courtesy of the North Carolina Division of Archives and History.)

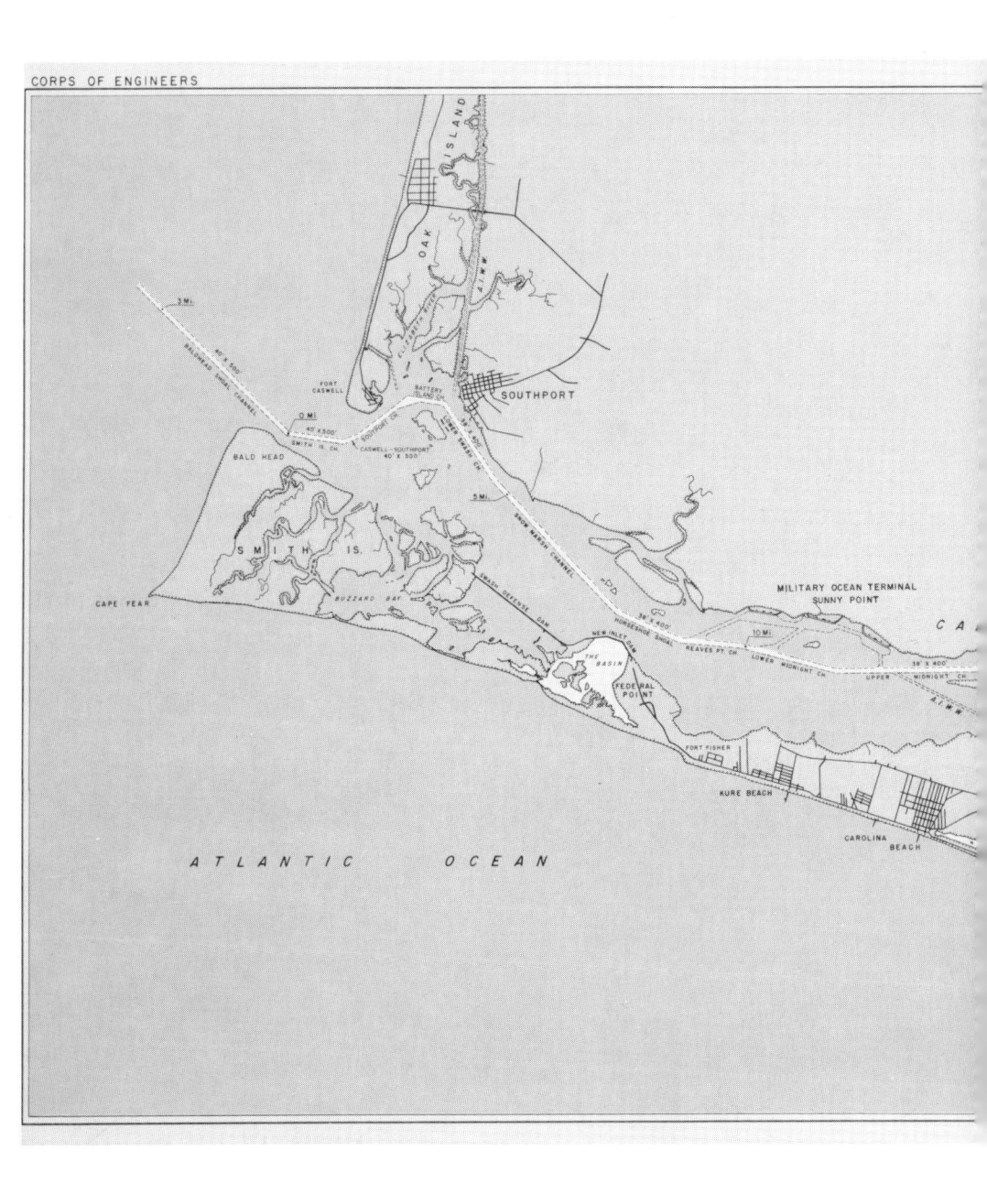

Map of the Port of Wilmington.
(U.S. Army Corps of Engineers.)

WILMINGTON HARBOR,
NORTH CAROLINA

CORPS OF ENGINEERS   WILMINGTON, N.C.
MAP REVISED SEP 1980

Lithograph representing the city of Wilmington, 1776–1876.

(Courtesy of New Hanover County Museum of the Lower Cape Fear.)

James Sprunt of Alexander Sprunt & Son, Wilmington's largest cotton exporting house and one of the largest such businesses in the United States during the last quarter of the nineteenth century.

(Courtesy of the North Carolina Division of Archives and History.)

Four vessels loading cotton at the wharves of Champion Compress and Warehouse Company of Alexander Sprunt & Son, late 1800s.
(Courtesy of the North Carolina Division of Archives and History.)

Paddle wheeler loading rosin at the foot of Water Street, Wilmington, late 1800s.
(Courtesy of the North Carolina Division of Archives and History.)

River steamboat *Wilmington*, owned by Captain J. W. Harper.
(Courtesy of the North Carolina Division of Archives and History.)

Floating pen for flatboats and rafts.
(Courtesy of New Hanover County Museum of the Lower Cape Fear.)

for the goods while the ships were cleaned and the crews isolated. Vessels arriving from uninfected ports passed freely.[65]

Yellow fever did not ravage Wilmington again during the war, but the town's inhabitants were nervous in the wake of their experience of 1862. Dr. Alexander R. Medway complained that rumors and vague allusions to disease had a deleterious effect on the public confidence. After reports of yellow fever in Bermuda and Nassau in 1864, a company of men was detailed to quarantine duty at Fort Anderson. All suspect blockade runners unloaded at the fort. No soldiers were allowed to leave the fort on furlough. Though a few cases of yellow fever were found at Fort Anderson and in Wilmington, the lateness of the fall season forestalled the appearance of the disease in epidemic proportions. Still, between the fever and the Yankees, there was a "queer feeling abroad," observed the *Journal*.[66]

One of the most successful blockade runners working out of the port of Wilmington was the *Advance*, a state-owned vessel. North Carolina's Adjutant General James G. Martin persuaded Governor Zebulon Vance to authorize the state to engage in blockade running in order to furnish North Carolina soldiers with badly needed supplies. The governor directed Captain Thomas M. Crossan, a former naval officer, to find a suitable ship, and appointed John White of Warrenton, North Carolina, as the state's purchasing agent abroad. While White engaged the English firm of Alexander Collie and Company to handle the affairs of the state, Crossan procured the *Lord Clyde*, renamed the *Advance*, a swift steamer capable of making seventeen knots.[67]

The *Advance* entered the mouth of the Cape Fear River on June 26, 1863, on her maiden voyage, and subsequently completed ten or eleven round trips before being captured a year later by the *Santiago de Cuba*. The success of Vance's venture on behalf of the state was undeniable, and the governor was justifiably proud of the *Advance*. Among the cargoes brought to North Carolina were large quantities of machinery supplies, 60,000 pairs of cotton cards, 10,000 grain scythes, leather for 250,000 pairs of shoes, 50,000 blankets, cloth for 250,000 uniforms, 12,000 overcoats, 2,000 Enfield rifles, 100,000 pounds of bacon, 500 sacks of coffee, $50,000 worth of medicine, and large quantities of lubricating oil. At the end of the war the state, which under Governor Vance supplied its own troops, had on hand 92,000 uniforms and considerable stores of blankets, leather, and other goods.[68]

The state's foray into blockade running produced conflict between the government of North Carolina and that of the Confederacy. Vance complained to Secretary of War Seddon that the Confederate representative in

England, James M. Mason, impeded the efforts of North Carolina agents in that country. Military-enforced quarantine delays in Wilmington disrupted the *Advance*'s sailing schedule. Also objectionable was the seizure of the *Advance*'s coal by the military authorities. Wrote Vance, "It is a little remarkable to me, that the entire importing operations of this State, which have been so successful and so beneficial to the cause, seems [sic] to have met with little else than downright opposition rather than encouragement from the Confederate Government."[69] Particularly obnoxious to Vance was the Confederate regulation that required all blockade runners, whether publicly or privately owned, to carry one-half of their cargo "on Confederate account." Vance, contending that the policy restricted his efforts to supply North Carolina's troops, and that carrying that much cargo for the Confederate government would mean incurring a loss on every voyage, believed that Wilmington was "more effectively blockaded from within than without." The governor asserted that he was willing "to fire" blockade runners partially or wholly owned by the state "rather than to submit to the quota established by the Confederacy."[70]

Nevertheless, Vance persisted, eventually selling one-half interest in the *Advance* but purchasing an interest in three other steamers, the *Don*, *Annie*, and *Hansa*. They were augmented by the Collie steamers, *Edith*, *Constance*, and *Pet*. The *Advance* was "regarded in an affectionate way by a half-million people," and North Carolinians, soldiers and civilians alike, lauded the governor. Wrote one soldier from Wilmington, "Our noble governor . . . richly merits the love and confidence which a united people have so cheerfully given him for his untiring energy to clothe our soldiers and administer to the wants of the people generally."[71]

The Confederate government also resorted to blockade running, though not as successfully as the state of North Carolina. Both the army and navy stationed cotton agents in Wilmington. By 1863 the Ordnance Bureau of the Army was running five steamers—*Cornubia*, *R. E. Lee*, *Merrimac*, *Phantom*, and *Eugenie*—out of Wilmington to St. George, Bermuda. The steamers completed twenty-two round trips through August of that year. They brought in small arms at the rate of ten thousand a month, saltpeter, lead, ordnance stores, and medicine. Then, in rapid succession, Union blockaders captured or destroyed three of the blockade runners, rendering the Ordnance Department's importation service ineffective thereafter. The losses occurred at a most inopportune time, following the defeats at Vicksburg and Gettysburg, when the Confederacy desperately needed additional munitions.[72]

The Confederate government found itself at a disadvantage in competing with private interests, particularly after mid-1863, when virtually the entire east coast trade devolved upon Wilmington following the siege of Charleston. Privately owned steamers so filled the Cape Fear River that they interfered with the defense of the harbor. While the War Department's agent had difficulty securing cotton for exchange, private interests experienced no problems. Nor did the quarantine regulations trouble them greatly. One writer suggested that quarantine officials were bribed by private concerns to escape confinement. And a Navy Department official complained he had "no allowance for propitiating the municipals."[73]

Wilmington's blockade-running trade principally involved the English possessions of Nassau and Bermuda. Wilmington was the closest Confederate port to those islands, lying 580 and 674 miles distant respectively. The commerce with Nassau and Bermuda constituted an indirect trade with Europe, particularly Great Britain. Although a royal proclamation ostensibly recognized the Federal blockade, British authorities failed to interfere with blockade running except to deny the protection of the British flag to those apprehended (unless they were British). Thus the islands became sources of huge quantities of goods—war matériel as well as luxury items—for the Confederacy.[74]

Halifax, Nova Scotia, was used infrequently by Wilmington blockade runners. The greater distance necessitated more coal, hence smaller cargo space, and greater exposure at sea, which elevated chances of capture. Additionally, United States agents in Nova Scotia could telegraph the time of departure of Confederate vessels, thus increasing the chances of anticipating and intercepting them. There also was less sympathy for the Confederate cause in Nova Scotia. Nevertheless, some of the blockade runners set out from Canada, including the ill-fated *Condor*, on which the Confederate spy Rose O'Neal Greenhow lost her life in 1864.[75]

The two inlets to the Cape Fear River, the shallow bars, and Frying Pan Shoals, all of which had militated against shipping before the Civil War, combined to render Wilmington an ideal center of blockade-running commerce. Guarding the two ingresses to the river, the Federal fleet had to cover a fifty-mile arc and at the same time remain beyond the range of the guns of Fort Fisher, which covered New Inlet, the favored of the two entrances by the blockade runners. Protecting the main bar were Fort Holmes on Smith Island and forts Caswell and Campbell on the mainland, though none possessed the firepower of Fort Fisher.

Blockade runners were mostly foreign, usually English-built, vessels. At the beginning of the war virtually any ship that appeared seaworthy and maintained sufficient speed was utilized. However, as the war progressed, vessels were built in England expressly for the purpose of running the blockade, which gave Wilmington "quite a Yankeeized appearance." Consequently they were far better prepared for the dashes from the Southern ports to their foreign destinations. They were speedier and lay lower in the water so that only their wake was visible on dark nights.[76]

Representative of the earlier craft was the *Robert E. Lee*, purchased by the Confederate government in 1862. She had been the packet *Giraffe* between Glasgow and Belfast, a narrow, side-wheeler steamer that could make thirteen and a half knots. Exemplary of the later blockade runners was the *Night Hawk*, owned by a company of Liverpool merchants. A side-wheeler of some six hundred tons, rigged as a fore-and-aft schooner with two funnels, she was 220 feet in length, 21½ feet across the beam, and 11 feet in her hold. The *Night Hawk* was fast and sufficiently light-draft to cross the New Inlet bar easily yet sturdy enough to withstand rough seas between Wilmington and Nassau or Bermuda. One of the largest and fastest blockade runners was the *Colonel Lamb*, built in 1864. A 1,788-ton paddle steamer, 281 feet long with a 36-foot beam and 15-foot hold, the *Colonel Lamb* attained almost seventeen knots on a trial run.[77]

An outward-bound steamer dropped into the main channel of the Cape Fear to proceed from Wilmington to the bar to await a propitious time to attempt to run the blockade. Constantly facing desertion by runaway slaves, draft evaders, and others who might take valuable information to the enemy as well as deprive the Confederacy of needed labor, the military posted sentries to patrol the wharves of Wilmington to prevent persons from illicitly boarding the blockade runners. At Smithville authorities continued the prewar practice of fumigating or "smoking" outward-bound vessels as an additional precaution. It was a "cruel process" in its effects on stowaways and not a little shocking for one to behold the dangerous application of a smoking apparatus to a cargo of cotton. Its efficiency was apparent to one observer, however, for after an hour or more, "an unfortunate wretch, crushed almost to death by the closeness of his hiding place, . . . and smoked the color of a backwoods Indian, was dragged by the heels into daylight, ignominiously put into irons and hurled into the guard boat."[78]

Still, the problem of unwanted passengers remained. According to one soldier, "Scarce a steamer went out without some stowaways, whom it was not always possible to smoke out." Usually they were sheltered by one or more of the crew, easily tempted by a small bribe. On one occasion, when the *Banshee* attempted to elude a pursuing blockader, cotton was cast overboard to lighten the vessel's load. In the process a runaway slave was discovered, somehow having managed to avoid detection on board and having endured the fumigation process. One blockade-running captain reportedly found the answer to the problem of stowaways: he set three or four adrift in an open boat with a pair of oars and a few days' provisions of bread and water.[79]

Pilots, always indispensable to the shipping of the port, found themselves in greater demand during the war. After the fall of Hatteras in August 1861 and the defection of some of the residents of the Outer Banks to the Union cause, the Richmond *Examiner* questioned the loyalty of North Carolina pilots as a whole. A resident of Smithville leaped to the defense of those in the Lower Cape Fear, noting the disruption to their livelihood but claiming that their attachment to the Confederate cause was unquestionable. Indeed, that appeared to be true, judging from the course of events, though the extraordinary wages paid for blockade running may have helped to cement their allegiance to the Confederacy.[80]

Pilots declined in number and ability during the course of the war. Captured pilots were rarely released or exchanged. By the end of the conflict, according to Thomas Taylor, the "so-called pilots were no more than boatmen or men who had been trading in and out of Wilmington and Charleston in coasters" before 1861. That ships were "cast away through the stupidity of the pilot" was not an uncommon accusation.[81] Even old hands came under fire. In a long, detailed missive to the *Journal*, Thomas Cubbins blamed the loss of his vessel *Wild Dayrell* on the incompetence of pilot James Burris. But Burris, a pilot on the Cape Fear for almost forty years, entered a disclaimer, contending that the captain was unaware of their exact location when they struck the coast, had desired Burris's services when they were still running down the coast rather than when crossing the bar, and then had failed to follow the pilot's prudent advice.[82]

The demand for pilots, whatever their ability, increased in proportion to their diminishing numbers. Rival companies competed for pilots to the detriment of public service. In 1864 the Navy Department established a branch of the office of Orders and Detail at Wilmington, headed by Captain John Wilkinson, who assigned pilots to the blockade runners, a move that greatly enhanced the efficiency of that service. Wilkinson believed that afterward "blockade runners were never delayed for want of a pilot, and the casualities [loss of ships] were much diminished." Still Secretary of the Navy Mallory was criticized for not officially incorporating the pilots into the navy.[83]

Inward-bound blockade runners usually made for the coast about thirty to forty miles above or below the entrance to the Cape Fear River, depending upon the inlet they wished to use. Hugging the coastline, which left them barely visible against the landscape, and running so close to shore that the breakers muffled their noise, the steamers feared the hazards of navigation more than the enemy fleet. The Confederates had extinguished all lighthouses and range lights on the coast at the beginning of the war. Only when the bars were in sight did the steamers signal for the Confederates ashore to set up navigational aids from inside the river. Even at the end of the war, when the blockade was at its peak strength, the problem of crossing the bar was more acute than that of passing through the enemy fleet.[84]

Critically important to the pilot were the range lights, for the compass bearing of an object did not enable a pilot to steer a vessel with assurance through a narrow channel. Range lights answered the need admirably. Thus every blockade runner carried a signal officer. The range lights were set inside the channels after signals were exchanged between the incoming runner and the shore. The lights were removed immediately after serving their purpose. The constant shifting of the channel, caused by storms or freshets on the river, occasioned the shifting of the range lights as well.[85]

Late in the war the Confederate government attempted to improve the signal service by reestablishing a light on Bald Head Island and by extending the signals farther down the coast. Previously incoming runners relied on the fires of salt works along the coast for guidance until they reached the bars. When Captain Wilkinson was charged with the duty of improving the signal service in 1864, he required each incoming vessel to contribute a barrel of sperm oil for illuminating the additional stations. Accordingly, more ships were seen in Wilmington in April 1864 than at any time since the beginning of the war, and "none get aground since the lights have been properly displayed," wrote one soldier.[86]

The "mound," or artificial elevation at Fort Fisher, saved numerous blockade runners. Not only was it a landmark along a "monotonous coast," appearing plainly and distinctly against the sky in clear weather, but it also mounted range lights and artillery for the protection of the Confederate vessels. The men at Fort Fisher maintained a constant watch. Blockade runners never displayed a signal without receiving an immediate reply and the setting of the lights.[87]

That Wilmington remained open to blockade runners was due in no small measure to Fort Fisher and its commanding officer, Colonel William Lamb. Soon after taking command of the fort in 1862, Lamb recovered four Whitworth rifle guns from the wreck of the blockade runner *Modern Greece*. Those extremely accurate pieces had a range of five miles and greatly impressed the Federal blockaders. Mounted at Fort Fisher, the Whitworths gave the blockade runners additional protection, causing the blockade squadron to retreat about two and a half miles from their original positions. Lamb was immensely popular among the blockader runners, who regarded him as a guardian angel. Wrote Thomas Taylor of the *Banshee*, "It was no small support in the last trying moments of a run to remember who was in Fort Fisher." Taylor and other captains expressed their appreciation by lavishing presents upon Lamb's family.[88]

The reputation of the Whitworths occasioned the transfer of three of them to other commands. Lamb lost the fourth when some of his men attempted to save the *Hebe*, run ashore in August 1863 to prevent its capture. Under the protection of their Whitworth and other artillery the Confederates attempted to salvage the vessel, but were driven off by Federals with a similar motive. General Whiting immediately sought a replacement, claiming to his superiors, "I have met with a serious and heavy loss in that Whitworth, a gun that in the hands of the indefatigable Lamb has saved dozens of vessels and millions of money to the Confederate States." Eventually, with the aid of Thomas Taylor, a battery of six Whitworth guns was presented to Colonel Lamb, "and good use he made of them."[89]

The regularity of the runs through the blockade was a source of embarrassment to the United States. Northern newspapers referred to the *Robert E. Lee* and the *Kate* as "packets." Wilmington blockade runners were early rivaled by those leaving Mobile and New Orleans for Havana, which made more frequent calls than the regular packets between New York City and the Cuban capital. By 1863 most of the traffic had shifted to the Atlantic coast. On board the blockader *Florida* off Wilmington, William F. Keeler wrote that he wished some system could be arranged for the Confederate runners to bring the mail, for they were more frequent and reliable in their passage than the Union mail calls.[90]

Although speed was eagerly sought and deemed essential by some, many relatively slow craft enjoyed much success. The *Pet*, said to reach only eight knots, made over forty runs through the blockade. The *Scotia* and *Greyhound* were likewise slow but seemed to lead "a charmed life." The success of blockade running fell mainly upon shoulders of the captains, and secondarily the pilots. Captain John Wilkinson could take virtually any vessel through the blockade with impunity, but other commanders simply collapsed under pressure. Courage, ingenuity, and luck usually spelled the difference between safety and capture.[91]

Of the principal Confederate exports—cotton, tobacco, and spirits of turpentine—the first was without doubt the most significant. Cotton, whether privately owned or belonging to the state or Confederate governments, seemed to be stored throughout Wilmington. Blockade runners, however, loaded cotton on Eagles Island across from Wilmington, where the steam cotton presses were located. The steam presses reduced the size of the bales of cotton to allow more to be transported on the ships. Over thirty thousand bales were exported from Wilmington during the first nine months of 1863.[92]

The steamers were specially constructed to carry the cotton. The compressed fiber was stored in the ships' holds by expert stevedores, who packed the cargo so tightly that "a mouse could hardly find room to hide." After the hatches were secured, bales of cotton were placed fore and aft in every available spot on deck, leaving room only for approaches to the cabins, engine room, and forecastle. Another tier was then added, after which the vessel, "with only her foremast up, with her low funnel, and gray painted sides, looked like a huge bale of cotton with a stick placed upright at one end." Cargoes usually ranged from three to eight hundred bales, though the *Ella and Annie* carried over 1,200 and the *Hero* took 1,745 to Nassau on one trip.[93]

While cotton formed the backbone of the export trade, it by no means proved the royal trump card many Southerners thought it would be. "King Cotton" did not provide sufficient economic leverage to force European countries to grant diplomatic recognition to the South or to bring the North to its knees. In fact, Europe was not assuredly the destination of all the cotton that reached Nassau and Bermuda. Southerners complained that their exports found their way to the United States. But eventually indignation gave way to resignation. Midway through the war the *Journal* recognized, "Once out and we lose control of it."[94]

Nonetheless, cotton financed a staggering variety and quantity of imports. Confederate vessels brought war matériel to port. Aboard the *Cornubia* in August 1863 were 228 cases of Austrian rifles, 459 cases of Austrian and Enfield rifle ammunition, 310 pigs of lead, 52 bales of cartridge paper, and 200 boxes of musket cartridges. Despite its significance, however, government freight was small in volume compared to private commerce. Private trade also included munitions but emphasized luxuries—fine English brandies, choice foreign wines, potted meats, preserves, jellies, anchovy paste, loaf sugar, tea, coffee. The cargoes of the *Douro* and *Eagle* in 1863 included 50 kegs of bicarbonate of soda and 120 pairs of Ladies Congress gaiters.[95]

One of the most unusual cargoes brought through the blockade was a magnificent Arabian thoroughbred, shipped by a representative of the Confederate government in Egypt to Nassau as a gift to President Jefferson

Davis. Thomas Taylor put the horse on his *Banshee No. 2*. Upon its arrival in the Cape Fear the health officer insisted on quarantine for the vessel, but Taylor contended that the horse might die during the wait. The health officer telegraphed Richmond for instructions and was told to have the *Banshee No. 2* sent to Wilmington, unload the horse, and return to quarantine.[96] Once at Wilmington, however, the crew of the *Banshee No. 2* went ashore. Taylor apologized to General Whiting but insisted that there was no need for him to undergo quarantine at that juncture. Whiting agreed, so Taylor loaded his vessel at Wilmington and steamed downriver on an outward-bound voyage—past a fleet of steamers in quarantine "whose crews were gnashing their teeth [at the sight of us]." On his return to the river Taylor found some of the same vessels still at quarantine. As a result of the horse and the quick round trip Taylor made an extra $100,000 to $150,000 for the owners of the *Banshee No. 2*.[97]

At the outset of the war few restrictions inhibited the blockade-running trade. Before the end of 1861 North Carolina Governor Henry T. Clark by proclamation forbade the export of bacon, pork, beef, leather, blankets, shoes, and woolen goods unless sanctioned by Confederate authorities. The Confederate government followed Clark by forbidding the export of cotton, naval stores, sugar, and other products to the United States. Otherwise, as long as appropriate export taxes were paid, a policy of free trade obtained.[98]

Still criticism of blockade running, at least the private traffic, mounted among the military in Wilmington. The secretary of Flag Officer Lynch felt it had engendered a "mountain of corruption and rascality." A naval officer agreed that it was an "unlawful traffic without profit or advantage to the body politic." The trade was "demoralizing in the extreme and an immense fraud on the gallant men in the army," a "pernicious system" that drained the country "for the benefit of speculators [,] extortioners and foreigners." However, the *Journal* observed that blockade running was simply an economic exercise conducted on the basis of rational profitability. It was "useless to attack the men engaged in any business not prohibited by law." If any alteration was contemplated, government regulation was the answer.[99]

Blockade running of course had its defenders, including those who found it paradoxical that a commercial town and seaport complained of an increase in its shipping. The trade profited Confederate producers, mainly of cotton, provided employment for large numbers of diverse people, some of whom might otherwise become objects of charity, and prepared Southern men for naval service if necessary. The blockade runners brought war matériel to the Confederacy and carried mail and envoys for the Southern government. Accumulated capital from the enterprise found its way into such crucial investments as railroads and government bonds. Useful ties were established between merchants in the Confederacy and in Europe. Altogether the benefits vastly surpassed the inconveniences of blockade running.[100]

Shipping remained undisturbed until private profit-taking began to interfere with the Confederate war effort. General Whiting began to complain to his superiors of the inattention to the needs of the government. In 1863, the *Merrimac*, a vessel used by the Confederacy, was unable to secure sufficient cotton to leave port because the railroad gave priority to private carriers of cotton whose agents could pay higher freight rates. Whiting sought permission from the Secretary of War to appropriate private cotton, subject later to full reimbursement, in order to obtain a full cargo for the *Merrimac*, but Seddon refused. The secretary suggested instead that Whiting use his authority to require the railroads to transport government cotton.[101]

When General Whiting complained to the War Department of the evils attending blockade running, the stock response was that he had no authority to intervene unless the loyalty of the parties was suspect. Eventually Whiting used that pretext along with the regulations forbidding trade with the United States and governing quarantine to bring shipping under strict army control. On September 1, 1863, he issued a lengthy set of orders that forbade the importation of United States goods except for munitions and medicine, required government approval of outward-bound passengers, established a curfew for sailors in port, required quarantine of vessels coming from Nassau, and mandated military approval of clearances from the port.[102]

The increasing interference with government blockade running along with the importation of luxury goods eventually evoked full-scale trade regulations in 1864. Congress prohibited the importation of such luxuries as furs, carpets, glass, and jewelry. Legislation also forbade the exportation of cotton and naval stores "except under such uniform regulations as shall be made by the President of the Confederate States," which meant in practice that each blockade runner was required to reserve one-half of its cargo space for government shipments on inward and outward passages. The government regulations shocked those in Wilmington. A local merchant predicted that blockade running would be stopped "almost entirely." Yet the trade continued, even heightened, due to the extraordinary profits to be made.[103]

Profits indeed were stupendous. Purchased at six cents a pound in the South, cotton brought ten times that much in England. A steamer carrying eight hundred bales of cotton might earn $420,000 on a successful round trip. Thomas Taylor, agent for a firm of Liverpool merchants, contended that the *Banshee*, captured after eight runs, paid her shareholders 700 percent on their investment. In writing of the departure of the *Dee*, James Randall commented that it should return in two weeks. Some made a round trip in eight days. The *Antonia* made nearly forty trips, the proceeds of which would "mail her with gold."[104]

The risks of running the blockade commanded commensurate renumeration for the officers and crew. Payment was made in British gold or United States dollars, half in advance as remuneration in the event of capture or loss. Additionally, officers in those wildly speculative times shipped articles on their own accounts to supplement their pay. Captains frequently carried bales of cotton for themselves. One master arrived in Wilmington with a cabin full of shoe thread. A speculator promptly bought the entire amount, which netted the captain an $8,000 profit in a matter of minutes. Thomas Taylor could not sell his toothbrushes in Wilmington, so he sent them to Richmond, where they sold at seven times their cost.[105]

For its part the Union experienced great difficulty in blockading effectively the Cape Fear and the port of Wilmington. At the beginning of the war the United States had only forty-two vessels in commission. Faced with the impossible task of stopping traffic along three thousand miles of Confederate coast, the Federal navy utilized virtually any vessel capable of carrying a long gun. Stretched to the limit, the Union's naval resources were not capable of guarding Wilmington together with other major Southern ports—Norfolk, Charleston, Mobile, New Orleans. And based on the volume of antebellum trade, Federal authorities deemed Wilmington less important as a port than the others at the outset of the war.[106]

Moreover, the Cape Fear presented two entrances, the old bar and New Inlet, the latter happily (for the Confederates) not having been closed as planned just prior to the war. The Federal naval authorities understood the task facing them. Rear Admiral Samuel P. Lee, placed in charge of the North Atlantic Blockading Squadron in September 1862, reported to Secretary of the Navy Gideon Welles that blockading both entrances was difficult because vessels on one side of Bald Head Island and Frying Pan Shoals could not support those on the other. At the time of his appointment Lee had only forty-eight vessels under his command and but twelve—ten steamers and two schooners—to blockade the Cape Fear. He kept up a steady stream of requests for additional craft, and gradually his squadron grew. By the time he was replaced by Admiral David D. Porter in October 1864, at least forty-five vessels guarded the approaches to Wilmington.[107]

The squadron off Wilmington lay in the form of a crescent, actually three semicircles, facing the Cape Fear River, with the center just out of range of the heavy guns mounted at Fort Fisher and the outside fringe approaching the shore on both sides. At night steamers patrolled the shore as closely as possible. Further out a cordon of cruisers and detached gunboats guarded the coastal waters. Though a blockade runner might evade the interior lines, it might be captured at daybreak by the third division. Beyond the special precautions for Wilmington, Union ships regularly patrolled the waters between the port and Nassau and Bermuda. Safety was realized only when the blockade runner reached British waters off the islands.[108]

Although blockade runners acknowledged the energy and activity of the naval officers employed in the blockading squadron, the results for the Union were not satisfactory. In addition to the stealth of the Confederate vessels and the paucity of Union ships, frequent gale winds blew sailing craft off course and even challenged blockading steamers. The latter constantly needed refueling, usually going to Beaufort, North Carolina, for that purpose. Insufficient armament and poorly constructed vessels added to the Union's woes. As the war lengthened, so did the number of ships needing repair—worn-out machinery, broken pumps, leaking boilers.[109]

Successful Confederate runs disheartened the blockaders. Although rumors of Union invasion occasionally brought business to a standstill, blockade running usually proceeded on a regular basis. A British visitor noted in his diary, "I cannot suppose that in ordinary times there would be anything like such a trade as this at a little place like Wilmington, which shows the absurdity of calling the blockade an efficient one." William F. Keeler, on the blockader *Florida,* believed that Wilmington had a larger foreign trade in September 1863 than ever before. The blockade runners grew bolder by the day; the blockade grew weaker "till it amounts to almost nothing."[110]

Other factors added to the woes of the blockaders. A lack of communication found Union vessels occasionally firing on one another, mistaking their comrades for blockade runners. Or they might chase their own vessels, as did the *Saccasus,* which pursued the *Keystone State* an entire day and fired nine warning shots before ascertaining its identity. The Union also lost vessels that ventured too close to shore in pursuing blockade runners or trying to secure stranded steamers.[111]

Generally the blockading squadron routine was monotonous. The vessels remained at anchor during the day and might run in a little closer to the shore at night. The sailors passed the time by reading, writing, fishing, and playing dominoes. Wrote Keeler, "What a howl there would be through the country could all these things be seen by the public as we who are the actors see them." Periodically the blockaders would be sent to Beaufort for coal and provisions. Keeler, like his fellows, chafed under the inactivity. He yearned for action.[112]

The chase and capture of blockade runners not only relieved boredom and allowed Union sailors to enjoy moments of retribution against the English, who were hated for their support of the Confederacy; such action was also most remunerative. The blockade runner *Hope*, taken by the *Aelous* off Wilmington in October 1864, brought $13,164 to the master, $6,657 to the assistant engineer (more than four years' pay), over $1,000 for each seaman, and $532.60 for the cabin boy. The *Florida* netted $37,667 for its capture of the *Calypso*, $29,576 for the *Hattie*, and $7,146 for the *Emily*, a total of just less than $75,000.[113]

As the war progressed and the blockading squadron grew, increasing numbers of blockade runners were captured, sunk, or wrecked. Confederates and Federals battled furiously for stranded steamers. No better example suffices than the destruction of the *Ella*, a two-stacked side-wheeler, in 1864. The *Pequot* discovered the *Ella* on the afternoon of December 2, giving chase until nightfall, at which time it sent up rockets to alert the rest of the blockading fleet. Early the next morning the *Emma* found the *Ella* lying close to Bald Head Island. Seeking to escape, the *Ella* had run around. As the *Emma* prepared to send a boarding party to fire the *Ella*, the guns of Fort Holmes on Bald Head opened. A standoff ensued for two days. The *Emma*, joined by several other blockaders, bombarded the *Ella* from long range. At dusk on December 3 numerous small boats were sent to fire the runner, but a heavy wind thwarted the effort. On the morning of December 4 the Federal ships opened fire once more; Fort Holmes responded, driving the vessels farther offshore. The bombardment continued throughout the day. About 1:30 the following morning a small boat from the *Emma* set out under cover of darkness. Upon reaching the *Ella* the Federals poured turpentine throughout the vessel, set her afire, and quickly left. The *Ella* burned fiercely for three hours, during which time shells placed among her machinery exploded. The Federals finally had destroyed the ship.[114]

Yet the mission was not without value to the Confederates stationed at Fort Holmes. The *Ella* carried about 380 gallons of gin, 1,670 gallons of brandy, and 80 gallons of wine. Despite reports that the destruction of the *Ella* was "very complete," apparently a large quantity of the spirits was brought ashore, a bonanza for the soldiers in Fort Holmes. According to a soldier in Fort Caswell who described the scene, "men seemed perfectly crazy, and officers high in command were *beastly drunk*. . . . Men flocked from all directions to plunder and traffic. Nothing was heard but blasphemous oaths, and [the] perfect babel of eager voices of avaricious men."[115]

Soldiers from the forts often managed to recover stranded vessels, or at least their cargoes. They braved the danger of enemy fire on many occasions, assuming that the prize was worth the risk. The owners of the vessels little cared, for after a ship was wrecked they rarely obtained the goods destined for them. Actually few rules governed the salvage of vessels, public or private, though the practice, called wrecking or "racking," had been regulated by law before the war. And the soldiers did not always reap the benefits of their labors. Often they found that goods they had saved from stranded runners were requisitioned by the military.[116]

The defenders of Wilmington enjoyed moments of retribution for the destruction of the blockade runners. In January 1864 the Union lost the *Iron Age*, a fine 424-ton, 9-gun gunboat which grounded while trying to salvage the blockade runner *Bendigo*. The Confederates managed to take a 30-pound rifle and a 12-pound boat howitzer from the *Iron Age*. In August the Federal tug *Violet* grounded on a bar close to Fort Fisher and had to be destroyed. Two months later the blockade steamer *Peterhoff* came under fire and grounded. Subsequently heavy seas broke up the *Peterhoff* and washed it ashore, allowing the Confederates to gather "lots of valuables." Soon thereafter another blockading steamer ran aground under the guns of Fort Holmes from which the Confederates managed to get two cannon.[117]

Occasionally the Confederates reclaimed captured blockade runners. On her first trip to Charleston an English vessel built for the trade was captured by the *Tuscarora*. Renamed the *Columbia* and carrying seven guns, she grounded off Masonboro Sound in early January 1863 on her first mission for the United States Navy. Lieutenant Lamb with one gun and a detachment of infantry and cavalry forced the surrender of the *Columbia*, subsequently driving off four blockaders that attempted to aid the stricken vessel.[118]

The effectiveness of the Union blockade remains moot. According to United States Secretary of the Navy Gideon Welles, the Union navy captured or destroyed 295 blockade running steamers, 44 sailing ships, and 683 schooners throughout the war. Admiral Samuel P. Lee reported the capture or destruction off Wilmington of only one steamer during the last six months of 1862 but seventeen between July and December 1863 and forty-two during the eleven months ending in July 1864. Secretary Welles stated in his annual report for 1864 that "sixty-five steamers, the aggregate value of which, with their cargoes, will scarcely fall short of thirteen millions of dollars, have been captured or destroyed in endeavoring to enter or escape from Wilmington."[119]

From the Confederate perspective, Wilmington's harbor master declared that from May 20, 1863, to December 31, 1864, 260 vessels ran the blockade, while some 15 entered before that date and 10 arrived afterward. Surely, however, the figures understate the early arrivals, for at least seven steamers ran the blockade in December 1862. At the beginning of the twentieth century local historian James Sprunt claimed that 397 steamers ran the blockade from the beginning of the war until a year before the fall of Fort Fisher. A more recent estimate by historian Richard E. Wood contends that 230 vessels entered the port of Wilmington during 1863 and 1864.[120]

In the latest and most comprehensive study of Confederate blockade running, Stephen R. Wise lends support to those who contend for the success of the enterprise. He also documents Wilmington's preeminent position among the Southern ports. More than twice as many blockade runners entered and cleared Wilmington as they did Charleston, which in turn easily outdistanced Georgia and Gulf Coast ports. According to Wise, blockade running at Wilmington was confined almost entirely to 1863 and 1864. Less than 3 percent of the runs occurred before or after those years. All told, 270 vessels successfully departed Wilmington; 294 entered.[121]

Those figures may be considered in conjunction with a surviving list of 133 vessels running the blockade at Wilmington and Charleston from January 1, 1863, to mid-April 1864. Of these 50 had been captured, 44 had been lost or burned, 6 had returned to England, and one was worn out, leaving 32 running (one of which was on the Cape Fear in river service). The picture looked bleak. Thirty-eight, or over a fourth, of the blockade runners never reached the Confederacy. Another 12 were captured or lost before making one round trip; 16 before making two round trips.[122]

Still, the statistics are deceiving. Blockade running was spectacularly successful because many vessels made several trips through the Union squadron. The *Herald* and *Kate I* ran the gauntlet 17 and 14 times respectively before they were lost; the *Pet* and the *Banshee*, 9 and 8 trips respectively. In fact, of 590 attempted trips in fifteen and a half months, 498, or 84 percent, were successful. That rate of success probably obtained for the duration of the war. A later authority estimated that 87 percent of the runs by steamers in and out of Wilmington and Charleston throughout the war were successful.[123]

Blockade running ended upon the fall of Fort Fisher. A Federal assault on the fort finally occurred in late 1864 but ended in failure. A second attack took place on January 13, 1865, when Union warships, numbering fifty or more with six hundred guns, opened a fearful bombardment. The final assault on Fort Fisher began during the afternoon of January 15. After the naval bombardment ceased, Union troops rushed the Confederates, overwhelming the defenders by sheer numbers. Lamb and Whiting were wounded, the latter mortally. Command devolved upon Major James Reilly, who finally surrendered about ten o'clock in the evening to prevent further, and needless, bloodshed.[124]

While the Federal forces celebrated their victory with an impressive fireworks display, two blockade runners approached the fort. The renowned Confederate sea captain John N. Maffit, in command of the *Owl*, realized that something was amiss and sent a boat ashore. Upon learning of the capture of Fort Fisher, he weighed anchor and steamed to Nassau, passing through a blockade squadron that took no notice in the jubilation of the moment. Likewise the *Rattlesnake*, commanded by M. P. Ursina, returned to sea after seeing unfamiliar campfires around Fort Fisher.[125]

The last blockade runners to enter the Cape Fear were the *Charlotte*, *Stag*, and *Blenheim*. Leaving Bermuda before news of the fall of Fort Fisher had reached the island, they were decoyed and trapped by the Federals. Lieutenant William B. Cushing, aided by two blacks who knew the signal code of the blockade runners, lured the vessels inside the bar. Unsuspectingly, the blockade runners dropped anchor and began the usual celebration of a successful run. As the champagne corks popped, bluejackets appeared to place all under arrest.[126]

The contribution of blockade running to the Confederate war effort was critical. Though blockade running was necessarily grounded on private enterprise, it admirably served the Confederacy's wartime needs, making up the difference between home production and the demands of the military. Only by such means could the South have adequately fed, clothed, and armed its soldiers. At first relying on private enterprise, the Confederate government found that it had to mount a fleet of vessels to service properly its needs. After the destruction of most of those blockade runners, Confederate authorities simply stringently regulated private shipping for the benefit of the public. The closing of Wilmington and Charleston in 1865 effectively sealed the fate of the Confederacy.[127]

After the capture of Fort Fisher the Federals regrouped for an attack on Wilmington. The Confederates abandoned Fort Holmes, Fort Caswell, and Fort Johnston as untenable, falling back to Fort Anderson as the primary defense of Wilmington. The campaign to reduce Wilmington began on February 11. The Union ground advance along the west bank of the Cape Fear River outflanked the defenders of Fort Anderson, forcing their retreat to Town Creek. That position in turn was flanked, and the Confederates fell back to Wilmington, which was patently untenable after the appearance of Federal troops to the south and across the river. General Bragg then ordered the evacuation of the town and went into camp on the north side of the Northeast River.[128]

Federal troops occupied Wilmington on February 22. Federal military officials soon tried to restore some semblance of normal economic conditions. Merchants who took an oath of loyalty and obtained permits from the provost marshal began to sell stocks of goods on their shelves. Some firms were allowed to import goods through the blockade. On March 14, at a "Grand Rally of the People" called and led by Major John Dawson, Wilmingtonians publicly recognized the reality of their situation by pledging "loyal obedience and hearty support" for the United States. They sought the reopening of the town's commercial facilities "as may be compatible with military movements and the general interests of the country."[129]

Nonetheless, shipping and commerce remained strictly regulated and subject to the supervision of the Treasury Department of the United States government. On June 20, 1865, the government created a large military district consisting of New Hanover and several other counties in southeastern North Carolina. General J. W. Ames was placed in command of the district with his headquarters in Wilmington. He controlled a small force of soldiers for police purposes. With the advent of General Ames the formal occupation of Wilmington ended. The town and state prepared for Reconstruction.[130]

Chapter Five

THE POSTWAR TRANSITION:
A Struggle for Recognition

Wilmington emerged from the Civil War confirmed in the status of North Carolina's principal port. While its economic fortunes rose and fell with those of the state and the South, by its shipping Wilmington was also linked inextricably to national and international developments. Thus it retained a cosmopolitan air that contrasted sharply with the rural agrarianism and isolation of much of the rest of the state. Meanwhile, in the transition to a peacetime economy and a totally free society, the state legislature in March 1866 incorporated Wilmington as a city, to offer the prospect of improved municipal government.[1]

The port city quickly overcame the wartime destruction of its wharves and shipping facilities to dominate completely the ocean commerce of North Carolina. The smaller ports, reorganized as Albemarle, Pamlico, and Beaufort, had been idle for the most part during the war except for Union military operations, and never recovered their prewar trade. The combined foreign tonnage entering and clearing those three ports in 1875 was 1,245 and 1,467 tons respectively, compared to 7,839 tons and 10,179 tons in 1860. By the end of the century foreign trade through the smaller port was virtually nonexistent. Coastal trade was more resilient, though it hardly approached Wilmington's level of commerce.[2]

Wilmington's postwar export trade resumed briskly, as may be seen in Table 10. With the exception of rice its articles of commerce differed little from those of the antebellum years: the familiar triumvirate of wood products, naval stores, and cotton. Wood products recovered soon after the war. Five lumber mills, led by O. G. Parsley's Hilton complex on the

Table 10
Principal Postwar Exports, Port of Wilmington

	1860 Domestic	1860 Foreign	1866 Domestic	1866 Foreign	1869 Domestic	1869 Foreign	1872 Domestic	1872 Foreign	1875 Domestic	1875 Foreign
Spirits of turpentine (casks)	127,652	20,400	49,078	7,929	54,085	64,097	59,410	67,969	18,599	77,882
Crude turpentine (bbls.)	52,175	23,548	28,973	1,150	20,537	764	11,558	766	7,958	339
Rosin	440,132	57,425	325,233	18,218	506,821	37,657	423,394	196,766	186,938	291,812
Tar (bbls.)	43,056	6,120	36,984	746	57,909	1,468	32,368	4,919	30,540	16,619
Pitch (bbls.)	5,489	784	2,875	251	4,869	64	7,072	275	3,994	182
Cotton (bales)	22,851		24,492	162	38,449	50	46,735	707	53,123	18,140
Cotton yarn (bales)	1,561		1,115		28		48		1,260	
Cotton sheeting (bales)	1,750		493		489		1,258		1,984	
Peanuts (bu.)	99,743		26,133	22	118,274	110	103,650		[41,138]	5,000
Lumber (p.p. ft.)	9,126,176	9,882,078	10,264,809	12,106,267	18,177,420	3,834,223	16,553,716	6,710,436	3,916,066	5,904,541
Shingles	730,880	2,887,870	756,286	2,241,200	2,191,315	[971,791]	1,353,786	1,539,439	3,330,200	1,859,000
Staves	97,432	10,000	318,627	50,913	1,558,404	9,150	6,606			

Smaw's Wilmington Directory, 1867, 39. *Wilmington Journal*, Jan. 10, 1873; Jan. 7, 1876.

Northeast Cape Fear, lined the Wilmington waterfront in 1872. Adding to Wilmington's capacity were Joseph Abbot's mills at Abbotsburg, about fifty miles west of the city on the Wilmington, Charlotte, and Rutherford Railroad. A decade later seven saw and planing mills in the environs of Wilmington gave the city an aggregate capacity of forty-five million board feet annually. Although the export of staves had been abandoned by 1890, the shipment of lumber (40,289,205 feet) and shingles (7,316,912) had doubled prewar figures.[3]

Wilmington's wood products proved to be the most popular if not the most valuable of the city's exports. Domestically Boston, New York, Philadelphia, and Baltimore received the bulk of the lumber, shingles, and staves, but virtually every port with which Wilmington traded, from several in Maine to those along the Gulf of Mexico, were recipients as well. Abroad, Wilmington's wood was widely distributed in the West Indies and South America.[4]

The commerce of postwar Wilmington centered on the export of naval stores, as shown by Tables 10 and 11. During the Civil War, when the American trade in naval stores was interrupted, Europe depended for its needs mainly on areas in northern France. The Franco-Prussian War in 1870–71 caused the French supply to run short, opened the American market, and created a speculative mania that eventually collapsed, leaving the industry awash in low prices. The naval stores market never quite recovered from that debacle; neither for that matter did Wilmington's trade.[5]

Compounding the problem of lower prices was the potential exhaustion of the natural resource basic to the naval stores industry—the longleaf pine. According to a traveler in the Cape Fear-Pee Dee river area of South Carolina in 1872, "There are no more sound trees in that region. They have been boxed and reboxed till they are 'done for.' "[6] Actually that assessment was overly pessimistic. Trees remained. And the Wilmington market called upon the "Piney Woods" area ever farther into the hinterland as the Wilmington, Columbia, and Augusta Railroad brought naval stores to the port.

Scandinavians, mainly Norwegians, followed by Germans and British in that order, carried the bulk of Wilmington's naval stores. Relatively small vessels, 275 to 300 tons, were used in the trade. Cargoes ranged from 1,000 to 1,500 casks or barrels. However, in the first week of February 1876 the German bark *Shangai*, the Norwegian brig *Normen*, and the German brig *G.C. Nichols* left port with 3,792, 2,020, and 3,151 barrels respectively.[7]

Table 11
Naval Stores Exports

Year		Spirits of Turpentine (casks)	Rosin (barrels)	Tar (barrels)	Crude (barrels)
1860	Domestic	127,562	440,132	43,056	52,175
	Foreign	20,400	57,425	6,120	23,548
	Total	147,962	497,557	49,176	75,723
1866	Domestic	49,078	325,233	36,984	28,973
	Foreign	7,929	18,218	746	1,550
	Total	57,007	343,451	37,730	30,523
1870	Domestic	68,966	483,546	54,090	12,929
	Foreign	32,889	26,127	6,107	3,258
	Total	101,855	509,673	60,197	16,187
1874	Domestic	42,838	309,959	47,820	14,945
	Foreign	83,087	379,330	20,799	650
	Total	125,925	689,289	68,619	15,595
1880	Domestic	69,453	399,349	14,032	
	Foreign	33,272	48,361	39,409	3,356
	Total	102,725	447,710	53,441	3,356
1888	Total	61,626*	351,827	68,865	18,171

*114 casks of spirits of turpentine were also shipped.
Wilmington Journal, Jan. 3, 1861; Jan. 3, 1867; Jan. 10, 1873; Jan. 7, 1876; *Weekly Star*, Jan. 7, 1881; Feb. 21, 1890.

Although Scandinavian bottoms transported the naval stores, cargo destinations dotted the shoreline of western Europe. London, Liverpool, and Bristol offered the best markets for Wilmington's naval stores. The spirits, rosin, tar, and crude turpentine also found their way to Amsterdam, Antwerp, Belfast, Bremen, Glasgow, Hamburg, Le Havre, Marseilles, Newcastle, Riga, Rijeka, Rostock, Rotterdam, Sète, Sunderland, Szczecin, and Trieste.[8]

Wilmingtonians were jealous of their reputation as the preeminent naval stores port in the United States. Naturally they bristled when a challenge was issued to their supremacy from Charleston or Savannah. Newspaper editorials, prospectuses, and trade commentaries alike offered figures to document Wilmington's eminence.[9] And indeed, as Table 12 shows, North Carolina seemed to enjoy an edge.

Compensating for the declining market for naval stores was cotton, which maintained Wilmington's reputation as a port of consequence into the twentieth century. Cotton shipments from Wilmington increased steadily after 1865, as shown by Table 13. Some cotton had been brought to the Wilmington market before the war, but the port was destined to conduct a relatively small trade in that product until improvements in the navigability of the Cape Fear River allowed shipments directly to Europe.

Table 12
Naval Stores Exports, Wilmington, Charleston, and Savannah, 1882–83

Foreign

	Spirits of Turpentine	Rosin	Tar	Crude	Pitch	Total
Wilmington	54,483	384,534	23,297	692	6	463,012
Charleston	54,883	205,634				260,517
Savannah	37,340	109,670				147,010

Domestic

Wilmington	32,567	98,918	52,241	2,496	7,794	194,016
Charleston	17,188	89,509				106,697
Savannah	49,454	303,500				352,954

Totals

Wilmington	87,050	483,452	75,538	3,188	7,800	657,028
Charleston	72,071	295,143				367,214
Savannah	86,794	413,170				499,964

Weekly Star, Oct. 5, 1883.

Table 13
Cotton Exports in Bales

Year	Domestic	Foreign	Total
1866	24,492	162	24,654
1868	31,828		31,828
1873	35,016	4,634	39,650
1875	53,123	18,140	71,263
1880–81	50,042	69,810	119,852
1884–85	28,282	65,862	94,144
1887–88	47,120	121,903	169,023

Directory of the City of Wilmington, 1889.

Foreign shipments of cotton were insignificant until the mid-1870s and did not surpass domestic exports until about 1880, when the Corps of Engineers had virtually finished the first stage of deepening the Cape Fear bar and channel. Subsequently the foreign trade in cotton was paramount, comprising two-thirds or more of the exports. The bulk of Wilmington's overseas cotton went to Liverpool (48,372 of 57,762 bales in 1883), followed distantly by Bremen and then a host of other ports including Amsterdam, Barcelona, Cranstadt, Genoa, Ghent, Hamburg, and Le Havre.[10]

The cotton export season opened in September. In 1889, the Spanish vessel *Borenquen*, arriving September 12 and clearing September 21 with 2,470 bales of cotton and 1,200 barrels of rosin, was the first cotton export steamer to appear that year. The British steamer *Picton*, entering on September 12 and clearing six days later with 7,459 bales of cotton, inaugurated the 1890 season. The bulk of the foreign cotton left port by January, though ships continued to call in March and a few might appear as late as May and June.[11]

While foreign exports boomed, the domestic trade in cotton leveled off in the 80s. During the decade and a half after the Civil War domestic exports barely more than doubled. During depressed years, for example 1884–85, they barely totaled more than 1866 exports. Cotton destined for United States ports was shipped throughout the year, even during July and August, though most of the crop had disappeared by the end of March.[12] By the 1880s virtually all Wilmington cotton in domestic shipping went to New York.

Though a number of merchant houses lined the waterfront of Wilmington, none was more significant to the port's cotton trade than Alexander Sprunt & Son. Alexander Sprunt, a native of Scotland, settled in Wilmington in 1852. A son, James, gained firsthand experience in the cotton export trade while engaged in blockade running during the war. After the war, when the business was organized, Sprunt concentrated on naval stores. Following the decline of the naval stores market and the death of Alexander Sprunt, who was succeeded by James, the company began expanding rapidly in cotton, becoming "probably the largest cotton exporting house in the United States," according to historian J. R. Killick.[13]

The Sprunts initiated radical changes in the system of marketing cotton in North Carolina. Before 1875 cotton moved from the farmer to a nearby factor, who in turn sought a buyer in Wilmington. That commission merchant sent the cotton north, where it might be sold to a northern mill or reexported to Europe. Basically the procedure was inefficient and expensive. During the next quarter century the Sprunts sought to acquire cotton in the cotton-growing regions of North and South Carolina, constructed warehouses between their wharves on the river and the railroad termini, gained control of Wilmington's cotton compresses, and instituted a direct European trade in cotton. By providing better financing and service for their agents who purchased cotton, the Sprunts even managed to make inroads into the cotton destined for Charleston and Norfolk.[14]

Cotton compressing was essential to the efficient shipping of the fiber. The Sprunts organized the Champion Cotton Compress Company in the late 1870s and eventually assumed control of the older Wilmington Compress and Warehouse Company, which had been started in 1875. Located in the southern part of the city on Nutt Street and vicinity, and connected by rail to the interior of the state, the compress operation was continually enlarged. The loading docks of Champion Compress accommodated four steamers or five sailing packets simultaneously. By 1908 Alexander Sprunt & Son operated six presses, employing a thousand workers in a plant termed one of the most efficient in the South.[15]

Also crucial to the growth of Alexander Sprunt & Son was the development of a direct European trade, which the firm pioneered in the 1880s. The British steamer *Barnesmore* arrived in 1881 in an unsuccessful experiment to start a trade with Liverpool. The Sprunts loaded the *Barnesmore* with 3,458 bales of cotton, 673 barrels of spirits, and 550 barrels of rosin. The venture was disappointing largely because the Cape Fear bar and channel were not yet deep enough to accommodate ships of the necessary size to make a transatlantic crossing profitable.[16] The Sprunts persisted. After the death of the elder partner in 1884, James Sprunt visited England and the continent, crossing the Atlantic some twenty-three times to establish sales offices in commercial centers which would supply the European cotton mills. About 1888 he began a direct trade with Reval, Russia. Credit for the enterprise came from Laird and Gray, New York bankers who were agents for the Canadian Bank of Commerce. Sprunt soon transformed his company and Wilmington into a potent force in the Atlantic mercantile world.[17]

At the outset the Sprunts were one of several cotton exporting firms in Wilmington. Among their competitors were Owen Fennell, Jr., Hall & Pearsall, Calder & Bros., F. W. Kerchner, Williams & Murchison, Woodie & Currie, Worth & Worth, McNair & Pearsall, S. P. McNair, and E. J. Lilly. In addition several general commission merchants, including Rudolph E. Heide, who came to American from Denmark, fought in the Confederate army, and settled in Wilmington after war, might have handled cotton. By the 1890s, however, the Sprunts controlled the cotton export trade of Wilmington. Starting in 1881 with the shipment to Liverpool, by 1890 the firm shipped two-thirds of all the cotton that left the port.[18]

Overall, however, as a cotton port in 1870s Wilmington lacked the shipping facilities to compete successfully with other Atlantic and Gulf Coast cities. Table 14 indicates the importance of New Orleans, which was distantly followed by Galveston, Savannah, Norfolk, and Charleston. The shallow Cape Fear bar and channel militated against the passage of larger ships and a profitable transatlantic trade. High insurance and freight rates also adversely affected cotton receipts. Merchants worked tirelessly and with some success (due to increased volume) to reduce the charges. More efficient methods of loading and unloading the "soft" cotton helped as well. Yet twenty years later Wilmington as a cotton port had not materially improved its position vis-à-vis competing ports. Cotton may have been the mainstay of the port's trade, but Wilmington conducted a comparatively small business.[19]

The appearance of peanuts in North Carolina agriculture before the war betokened a growing industry and export for the Lower Cape Fear. In the two decades following reunion North Carolina peanuts were grown principally between Beaufort and the South Carolina line. Most of the crops in that area were marketed in Wilmington and exported to New York and Philadelphia. By 1883 four peanut cleaners in Wilmington reflected the importance of the trade. As in the case of rice, the tariff was crucial to the development of the American industry, principally as protection from the competition of African imports.[20]

Noticeably absent from Wilmington's major exports was rice. The postbellum rice industry struggled but never attained its prewar status. Not

Table 14
Cotton Exports (Thousands of Bales), Selected Ports, 1875–1900

	1875	1880	1885	1890	1895	1900
Wilmington	15	37	66	112	202	275
Norfolk	67	254	296	266	192	46
Charleston	265	315	340	240	341	NA
Savannah	426	425	390	535	537	726
New Orleans	995	1,398	1,336	1,825	2,088	1,706
Galveston	225	294	230	456	1,349	1,569

Evans, *Ballots and Fence Rails*, 194 (figures rounded to nearest thousand).

only was rice production exceedingly labor-intensive and therefore costly, but the rice planters were unable to adapt to the use of free labor—to calculate the costs and benefits of the wage system as opposed to bonded labor. According to the editor of the *Wilmington Review,* "It is a well-known fact that of the old planters on the Cape Fear River, who had the temerity to undertake the planting of rice with free labor as it existed in 1865, 1866, 1867 and 1868 not one succeeded."[21]

Rice production did experience a brief revival about 1880. The discovery that certain strains could be grown in the uplands as far away as the Piedmont and the protection offered by the federal tariff contributed to the renewed interest in the grain. Barely 10,000 bushels were brought to the Wilmington market in 1875, not nearly enough to feed residents of the port. But by 1878, 40,000 bushels appeared, and in 1881, 124,000 bushels were harvested in the Cape Fear area, about two-thirds of the antebellum total.[22]

Wilmington was the major market for rice in the state. The port received rice from Washington, Beaufort, New Bern, Goldsboro, Warsaw, Mount Olive, and Wilson as well as from some twenty-two planters who in 1882 grew rice along the Cape Fear. Most of the rough grain was sent to northern mills and to South Carolina. Some was cleaned by the Carolina Rice Mills in Wilmington, started in 1881 by local entrepreneurs Norwood Giles and Pembroke Jones. That rice was shipped principally to New York, Boston, and Philadelphia.[23]

Although the commercial production of rice in the United States shifted to the Mississippi delta region during the last quarter of the nineteenth century, the grain continued to be grown in the Lower Cape Fear. William Larkins and Andrew Flanner operated a rice mill in 1887 at their recently purchased Point Peter plantation at the confluence of the Northwest and Northeast rivers. Storms in the fall of 1893 reportedly damaged rice crops along the Cape Fear River. Rice was protected by the tariff, particularly the Dingley law of 1897, and prospects in that year were "bright for a large yield of rice" in the Wilmington area.[24]

Enhancing Wilmington's potential as a port was its manufacturing capacity. However, the postwar industrialization that so characterized the nation and Piedmont North Carolina made less of an impression upon the Lower Cape Fear, geared as it was to extractive industry and its ancillary manufacturing enterprises of naval stores and wood products. Newspaper editors and progressive businessmen eloquently intoned the "New South" philosophy, in which progress was equated with the number of miles of railroad track and the number of spindles in cotton manufactories, but in North Carolina's coastal plain traditional agrarianism proved almost insurmountable.

True, in some towns—for example, Wilmington and New Bern—the cotton textile industry gained a foothold. Several prominent local businessmen started the Wilmington Cotton Mills in 1874. Completed the following year, the mills employed 125 operatives to manufacture over 3,000 yards of cloth daily. As one historian aptly wrote, the project "survived but scarcely thrived." In 1878 the company admitted bankruptcy and appointed a trustee to sell the property, stock, and franchise of the corporation to pay its debts. It brought $58,000 at public auction.[25]

Upon its reorganization in 1878 with a reduced capitalization, the Wilmington Cotton Mills gained a new lease on life. In the early 80s it produced annually 200,000 yards of cloth, mainly print and batting, which were sent to the north for finishing. By the end of the century the operation had added a dyehouse and finishing machinery to produce a wide range of fabrics in Wilmington. A second manufactory, the Delgado Cotton Mills, joined the Wilmington Cotton Mills in 1899.[26]

Much of the manufacturing growth of Wilmington remained linked to the extractive industry of the region and the operation of the port. The Wilmington Manufacturing Company, incorporated in 1867 to produce casks for spirits of turpentine, the Steam Cooperage Manufactory of Strauz & Rice, and the five lumber mills that lined the Wilmington waterfront in 1872 were exemplary. So, too, in 1883 were the four grain and two flour mills, eight turpentine and two rosin distilleries, the Cape Fear Tobacco works (employing sixty in making plug, twist, and smoking tobacco), the Carolina Rice Mills, the Southern Ore Company, the dry dock, the two marine railways, and the three machine shops and foundries to be found in the environs of Wilmington.[27]

Stimulating lumbering was the wood preservation industry. Railroad cross ties and utility (telegraph, then telephone and electrical) poles required continuous replacement. Creosoting ordinary timber provided the means to counter wood deterioration, leading to immense savings of lumber and labor. In 1886, a decade after the Louisville and Nashville Railroad began experimenting with the process, Ludwig Hansen and Andrew Smith with other investors founded the Carolina Oil and Creosote Company in Wilmington.[28]

The Carolina Oil and Creosote Company added greatly to the demand for timber in the Lower Cape Fear, not just for fat lightwood from which creosote was derived but also for ordinary woods that previously possessed little economic value. In June 1887 the *Wilmington Review* carried the story of a resident living along the Northeast Cape Fear in Duplin County who had been gathering timber for the creosote company since the previous October. He was sending to Wilmington four rafts of old spruce pine, "hitherto the most useless timber in the state." According to the paper, he had "a large quantity of this sort of timber . . . and what has been an eyesore has now become the most profitable property in his possession."[29]

Fertilizer production emerged as a leading Wilmington industry in the latter years of the nineteenth century. Almost coincidentally it originated in the need for a substitute for ballast brought by ships in the West Indian lumber trade. From the inception of Wilmington in the eighteenth century vessels often arrived in ballast, wishing to load in port but not having cargoes to sell in the Cape Fear. After the Civil War several investors in the West Indian lumber trade decided to import guano in hopes of making the return voyage from the islands profitable and at the same time stimulating a fertilizer industry in that area that might prove remunerative.[30]

Although an initial effort in 1867 to establish the Cape Fear Guano Company failed, mainly due to postwar financial distress, two years later the same businessmen organized the Navassa Guano Company, named for the Caribbean island between Haiti and Jamaica from which the guano came. Subscribers to the Navassa Guano Company included South Carolinians and planters from as far away as Edgecombe County, North Carolina. By locating the company at Hilton, a site just north of Wilmington, the organizers took advantage of the three rail facilities that converged on the port. The Navassa company almost immediately proved a success. Demand outstripped its capacity to supply "during the dullest season," according to the *Journal*.[31]

The fertilizer industry became increasingly important in the Wilmington economy and played a vital role in the port's trade in the twentieth century. By 1896 three additional fertilizer firms had joined the Navassa Guano Company in Wilmington: Powers, Gibbs & Co., Sans Souci Fertilizer Works, and Acme Fertilizer Company. The four companies, producing seventy thousand tons of fertilizer annually, marketed their product in Virginia, Tennessee, South Carolina, Georgia, and Alabama. Again Wilmington competed with southern ports. Its fertilizer production approximated that of Savannah but lagged behind that of Charleston.[32]

Shipbuilding continued apace in Wilmington as well as along the Cape Fear River, from Fayetteville to Bald Head Island, and its tributaries. Steamers (paddle and screw), tugs, snag boats, schooners, sloops, sharpies, and yachts slid down the ways. The 300-ton *Marion S. Harriss*, built for Wilmington commission merchant George Harriss and intended for the West Indies trade, may well have been the largest. Steamers *Colville* and *River Queen*, 140 and 132 tons respectively, doubtlessly topped their class. Most Wilmington-built vessels were well under 100 tons. By 1900 Captain S. W. Skinner's marine railway was the only major private boat contractor in the port, though he had been joined by the Army Corps of Engineers who operated a boatyard for repairing their vessels.[33]

At the end of the century the creosoting works, cotton compresses, cotton mills, marine railways, and machine shops were supplemented by the American Pine Fibre Company, which manufactured bagging; the Industrial Manufacturing Company, which produced dishes; and the North Carolina Cotton Seed Oil Mills. Counting large as well as small industrial concerns, according to census definition in 1900, Wilmington contained 131 manufacturing establishments, whose output was valued at almost three million dollars.[34]

In conjunction with river and ocean commerce, railroads helped to form the lifeline of Wilmington's trade in the latter years of the nineteenth century. In some instances, particularly truck farming, which burgeoned in eastern North Carolina after the Civil War, the railroads were the principal carriers. More important, however, the railroads served, and were expected to serve, as conduits of naval stores, wood products, cotton, and other bulky products to Wilmington, from whence such goods would be shipped to northern Atlantic ports, the West Indies, and Europe.

Three railroads converged upon Wilmington within a decade of the conclusion of the war—the Wilmington and Weldon, the Wilmington and Manchester, and the Wilmington, Charlotte and Rutherford—all of which, along with their side tracks or spurs, were designed to tap specific areas of interior trade. After its completion in 1840, it was thought that the Wilmington and Weldon would attract produce of the Roanoke Valley, particularly cotton, that ordinarily went to Petersburg and Norfolk. Yet the road was never as successful as North Carolinians and Wilmingtonians had hoped in diverting trade from Virginia.

Like the Wilmington and Weldon, the Wilmington and Manchester was intended to draw trade from a competing port, in this case Charleston, South Carolina. The railroad emerged from the Civil War in a debilitated condition. It went into receivership in 1868, appearing two years later as the Wilmington, Columbia and Augusta Railroad, whose link to the South Carolina capital, completed in 1875, raised the expectations of Wilmingtonians. Actually the effort insofar as cotton was concerned was mainly unsuccessful, for Charleston afforded farmers a well-developed market for their crop.[35]

With its eastern terminus on Eagles Island, the Wilmington, Columbia and Augusta traversed 189 miles through Brunswick and Columbus counties in North Carolina and into Marion, Darlington, Sumter, and Richland counties below the border. Although little cotton was diverted from the Charleston market, the Wilmington, Columbia and Augusta did lure a considerable quantity of naval stores and lumber from the northeastern area of South Carolina, for Wilmington proved a better naval stores market than Charleston.[36]

Following the Civil War the Carolina Central Railway Company, which purchased the Wilmington, Charlotte and Rutherford in 1873 and reorganized as the Carolina Railroad Company in 1881, was probably Wilmington's most important rail link. Many entertained hopes that the Carolina Central would be extended through Asheville to the Tennessee line and thus offer a western connection as far as the Ohio River Valley. Although the link to the west failed to materialize, by 1900, when the Carolina Central became part of the Seaboard Air Line system, its main trunk extended 264 miles to Rutherfordton with branch lines covering another 11 miles.[37]

Rather than the Carolina Central, the Cape Fear and Yadkin Valley Railroad proved to be Wilmington's most feasible connection with the west. The Cape Fear and Yadkin Valley originated in the consolidation of the Western Railroad Company and the Mount Airy Railroad Company in 1879, which was permitted to build to Wilmington in 1881. By 1890 the railroad had been completed. The 248-mile main line connected the port with Mount Airy in Surry County. Three branch routes, including one from Fayetteville to Bennettsville, South Carolina, encompassed another 89 miles.[38]

Supplementing the major roads was the Wilmington, Onslow and East Carolina, running from New Bern in Craven County through Jacksonville in Onslow County to the port. Onslow planters had tried as early as 1870 to secure a rail connection from Jacksonville or some point on New River to the Wilmington and Weldon, but their efforts were premature by two decades. The first train from Jacksonville to Wilmington arrived in February 1891. Two years later the New Bern route was opened, by which time the 87-mile road had become the Wilmington, Newbern and Norfolk Railroad.[39]

Most of Wilmington's railroads eventually were subsumed by the Atlantic Coast Line Railroad, which located its general offices in Wilmington.

The name originated about 1871 upon the unification of management policies of several railroads in Virginia, North Carolina, and South Carolina, and was later formalized by the creation of a holding company. By the beginning of the twentieth century the Atlantic Coast Line had constructed an extensive office and warehouse complex in Wilmington abutting the river at Red Cross and Front streets. The Wilmington and Weldon, the Wilmington, Columbia and Augusta, part of the Cape Fear and Yadkin Valley, and the Wilmington, Newbern and Norfolk railroads became Atlantic Coast Line properties. The Carolina Central fell under the control of the Seaboard Air Line.[40]

Although the railroad was a potential competitor of inland and coastal water transportation, it was not until the postbellum years that the rails mounted a formidable threat, mostly in the form of passenger and mail traffic in addition to carrying truck produce. It seems clear that shipping benefited more from railroads than vice versa, for the railroads brought the needed export items of cotton, naval stores, and lumber to the port. Moreover, trains complemented shipping in the wake of a burgeoning fertilizer industry in Wilmington, making the importation of guano profitable by providing a cheap, easy means of selling it in the interior.

Favored as they were by extensive watercourses and a railroad network, Wilmingtonians failed to appreciate the need for improved highways into the interior that might contribute to the city's growth. Road supervision and construction changed little from the previous century. And in the aftermath of the Civil War poverty-stricken conditions were not conducive to internal improvements underwritten by government. As a result, according to a correspondent to the *Journal* in 1870, the roads in New Hanover County were "in a most desperate condition."[41]

Inadequate bridges—or, where they existed, toll bridges— reinforced the difficulty and expense of land travel. Most of the bridges in New Hanover County had to be rebuilt after the war. The state resorted to the time-honored practice of establishing toll bridges or ferries across the Northeast Cape Fear above Wilmington and across the Brunswick River to Eagles Island and from the island to Wilmington. Toward the end of the century the local authorities toyed with the idea of free bridges and ferries (passage paid by tax revenues) and began to spend more money to improve roads. Yet it remained for the automobile in the twentieth century to create a demand for better roads.[42]

Still contributing greatly to Wilmington's local market was river shipping, though it may have declined in relative importance after the war. The two branches of the Cape Fear remained crucial arteries of interior trade for the port. Rafts and flatboats continued to bring down lumber, naval stores, and cotton. The mode of freightage had changed little. Dependent upon water levels and currents, it was tedious and uncertain. And rafting was not always an idyllic exercise of floating down the river. In January 1881 a strong tide and wind on the Northwest Cape Fear carried five timber rafts coming from Bladen County into the Brunswick River. Two men drowned; the others managed to make their way to shore. All the rafts were later found among the jetties below Wilmington. Even when moored the rafts were not altogether safe. Tied up at a wharf at the foot of Princess Street, a raft carrying 245 barrels of rosin belonging to W. T. Autry of Sampson County was struck by the tug *Wm. Nyce*, which was towing a schooner downriver. The raft was demolished and the rosin sank like "lead." The accident was described as one of the "unavoidable mishaps" which was bound to occur in a crowded harbor.[43]

Only steamers provided reasonably reliable service on the river. For the run between Wilmington and Fayetteville the Express Steamboat Company was incorporated in 1865 to promote "the commerce and industries" of Wilmington. By 1867 five companies, not to mention private individuals, offered steamer service between Wilmington and Fayetteville. Obstructions in the river, however, continued to threaten or impede boating traffic. The *Governor Worth* hit a snag and sank in 1881, only to be raised four months later.[44]

Traffic on the Northwest Cape Fear probably increased in the 1880s after Congress appropriated funds in 1881 to improve the navigation of the river. In preparation for the Corps of Engineers to dredge a channel the government had to settle the claims of the Cape Fear Navigation Company. That company in 1870 had attempted to collect tolls on the Northwest Cape Fear and apparently by intimidation had deterred traffic on the river. Immediately after the $10,000 government buyout of the company in 1881 a new line of steamers was put on the Northwest Cape Fear, and the *Wilmington Post* extolled the "fruits of . . . a free river."[45]

Acting on a $30,000 appropriation in 1881, the Corps began clearing the river below Fayetteville, work that included some dredging and constructing of jetties or dikes to improve the water flow. In 1885 Congress called for a four-foot channel from Wilmington to Elizabethtown, approximately seventy miles upriver, and a three-foot channel from Elizabethtown to Fayetteville. The Corps continued its efforts to the end of the century, but the work was never as productive as hoped. Despite dredging, snagging, and jettying, freshets quickly devastated the best efforts of humans (as early Cape Fear improvement companies had discovered).[46]

As the attempts to improve the navigability of the Northwest Cape Fear moved forward, so did steamer passenger, freight, and mail traffic. During the 1880s the Express, Cape Fear and People's, and Bladen companies provided daily (except Sunday) service. In addition to towing lighters, the *D. Murchison* and *Wave* carried 1,000 and 800 barrels respectively for the Express Company. The *Gov. Worth, North State,* and *A.P. Hurt* could transport 2,200, 700, and 400 barrels respectively for the Cape Fear and People's Company; the *Bladen* and *John Dawson,* 500 and 350 barrels respectively for the Bladen Company. All had a load draft of less than four feet.[47]

Steamer traffic between Wilmington and Fayetteville diminished toward the end of the century in consequence of the competition offered by the railroads, particularly the completion of the Cape Fear and Yadkin Valley in 1890. In 1894 the Express Company operated the *Cape Fear* and the *A.P. Hurt,* but laid off the *D. Murchison.* By 1900 only the Cape Fear Transportation Company and the Merchants and Farmers Steamboat Company were running steamers regularly from Wilmington on the Northwest Cape Fear River. The former had secured the *A.P. Hurt* and the *D. Murchison,* and chartered other steamers when needed.[48]

Steamer activity heightened on the tributaries of the Northwest Cape Fear after the Civil War. Captain R. P. Paddison pioneered efforts to open Black River to Wilmington traffic. His *Little Sam* make triweekly trips between Point Caswell on the river and Wilmington in 1870, advertising "moderate" freight and passenger fares. Five years later Paddison ran the *North East* on the same route, and even included excursion parties when time permitted. "Commodore" Charles Howe in 1875 put the *Little Adrian*, named for Aldrich Adrian of the Wilmington firm of Adrian & Vollers, on the upper reaches of Black River in Sampson County.[49]

Howe and Wilmington businessmen also secured a charter from the legislature in the session of 1876–77 to incorporate the Black River Navigation Company. The statute granted the company a monopoly on traffic above Point Caswell on the condition that it clear the upper reaches of Black River to render steamboat navigation safe. Apparently the difficulty of clearing the river was too great for the incorporators, particularly in light of the meager returns from the naval stores industry in the area. Thus the company centered its attention on the lower part of Black River, acquiring the steamer *Isis* and putting her on a regular run to Wilmington in 1879 under Captain S. W. Skinner.[50]

Short railroads were contemplated to complement the steamer trade. Efforts to build a narrow-gauge railroad from Clinton, the seat of Sampson

County, to Point Caswell on Black River, where steamers could load produce for Wilmington, led to the incorporation of the Wilmington, Point Caswell and Clinton Railroad and Steamboat Transportation Company in 1883, but the road was never built. Instead, the Wilmington and Weldon constructed a branch line from Warsaw to Clinton.[51]

During the 1880s commerce on Black River heightened to the extent that four steamers and five flats operated regularly in mid-1886. Inhabitants of Bladen, Pender, and Sampson counties petitioned Congress for appropriations to improve the navigability of the river. They claimed that annually $750,000 worth of produce—cotton, naval stores, lumber, shingles—was taken to market via Black River, an amount that could be doubled with the enhancement of river transport facilities. Upon investigation Captain W. H. Bixby of the Corps of Engineers recommended that the government undertake a project to clear thoroughly a channel of natural depth over seventy miles in length from the mouth of Black River to the vicinity of Lisbon, a small Sampson County community on the Great Coharie, a tributary of Black River.[52]

Subsequent dredging by the Corps of Engineers, extending well into the 1890s, brought increased activity and prosperity to the Black River region and Wilmington. Though naval stores receipts in Wilmington began to decrease in the late 1880s, the improvements to the navigability of Black River brought forth a greater flow of those products from that area. A year after the panic of 1893 traffic on Black River continued to surge. The steamer *Lisbon* of the Black River Line had more freight than she could carry, showing that "times are not so hard in the huckleberry country as in other sections."[53]

The commercial potential of the Northeast Cape Fear River was not neglected following the Civil War. The General Assembly chartered the New River Canal Company in 1872, in what proved to be an unsuccessful effort by Onslow County residents to link New River and the Northeast Cape Fear. Other efforts in the 1870s to utilize the waters of the Northeast Cape Fear involved the construction of canals to shorten the distance of navigating the winding, twisting river to the Wilmington market. Surveys to that end were made by the Duplin Canal Company in 1874; eight years later the company continued to hold annual meetings, resolving to operate on a "cash" basis to avoid the death-grip of indebtedness.[54] None of these efforts, however, seems to have materialized in a viable canal.

Steamer traffic on the Northeast appeared after the Civil War, though it was insignificant compared to that on the Northwest Cape Fear. In April 1879 the *Clinton* brought seven hundred barrels of rosin from Bannerman's

Bridge in Pender County to Wilmington. That small stern-wheel steamer continued to run on the Northeast for another two years before sinking at her wharf in Wilmington in 1881. That year Captain B. M. Roberts of Wilmington, in his little steamer *Busy Bee*, towed a flat up Holly Shelter Creek about nineteen miles from its junction with the Northeast Cape Fear, the first time a steamer had entered that creek. Roberts hoped to make regular freight runs between Holly Shelter Creek and Wilmington.[55]

The late 1880s found the United States government funding work by the Corps of Engineers to improve the navigability of the Northeast Cape Fear. A report in 1888 by Captain W. H. Bixby, U.S. engineer in charge of river and harbor improvements, noted the wealth of material and agricultural resources along the river that might be tapped by improved trade. Subsequently congressional appropriations allowed the Corps to clear the river for steam navigation from Chinquapin, about seventy-eight miles from Wilmington, down to Bannerman's Bridge, below which there was a six-foot channel to the port.[56]

Wilmington's downriver commerce centered upon Smithville, incorporated as Southport (the Port of the South) in 1887. Southport expected to reap valuable commercial benefits from the improvement of the bar and river channel after the war, particularly by way of shipping from South America and the West Indies, and as a distribution point for coal from the north and west. Various schemes were hatched to link the town by rail to Wilmington and the interior, but all efforts proved abortive. Southport remained a village in the shadow of the busy port of Wilmington.[57]

Steamer travel between Wilmington and Southport (Smithville) resumed immediately after the Civil War, but was confined mainly to passenger traffic. The Wilmington and Smithville Steamboat Company, chartered in 1871, ran the *Waccamaw* between the river towns. The following decade the *Passport* and the *Minnehaha*, 250- and 200-passenger capacity respectively, awaited the traveling public on the lower Cape Fear. A favorite stop between Wilmington and Southport during the summer season was Carolina Beach, an ocean resort about fifteen miles below Wilmington. During the 1890s the New Hanover Transit Company's *Wilmington*, captained by John W. Harper, gave daily (except Sunday) service. At the turn of the century two other companies ran steamers on the lower Cape Fear River.[58]

Some commercial activity linked Wilmington and the smaller streams of Brunswick County below Southport. River craft brought produce to market and returned with general merchandise for the country inhabitants. Encouraging that activity was the improvement in the navigability of the local waters. Although state law traditionally required residents along navigable watercourses to keep the rivers and streams open, federal funding underwrote much of that work after the war. The water-borne commerce between Wilmington and Brunswick County centered on Town Creek, Lockwoods Folly River, and Shallotte River. After a drawbridge was built in 1889 on Town Creek a short distance from its mouth, the steamer *Acme* operated regularly between Wilmington and the "upper bridge" on Town Creek, about thirty miles from its mouth. In 1890 one vessel made scheduled runs on Lockwood Folly River; two others made frequent trips on the river. More active was shipping on Shallotte River, where coastal schooners used the river at high tide to carry naval stores, lumber, cotton, and other goods to Wilmington.[59]

Wilmington's coastal trade followed antebellum patterns, focusing as it did on New York. Six of nine commercial steamships calling at the port in 1865 connected Wilmington and New York. Two linked the North Carolina port and Philadelphia; one, Boston. Nonetheless, efforts of the Wilmington and Charlotte Ocean Steamship Company and the Wilmington and Atlantic Steamship Company, incorporated mainly by Wilmington businessmen who intended to run a regular line of steamers between Wilmington and New York or other ports, met a quick demise. Apparently a line of steamers to Baltimore, pioneered by the *Raleigh* in 1883, was also short-lived. Still some cotton was sent to the Maryland port as pre-Civil War interest in a Baltimore trade carried over to the 1870s.[60]

Of the several steamship lines connecting Wilmington with Atlantic ports in the United States, the New York and Wilmington Steamship Company, known locally as the Clyde Line, was by far the most successful. Running the *Gulf Stream* (998 tons), *Regulator* (847 tons), and *Benefactor* (844 tons) in 1883, the Clyde Line maintained a semiweekly freight service. Table 15, showing Wilmington's imports and exports via the Clyde Line during 1882, reflects the general nature of the port's commerce: lumber, naval stores, cotton, and rice left for New York; merchandise and foodstuffs, supplemented by hay and corn for area farmers concentrating on more remunerative crops, returned to Wilmington. At the end of the century the Clyde Line remained Wilmington's only regularly scheduled commercial shipping carrier beyond North Carolina. At that time five steamers moved freight and passengers among New York, Wilmington, and Georgetown, South Carolina, the last having been added to the Clyde's schedule.[61]

The West Indian trade, mainly based on the island demand for lumber, resumed on an irregular basis after the Civil War. The growing European commerce in naval stores and cotton may have diminished Wilmington's

Table 15
Wilmington Imports and Exports via the Clyde Line, 1882

Exports		Imports	
Cotton (bales)	58,655	Syrup (bbls.)	1,379
Lumber (ft.)	5,640,707	Sugar (bbls.)	6,195
Shooks	2,935	Bacon (boxes)	10,318
Shingles	1,292,000	Lard (pkgs.)	1,570
Naval stores (bbls.)	95,607	Corn (sacks)	114,503
Spirits turpentine (bbls.)	27,400	Oats	7,251
Rice, cleaned (tierces)	3,950	Hay (bales)	25,328
Rice, meal (sacks)	4,396	Liquor (pkgs.)	686
Rice, rough (sacks)	4,131	Oil, lubricating (bbls)	144
Molasses (hhds.)	130	Coffee (sacks)	5,913
Peanuts (sacks)	1,197	Ties (bundles)	3,162
Pig Iron (tons)	174	Bagging (rolls)	15,875
Yarn (bales)	366	Cement (bbls.)	600
Merchandise (pkgs.)	7,676	Water pipe (pieces)	916
		Brick	10,200
		Sulphur (tons)	437
		Railroad iron (rails)	2,785
		Merchandize (pkgs.)	143,601
		Shoes (cases)	3,776
		Barrels	21,346
		Guano (sacks)	40,510

Sprunt, *Information and Statistics Respecting Wilmington*, 113.

dependence upon the islands for export purposes, but the incorporation of the Wilmington and West Indies Navigation Company in 1893, chartered for passenger and freight service, attested to the continuing trade with the islands. Of Wilmington's foreign traffic in 1895, 45 of the 80 vessels entering the port arrived from the West Indies; 84 of the 136 clearing left for the islands.[62]

American-owned vessels monopolized coastal shipping because the United States government refused to allow foreign competition in that realm of commerce. However, Wilmington's coastal trade, dominant during the Reconstruction era, was thereafter challenged by an overseas commerce in which American ships played a very minor role. Of the total value of Wilmington's foreign exports in 1882, $5,793,188, only $155,722, or 3 percent, was taken out by American-owned shipping.

Throughout the postwar era exports continued to overshadow imports in tonnage and value. During the year ending June 30, 1895, imports amounted to $87,921; exports, $6,590,264—90 percent of which was cotton destined for the United Kingdom and Germany. Naval stores (7 percent) and wood products (3 percent) comprised the remainder of the exports. As in the colonial era the imbalance between exports and imports militated against trade. Many vessels arrived in ballast—17 of 80 in foreign trade in 1895, indicative of the weak market for foreign (and American) goods in Wilmington.[63]

Improving the navigability of the Cape Fear, particularly below Wilmington to the bar, was the key to the continued commercial importance of the port, particularly in foreign trade. During the Civil War the obstacles to navigation at the mouth of the Cape Fear proved to be a blessing to Wilmington and the Confederacy. Frying Pan Shoals, the relatively shallow river bar, and New Inlet rendered a successful Federal blockade virtually impossible. The failure to close New Inlet in the late 1850s was fortuitous, for it was the preferred entrée to the river by blockade runners. Indeed, Wilmington reached its zenith of commercial importance and prosperity during the war years. The end of the Civil War, however, again found the shoals and shallow bar a hindrance to shipping. This realization was intensified by the fact that larger, deeper draft ships were being constructed. Not only would they find the bar difficult to cross, but the vessels would encounter a twisting, shoaling river channel with snags as they sought to reach Wilmington. Wrote one pessimistic observer in 1869, "Because the Cape Fear seems to be gradually filling up, and vessels of a large class cannot enter our port, and because the produce of the State is seeking ports in other states, while the trade and commerce of our own *languishes,* many people suppose that North Carolina is doomed and may sooner or later yield to the law of circumstance [and] merge her territory into Virginia and South Carolina."[64]

Wilmington businessmen led by Henry Nutt sought congressional help in renewing prewar efforts to close New Inlet and deepen the channel. Spearheading the fight in Congress was North Carolina Senator Joseph C. Abbot, a "carpetbagger" who had fought for the Union, been cited for gallantry in the capture of Fort Fisher, and settled in Wilmington to edit the Republican newspaper *Wilmington Post.* Congress responded to the pressures of the North Carolina delegation in 1869 by authorizing a preliminary examination of the river the following year. The ensuing report favored the resumption of the prewar works. Between 1870 and 1882 Congress appropriated $1,502,500 for the improvement of the lower Cape Fear

River and bar. The work involved three objectives: removing obstructions in the river, closing New Inlet and nearby swashes, and dredging a 12-foot channel.[65]

Eliminating obstacles in the river challenged the Corps. The Engineers removed Confederate-laid obstructions about three miles below Wilmington. Some five miles farther downriver the Corps had to contend with the "logs," supposedly a shoal of relict timbers. As a dredge boat began to remove the trees in 1874, it discovered that the "logs" actually were an old cypress swamp. Some of the extracted stumps measured eight feet in diameter. The clearing process was lengthier than anticipated, though by March 1875 a dredge boat made its sixth and last swing through the "logs," clearing a channel 245 feet wide and 12 feet deep at low tide.[66]

Of the two inlets to the Cape Fear River—New Inlet and the one between Bald Head and Oak Island—the former was the logical one to estop. Easternly winds drove the floodtides and accompanying sand through New Inlet. The tide ebbed through the old channel, leaving sand in the harbor and mouth of the river from New Inlet south some twelve miles to the old bar. Furthermore, while the old bar could be dredged, New Inlet had a floor of rock that militated against obtaining more than a 12-foot depth.[67]

Not all appreciated the decision to close New Inlet. The small coastal sailing craft or "corn-crackers" from Onslow and other coastal counties would be forced to round the cape, an additional fifty-mile trip, and would have to contend with Frying Pan Shoals in order to enter the river. A petition opposing the New Inlet closure circulated in Wilmington in 1876. Three years later the area's congressional representative, Daniel L. Russell, having strong ties with Onslow County, protested the move.[68]

The work went forward, however. But closing New Inlet proved a formidable task, requiring several years to complete. During the process the Corps left a gap in the dam to admit small coastal schooners. In June 1879 the Corps finally closed the aperture, and Henry Nutt was given the honor of being the first person to walk across the dam. The Rocks, as the structure was known, was a monument to the skill of the Corps. But another two years elapsed before its completion. When workmen finished the dam in July 1881, it was 4,800 feet in length with an average height of 37 feet and a base that varied from 75 to 120 feet.[69]

Storms continued to play havoc with the Corps's efforts. One in 1877 opened a breach in the breastworks between Zeke and Smith islands. Closed in the summer of 1881, the opening reappeared after a succession of storms in the fall of that year. Eventually three swashes emerged. The

Corps moved slowly but steadily, using stone quarried along the banks of the lower Cape Fear River to close the gaps. By 1891 a 12,400-foot "swash defense dam" had been completed to separate the Atlantic Ocean and the Cape Fear River.[70]

Dredging the river channel began in earnest after the closing of New Inlet. In its Rivers and Harbors Act of 1881 Congress mandated a channel 270 feet wide and 16 feet deep from Wilmington to the bar. Work proceeded slowly on the new congressional proposal. By June 30, 1887, a total of $1,773,946 had been spent on the lower Cape Fear projects. The Corps also attempted to straighten Horseshoe Bend opposite New Inlet, the worst turn in the lower part of the river, a project completed in 1890 and named Snow's Marsh Channel.[71]

As the Corps struggled to establish and maintain a 16-foot channel, Congress in its appropriations bill of 1890 envisioned deepening the channel to 20 feet. The Corps finally realized its 1881 directive of a 16-foot channel, 270 feet wide, in 1892. Work to deepen the channel to 20 feet moved slowly, interrupted in 1898 by the war with Spain. By 1902, a depth of 20 feet and a width of 300 feet had been achieved at the bar. Elsewhere, on all the shoals, the figures were 18–20 feet and 185–222 feet.[72]

By the end of the decade ships drawing 19 feet could sail from Wilmington to the sea on one tide. In 1893 the *Holyrod*, bound for Bremen, cleared Wilmington at 18 feet, 4 inches, took on coal and cargo at Southport that lowered her draft to 20 feet, and still made to sea without incident. And in 1894 the Norwegian bark *Anna*, drawing 19 feet, 4 inches, left Wilmington. The efforts of the Corps in improving the river and bar were effective. Moreover, they proved to be the salvation of Wilmington as a deepwater port.[73]

Not only did the Cape Fear serve private commercial craft, it also entertained United States naval vessels in the 1890s. The man-of-war *Kearsage* and the monitor *Nantucket* anchored in Southport harbor in September 1893. The ships afforded an opportunity for the naval reserves of North Carolina, including the company in Wilmington, to gain firsthand experience on vessels at sea. A year after her commissioning in 1895 the cruiser *Raleigh*, named for North Carolina's capital, arrived in the Cape Fear. In 1899, following the conclusion of the war with Spain, the *Raleigh* returned to deliver some trophies of the conflict, including several Spanish cannon, to a delegation representing the state.[74]

Indeed Wilmington played a role in American foreign affairs, and ultimately in the war with Spain in 1898. As a strategically located port in a country sympathetic to the cause of Cuban independence, Wilmington became embroiled in the efforts of Cuban insurrectionaries to liberate their country from Spanish control. The rebels used American ports to obtain coal and cargoes of war matériel as well as to launch filibustering expeditions against the Spanish in Cuba.

After the Civil War, Wilmington's initial overt involvement in the fight for Cuban freedom occurred in the fall of 1869, when the steamer *Cuba,* a privateer in the employ of Cuban insurrectionaries, was seized by the United States marshal after putting into port. Ostensibly the *Cuba* arrived in distress—one engine was incapacitated and she needed coal. Armed with six guns and manned by a crew of a hundred, the vessel presented a formidable appearance. Supportive of the Cuban rebels, Wilmingtonians welcomed the *Cuba,* all the more enthusiastically because her officers were mostly Southerners who had served in the Confederacy. In reciprocation the commander and officers of the *Cuba* held a ball and dinner aboard their vessel for the ladies and gentlemen of the city. The vessel remained in port under government detention as late as November 1869.[75]

At the end of the century Wilmington became the focus of an effort by the Cuban Revolutionary Council in New York to aid the rebel cause by dispatching munitions from the port to the island. In September 1895 the Spanish minister to the United States, Dupuy de Lôme, warned the State Department that ammunition and rifles had been shipped from New York to a Charles Raymond in Southport, North Carolina. He claimed that the 99-ton steamer *Commodore,* which had sailed from New London, Connecticut, would pick up the cargo in Wilmington. The *Commodore* put in at Wilmington in mid-September for repairs and coal, according to her captain, John G. Dillon. Shortly thereafter two railroad cars were brought to a siding close to the point at which the *Commodore* was moored and their contents transferred to the vessel. The Collector of the Port William R. Kenan claimed that the ship's papers were in sufficient order to allow the *Commodore* to proceed to Cartagena, Colombia, but sought instructions from the Treasury Department.[76] As a result of deliberations of the Treasury and State departments, the U.S. attorney for the Eastern District of North Carolina, Charles B. Aycock, was directed to seize the *Commodore,* her captain, and her crew. Though Captain Dillon contended that the suspicious cargo consisted of mining implements and machinery, an investigation revealed munitions. In a preliminary hearing U.S. commissioner Robert H. Bunting discharged Captain Dillon and other members of the crew because there was insufficient evidence that the munitions were destined for Cuban rebels.[77]

As the government prepared to return the *Commodore* to Dillon, new evidence—or at least renewed pressure from de Lôme—prompted federal officials to order the retention of the ship. At a trial held in Goldsboro, North Carolina, before U.S. District Court Judge Augustus S. Seymour the government could produce no new substantive evidence. The defense maintained that the prosecution failed to show that the munitions would be used against a friendly power and that private commerce in munitions was legitimate. Seymour ordered the immediate release of the *Commodore* and her cargo. Still, the vessel lingered in Wilmington until the early months of 1896. A report from de Lôme that dynamite had been taken aboard the *Commodore* prompted a thorough but futile search for the explosives in January. The *Commodore* finally cleared for Charleston at eleven o'clock on the evening of February 14 to the cheers of a handful of people who stood at the wharf watching the departure. Indeed, throughout the affair, Wilmingtonians generally applauded the rebel effort in Cuba and supported the munitions-running *Commodore*—a "gallant ship" that "will carry with her the best wishes of every Wilmingtonian who loves liberty and independence," according to the local newspaper.[78]

In addition to the *Commodore* affair, several other filibustering expeditions on behalf of the Cuban rebels may have centered on the port of Wilmington in 1896 and 1897. The steamer *Horsa,* a fruiterer between New York and the West Indies which had been credited with landing one or more shipments of arms in Cuba, put into Southport in distress after an onboard fire. But the steam yacht *Camoose* and the sailing schooner *Silver Heels* appeared in Wilmington under highly suspicious circumstances. And residents along the Atlantic beaches near Wilmington felt sure that the coastal waters were being used for rendezvous by Cuban filibusterers.[79]

The support shown the Cuban rebels eventually became formal United States policy when the Congress voted to declare war against Spain in April 1898. The prospect of war with Spain prompted the federal government to refurbish Fort Caswell with the help of stevedores and laborers from Wilmington. The Navy Department also collected a list of all steamers on the Cape Fear River and its tributaries, including their tonnage and dimensions, and prepared instructions for arming the vessels with small-calibre cannon—one and six pounders.[80]

With the advent of war the Navy mined the entrance of the Cape Fear. Patrol boats were stationed above and below the mined area to escort vessels through the danger zone. Sailing craft and small boats drawing less than three feet of water might pass safely. All traffic was restricted to daylight hours. Any violations not only subjected shipping to damage by the mines but also to artillery fire from shore batteries. The Spanish danger passed quickly, however, and the mines were removed by the end of July.[81]

Wilmingtonians were duly alarmed by the prospects of Spanish raids. When the Clyde steamer *Oneida*, the first to pass through the mined area, was several hours late in reaching Wilmington, it was rumored that she had been beset by the Spaniards. Actually strong headwinds and the need for escort service explained the delay. Captain J. C. Mitchell of the government revenue cutter *Colfax* stationed at Wilmington tried to reassure the townspeople. He ridiculed the idea that the Spanish would attack Wilmington and praised the protection provided by the river fortifications as well as the mines at the mouth of the Cape Fear.[82] The war, in fact, was a brief one, ending in a decisive victory for the United States.

In addition to its naval presence in Wilmington the Federal government reestablished the Customs Service in the port at the conclusion of the Civil War. That agency superintended the lights off the coast (lighthouses and lightship), the revenue cutter, and the implementation of the nation's commercial legislation. Lighthouses and coastal navigational aids were crucial to the safety of Wilmington shipping and the commercial development of the port. After the war the government reactivated the Bald Head Island and the Federal Point lighthouses. The latter was discontinued in 1879, following the closing of New Inlet. The Bald Head light, visible for no more than fifteen miles at sea, proved inadequate. Its shortcoming became more evident after all shipping was routed through the channel between Oak Island and Bald Head.[83] During the last quarter of the nineteenth century the federal government improved the lighting mechanism of the Bald Head light to provide more effective guidance for mariners. Congress responded to recommendations from the Light House Board by appropriating funds in 1898 to erect a new lighthouse on Smith Island. A site was selected in 1900, and a construction contract let the following year. The new Cape Fear Light Station was activated in 1903 with a "first-order flashing-lens apparatus." The government retained the old lighthouse, demoting Bald Head "to a fourth-order fixed light."[84]

The first Frying Pan Shoals lightship, stationed in 1854, was removed at the outbreak of the Civil War, but late in 1865 a two-masted schooner was anchored at the tip of the shoals in ten fathoms of water. The storms that ravaged shipping off Cape Fear played havoc with the Frying Pan lightship and the buoys in the area. After a blow in 1883 the lightship was found at Myrtle Grove Sound, several miles north of her anchorage. Five years later another storm set the lightship adrift. In addition one watch buoy was dragged a half-mile; another disappeared. Commercial interests from

Charleston contended in 1890 that the signals (bell and horn) were ineffective except in calm weather and in close proximity to vessels, thus rendering Frying Pan Shoals still extremely hazardous.[85]

The United States revenue cutter *Colfax*, succeeding the *W.H. Seward*, was attached to the Customs Service at Wilmington in the late 1870s. Carrying seven officers, a pilot, and a crew of thirty, the *Colfax* cruised from Boddie Island, North Carolina, to Georgetown, South Carolina. Among its responsibilities were notifying mariners of sunken vessels that posed a threat to navigation and offering assistance to ships and seamen in distress, tasks performed admirably judging from its reports and many rescue efforts. Among the ship captains of the port of Wilmington, highly respected men in general, great esteem was reserved for those of the revenue cutters.[86]

Mitigating to some extent the danger of accidents off the coast was the establishment in 1882 of the Cape Fear Lifesaving Station, a branch of the United States Lifesaving Service, which had been created by Congress in the early 1870s. The Cape Fear Station was supplemented by the opening of the Oak Island Station across the river in 1891. In 1915 Congress merged the Lifesaving Service and the Revenue Cutter Service to form the United States Coast Guard. In 1937 the Cape Fear Station was deactivated in favor of that at Oak Island, which offered better protection for cutters and surfboats.[87]

Another federal agency that benefited shipping was the United States Army Signal Corps. Barely organized before the Civil War but maturing during that conflict, the Signal Corps was subsequently adapted to peacetime purposes. By a congressional resolution in 1870 the Signal Corps became responsible for meteorological observations and weather forecasting along the Atlantic and Gulf coasts. In additional to using commercial telegraph lines the Signal Corps in 1873 began to string wires to connect lighthouses and lifesaving stations, including a line from Norfolk to Cape Hatteras. Two years later the service was extended from Cape Hatteras to Wilmington and probably to Smithville, as the government had placed Signal Corps stations in both those towns.[88]

In many other ways the federal government protected and promoted shipping. Before the Civil War, Congress had prescribed safety regulations and inspections for steam vessels. It required the painting of the name of a vessel on both sides of the bow, and the draft on the stern and stern-post in order that overloading might be easily detected. The United States Hydrographic Office issued pilot charts that listed dangerous obstructions along the coast; in early 1894 there were six known vessels with spars and masts extending out of the water within forty miles of the Frying Pan lightship. Periodically navy cruisers dynamited wrecks that were hazardous to shipping.[89]

Complementing federal oversight of shipping were the commissioners of navigation and pilotage, who resumed their regulation of local commerce after the war. Legislation in 1870 abandoned the popular election of the commissioners, requiring instead that the mayor and aldermen of Wilmington annually appoint five persons to serve on the board, to be joined by two others appointed annually by the mayor and commissioners of Smithville. The commissioners of navigation controlled traffic from seven miles above the junction of the Northeast and Northwest on both rivers to the mouth of the Cape Fear beyond the bar. With the mayor and aldermen of Wilmington the commissioners exercised jurisdiction in the city over the disposal of rubbish in the river and the construction of wharves. Among the specific duties of the commissioners of navigation remained the appointment of a harbor master and the regulation of pilotage.[90]

The regulation of pilotage did not differ materially from that of the antebellum era. The commissioners licensed pilots for the bar and the river, supervised pilot stations and boats, and established fees. In 1883 some sixty-five pilots held licenses, divided about equally between the bar and the river, but legislation in that year required a reduction of the number of pilots to forty-five. Although each pilot was supposed to train at least one apprentice, there were no more than three or four apprentices in 1883. The commissioners also appointed trustees to administer the Pilot Fund, moneys set aside from pilot fees to provide financial assistance for aged pilots.[91]

Competition among pilots was keen. As pilotage was compulsory on all vessels over sixty tons, some measure of the pilotage business may be gleaned from the harbor master's reports for 1880 and 1882, which showed that 490 and 481 vessels of that size entered the port during those years respectively. Pilots having large decked boats possessed an obvious advantage over those in small open craft in spotting and reaching incoming ships. In fair weather pilots of smaller vessels might visit the Frying Pan lightship, whose location not only gave them an edge in detecting incoming ships but also allowed them to partake of the lightship's stores. Rumor held that rations ran low on the lightship in consequence of pilot visitations.[92]

The largest pilot boats, *Gracie*, *Uriah Timmons*, and *Oriental*, earned meritorious reputations for braving howling gales and the roughest seas. But, as sail yielded to steam in passenger and freight transport, so progress revolutionized pilot boats. The Pilot's Association of Southport in 1894 resolved to eschew sailing craft and bought two steam tugs, the *Alexander Jones* and the *Blanche,* from Captain T. J. Harper of Wilmingon.[93]

After 1868, the commissioners of navigation and pilotage were divested of their control over quarantine. Legislation in that year empowered the governor to designate a port physician for a quarantine station located in the vicinity of Southport. The port physician thenceforth determined quarantine procedures. An amendment to the law in 1879 directed the president of the state Board of Health to appoint two physicians resident in Wilmington to act in conjunction with the port physician or quarantine officer to establish and enforce health regulations for the port.[94]

The appointment of the port physician by the governor subjected the office to political pressures in the Reconstruction era. Republican Governor Curtis H. Brogden replaced Dr. F. W. Potter with Republican Dr. S. P. Wright, a "carpetbagger," which led a correspondent to the *Journal* to ask, "How dare this old political trimmer and trickster [Brogden] thus to tamper with the health and safety of the lives of our citizens?" After the Democrats took control of the gubernatorial office in 1877, Dr. W. G. Curtis was appointed port physician, serving in that capacity until the mid-1890s, when Republican political ascendance and the transfer of the quarantine station at Southport to federal authority ended his tenure, and once more embroiled the office in controversy.[95]

Whoever the physician or whatever the composition of the board, quarantine regulations for the port did not alter materially. All vessels arriving at the port were required to produce a clean bill of health according to standards set by the national Board of Health and to satisfy the Wilmington officials that no infectious disease was aboard. Vessels were cleansed and disinfected at the quarantine station and discharged their ballast there. All communication with ships riding quarantine was strictly prohibited. Ships not allowed to proceed to Wilmington could load and unload cargoes at the quarantine station, though all lighters, stevedores, and others concerned were considered under quarantine.[96]

Merchants and shippers of the port chafed under quarantine restrictions, but the threat of epidemic disease was too real to be taken lightly by the port physician and governing authorities. The port physician routinely imposed quarantine on all vessels coming from the south of Wilmington (the West Indies, Central and South America, and the southern coast of the United States) after June 1 (later May 1), and maintained the mandatory quarantine until November 1. Of course any vessel having sickness aboard or coming from a port where contagion existed underwent quarantine.[97]

Violations of quarantine, accidental or purposeful, were not uncommon. In 1891 the schooner *Florence* was towed into Southport in distress. The captain, thinking that he had a clean bill of health, since he was sailing from one United States port, Key West, to another, went ashore. However, the Wilmington quarantine still obtained because the vessel had sailed from a port south of Wilmington. The captain dutifully paid his fine. On the other hand, a Captain Partlow who was placed under quarantine mingled with the citizens of Smithville at dockside and with excursionists (presumably from Wilmington) on board the river steamer *Passport*.[98]

The need for a properly equipped quarantine station at Southport, combined with an outbreak of cholera in Europe and the ever-present threat of yellow fever, prompted the General Assembly to appropriate $20,000 in 1893 to improve the facility. Federal legislation in that year, however, granted the Marine Hospital Service control over all quarantine stations, exempting only those local facilities that had complied with minimum requirements of the United States quarantine laws. Since the Southport station was negligent in its compliance, the state of North Carolina had little choice but to turn its operations over to the Marine Hospital Service. After an inspection a federal appropriation of $25,000 was made to upgrade the station. Control of the state quarantine station in Southport was transferred to the federal government in 1895.[99]

The federal government also operated a marine hospital in Wilmington for seamen. Built in the late 1850s to replace the Seamen's Friend Society hospital and located on Nun Street between Sixth and Eighth Streets, the hospital's facilities were upgraded in the late 1890s. A separate building served as a tubercular ward, reportedly the only one of its kind in the country, to which patients could be sent from other marine hospitals. The hospital fell into disuse after the opening of James Walker Memorial Hospital in Wilmington in 1901, though the building subsequently served many other purposes before being demolished in 1958.[100]

Supplementing the medical care for the mariners in port were the services of the Seamen's Friend Society. Incorporated before the Civil War, the society offered comfort, shelter, and spiritual guidance to shipwrecked and destitute sailors. Although the society survived the war, it did not enjoy smooth sailing. During the economically depressed 1870s its revenues were so depleted that it barely met operating expenses. By its forty-fifth annual meeting in 1898 the society seemed to be on a sound footing, though its long-standing claim against the United States government for the use of its Home during the Civil War had yet to be satisfied. In 1899 the state legislature extended the charter of the society for an additional sixty years.[101]

Among the seamen supported by the Seamen's Friend Society were those whose vessels had been damaged by the storms that periodically ravaged the Carolina coast. In September 1883 the *City of Atlanta,* Charleston to New York, was disabled and towed first by the passing steamer *British Empire* and then by the revenue cutter *Colfax.* The schooner *Wyer G. Sargent,* bound from Laguana, Mexico, to New York with a cargo of mahogany and cedar, made port in distress in April 1887. Stormy weather had carried away the rudder head, damaged the foremast, and blown away the sails. That same year the *Lizzie Dewey,* sailing from Baltimore to Savannah with a load of guano, limped into port leaking after encountering a heavy gale that carried away part of her stern as well as her compass and wheel. In the wake of a hurricane in September 1893 eight ships were in Wilmington undergoing repairs; four were in Southport.[102]

At the end of the nineteenth century Wilmington remained the center of North Carolina's commercial shipping industry. Indicative of Wilmington's extensive overseas trade was the presence of foreign vice-consuls representing Great Britain, Spain, France, Germany, Denmark, Norway, Sweden, Brazil, the Argentine Republic, and Haiti. The British in 1866 obtained the services of Alexander Sprunt, founder of the commission house of Alexander Sprunt & Son, and after his death in 1884 James Sprunt, his son, who assumed control of the business. The younger Sprunt also served as Imperial German Consul for North Carolina from 1907 to 1912, and upon his resignation was awarded the Order of the Royal Crown by the emperor of Germany.[103]

Providing overarching supervision of Wilmington's trade were the Chamber of Commerce and the Wilmington Produce Exchange. The Chamber, reorganized in 1866, sought to institute "a uniform system for the government of trade and commerce" and to settle "amicably" matters of dispute relating to trade. The Produce Exchange, established in 1873, supplemented, if not supplanted, the Chamber of Commerce. Among its responsibilities was the determination of regulations to govern the inspection of cotton, rosin, and spirits of turpentine. The Produce Exchange more generally considered "such other matters as were calculated to be of benefit to the commerce of [the port of Wilmington], as well as the general commercial interests of the United States." By 1900 the Merchants Association of Wilmington and the Wilmington Tariff Association supplemented the Chamber and the Produce Exchange.[104]

Contemporaries characterized Wilmington as a "cheap" port. The principal expenses incurred by vessels were pilotage, compulsory for all ships above sixty tons, and towage. A $3.00 harbor master's retainer fee was optional, though if not paid might possibly result in higher charges later. (The first visit, if necessary, was $5.00; subsequent visits were $2.50.) Dock and wharf accommodations were satisfactory; warehouse storage was adequate; charges for compressing and stowing cotton approximated those in other United States ports. Provisions lacked the quality of those in most American ports but were moderately priced.[105]

Wilmington possessed other advantages as well. Freight for foreign destinations—cotton and lumber—might be found throughout the year. Marine insurance was as low as in any port below Wilmington along the Atlantic coast. Located south of perilous capes and shoals, especially Cape Hatteras, the passage to Wilmington subjected foreign ships to less danger and loss of time, thereby lowering marine insurance rates. And the waters of the Cape Fear River served to kill barnacles and facilitated the cleaning of ships' bottoms.[106]

Yet Wilmington's future as a port of consequence appeared problematic at the end of the nineteenth century. Increasing cotton exports and the burgeoning fertilizer industry were unable to offset a collapsing naval stores market and a declining wood products trade. Competition offered by neighboring Atlantic ports also portended trouble. While the trade of the port of Charleston declined toward the end of the century, that of Savannah evidenced a sustained high decennial growth, and that of Norfolk underwent a veritable explosion. As a result Wilmington's commerce began to suffer. Export tonnage, foreign and domestic, which peaked at 95,000 tons in 1880, dipped to 88,000 in 1890 and fell to 81,000 in 1900. Wilmingtonians failed to broaden their export base by securing a rail link to the Ohio Valley to tap the trade in grain and provisions. Efforts to obtain coal and iron by rail from eastern Tennessee, northwestern North Carolina, and southwestern Virginia also proved futile.[107] Wilmington perforce became a one-export port, depending upon cotton to undergird and maintain its economy.

Chapter Six

REVIVAL AND MODERNIZATION IN THE TWENTIETH CENTURY

At the turn of the century Wilmington remained North Carolina's most populous city and only significant port. However, cities in the industrial Piedmont soon eclipsed Wilmington in population, while the port continued to enjoy its distinction as a shipping center. The Cape Fear River served as Wilmington's "showplace" as well as the lifeline of the city. When President William H. Taft visited the port in 1909, he, like most dignitaries, received the customary river and harbor tour. After arriving by train on the morning of November 9, the President was escorted aboard the revenue cutter *Seminole*. Gaily bedecked ships of all descriptions and classes—three Navy torpedo boats, the tug *Sea King*, river steamers, launches, and yachts—accompanied the *Seminole* downriver to Southport.[1]

During these years the oversight of Wilmington's port activity remained virtually unchanged from the nineteenth century. Legislation in 1907 prescribed a five-man Board of Commissioners of Navigation and Pilotage, appointed to four-year terms by the governor of the state. Three of the board members were required to be residents of Wilmington, two of Southport. Legislation in 1921 altered the residence requirements to read four from New Hanover County. The board annually selected a harbor master and three port wardens. The harbor master maintained an open channel for ships using the Cape Fear, berthed vessels, and cleared Wilmington's public docks of obstructing ships and trash. The port wardens appraised damages to any vessel or cargo arriving in Wilmington or stranded within the bounds of the port, and collected fees set by law for that purpose.[2]

Throughout the twentieth century the Board of Commissioners of Navigation and Pilotage, altered to the Cape Fear Navigation and Pilotage Commission in 1985, continued to supervise pilotage, license pilots, and appoint Wilmington's port wardens. The Cape Fear Navigation and Pilotage Commission comprised five members, but only four were appointed by the governor (three from New Hanover County and one from Brunswick County). The fifth was the president of the Wilmington-Cape Fear Pilots' Association. The legislation of 1985 enlarged the powers of the commission to permit the members to set pilotage rates, which previously had been prescribed by law, and to work closely with the pilots' association.[3]

Impelled by North Carolina Senator Lee S. Overman early in the twentieth century, Congress continued to fund improvements to the navigability of the Cape Fear. In 1911 a new lightship replaced the old one which had been summarily removed. Following the Corps of Engineers' dredging the river channel, thirty-three new range lights were installed by November 15, 1913, to supplant older, less adequate luminants. Other aids mainly consisted of lighthouses at Bald Head and at Fort Caswell and numerous buoys positioned at the outer edge of Frying Pan Shoals, near and at the mouth of the Cape Fear River, and at critical points along the dredged channels of the river.[4]

Supplementing the navigational aids were the Revenue Cutter Service and the Lifesaving Service, combined in 1915 to form the United States Coast Guard. Stationed in Wilmington during the early years of the twentieth century was the cutter *Seminole*, which received numerous commendations for her rescue service as she patrolled the waters from Cape Hatteras to Charleston. During the four months from December 1, 1912, to March 31, 1913, the *Seminole* assisted nine craft, sail and steam, and destroyed a tenth, a dangerous derelict. Closer to shore the men of the Cape Fear and the Oak Island life saving stations, keeping a constant watch from lookout towers during the day and maintaining a beach patrol at night, likewise compiled an admirable service record.[5]

Through the Coast Guard, supervision of health and immigration policies, and various other agencies including the Customs and Army Corps of Engineers, the federal government maintained an active presence in the port. The responsibilities of the Coast Guard encompassed search and rescue, merchant marine safety, and aids to navigation (maintaining lighthouses, buoys, channel lights and markers). In addition Wilmington was the home port for a succession of Coast Guard cutters, from the *Seminole* to the icebreaker *Northwind*, which was decommissioned in January 1989 following forty-three years of service. Health regulations required the inspection of vessels subject to quarantine laws by a medical officer appointed by the Public Health Service. Sailors needing medical attention received care in Wilmington, or, in the case of extended treatment, in the Marine Hospital in Norfolk. The Department of Justice established a field office of immigration and naturalization in Wilmington, and an immigration officer boarded and inspected all foreign ships entering the port.[6]

Requisite to the growth of the port was the continued deepening of the bar and channel of the Cape Fear to permit ever larger ocean steamers to call at Wilmington. It seemed an endless endeavor. By 1907 the Army Corps of Engineers finally met its 1890 mandate to dredge to 20 feet (with the exception of Snow's Cut Marsh). Using five to six dredges, the Corps continued to deepen the channel along a swath that varied in width from 74 to 270 feet. By 1917, when World War I stopped the Corps's efforts, the depth of the channel stood at 26 feet (except for 23 feet at Snow's Cut Marsh) with a fairly uniform width of 300 feet.[7]

Meanwhile, repairing the Swash Dam and dredging a turning basin in Wilmington's harbor occupied the Corps. Storms in 1899 had greatly damaged the Swash Dam, reducing some areas to the low water mark. The Corps delayed major repairs to the dam until 1905, and completed its work three years later. The Corps undertook the construction of a turning basin in 1907. It had postponed the dredging, claiming that the project was too expensive and that mooring dolphins would be more economically feasible. But Wilmington merchants, led by Chamber of Commerce president Marcus W. Jacobi, emphasized the need to accommodate Wilmington's increased shipping. The port's harbor master justified the project by noting the recent grounding of twenty to thirty ships in the harbor. The Corps yielded, and by 1911 had completed a basin 24 feet in depth, 300 feet in width, and 5,300 feet in length.[8]

The deepening of the channel had a salutary effect upon Wilmington's commerce. The average tonnage of vessels using the Cape Fear was 1,462 in 1915 as opposed to 1,100 in 1905 and approximately 400 tons in 1885.[9] Although fewer ships engaged in Wilmington's trade, the larger vessels contributed to the increasing value of imports during the first decade and a half of the twentieth century, as may be seen in Table 16. The value of exports trebled between 1900 and 1908, then dipped slightly until World War I disrupted commerce.

Export tonnage had begun to slip noticeably at the turn of the century as the naval stores and wood products industries foundered. Only cotton

Table 16
Wilmington Shipping, 1900–1915

Fiscal Year June 30	Vessels Entered Foreign	Vessels Entered Domestic	Vessels Cleared Foreign	Vessels Cleared Domestic	Exports Value	Imports Value
1900	69	85	108	65	$10,975,511	$ 109,614
1902	56	83	88	78	11,102,171	258,358
1904	37	95	73	71	19,085,221	264,550
1906	33	96	60	78	18,466,929	381,890
1908	36	88	64	78	30,291,681	878,952
1910	42	60	39	100	20,922,398	2,355,253
1912	54	75	55	90	28,705,448	3,159,043
1914	52	75	35	92	25,870,850	4,174,745
1915	47	90	30	109	11,308,535	1,990,755

Sprunt, *Chronicles of the Cape Fear River*, 595.

remained as a major foreign export, and even the shipment of that fiber began to wane on the eve of the war. Fertilizer, a significant local industry that generated exports to the interior of the state and southeast, was unable to offset the downward trends elsewhere. The decline of agricultural and related industries on which Wilmington earlier had drawn for exports threatened its status as an international port.[10]

Cotton remained king in terms of Wilmington's foreign export trade between the turn of the century and World War I. It was due to that crop that Wilmington ranked ninth among United States Atlantic ports in the value of its foreign imports and exports. Still, in 1905 Wilmington stood a distant fourth, following Galveston, New Orleans, and Savannah, among United States ports in the export of cotton. Most of Wilmington's cotton, and 98 percent of the value of its foreign trade, went to Germany and England. Eighty-four percent of Wilmington's imports, mainly fertilizer materials, came from Germany and Chile.

The cotton export trade was led by Alexander Sprunt & Son, which achieved its height of eminence and wealth before World War I. By engaging in the cotton futures market, opening a Bremen agency in 1906, and establishing branches in Le Havre, Rotterdam, and Barcelona, the firm "brought the farmer and foreign spinner into practically direct personal relation," exulted James Sprunt. As a result exports and profits soared. Bremen, to which 320,000 bales of cotton were sent in 1907–08 and 100,000 bales in 1922, was the prime destination of the Sprunts. From Bremen cotton was distributed widely in central Europe. Following Bremen, the firm favored Liverpool, sending 140,000 bales to that English port in 1907–08. Chartering fifty steamers annually, James Sprunt, in November 1908, claimed that his firm had shipped 501,000 bales of cotton to foreign ports during the previous year. Profits rose from $60,000 annually, 1901–03, to $280,000 annually, 1907–10, and to $838,000 during 1918–19.[11]

While foreign trade was greatly skewed in favor of exports, domestic commerce evinced more balance. Coastal receipts amounted to $12,771,461 in 1905, originating mainly from fertilizer materials, oil, cement, cotton, turpentine, cotton bagging, and general merchandise. Coastal exports, valued at $12,942,564 in 1905, depended upon cotton, naval stores, shingles, and lumber. Generating the exports were Wilmington-based companies—the Sprunts, American Naval Stores Company, Navassa Guano Company, American Agricultural Company.[12]

The internal water commerce of Wilmington, that which was sent and received via rivers and streams (and, after its completion to the Cape Fear River in 1932, the Intracoastal Waterway), figured prominently in the port's trade. Receipts centered on timber, which comprised 65 percent of the tonnage and 40 percent of the value of the goods brought to Wilmington. Fertilizer comprised the preponderance of the exports to the interior in terms of tonnage and value.

Wilmington retained its connections with the lower reaches of the Cape Fear area early in the century. The shipping included a line of sharpies and small steamers between Wilmington and Little River, South Carolina. Sharpies also linked Wilmington with Lockwoods Folly and Shallotte. Some trade came from Elizabeth River in Brunswick County.[13] The nature of the traffic remained the same as in years past. Cotton, corn, hay, naval stores, lumber, fertilizer, and general merchandise made up most of the traffic. Table 17 contains an estimate of the tonnage and value of the trade.

In addition to freight traffic Captain J. W. Harper, proprietor of Harper's Line Steamers, kept the steamer *Wilmington* for passenger travel between Wilmington and Southport, with stops at all landings and at the resort of Carolina Beach. Harper, who had been running vessels on the Cape Fear since the post–Reconstruction era, transported as many as 75,000 people a year, about two-thirds of whom were summer patrons. Carolina Beach remained a favorite watering place; Southport was a delightfully restful haven or point of departure for fishing excursions. Local

Table 17
Estimated Traffic, Wilmington and the Smaller Rivers of the Lower Cape Fear

Route	Tonnage	Date	Value
Wilmington to Little River	10,488	1907	$497,568
Wilmington to Lockwoods Folly	5,000	c. 1910	200,000
Wilmington to Shallotte	5,000	1910	211,368
Wilmington to Elizabeth River	2,000	1910	23,000

Source: *Intracoastal Waterway*, 48.

people as well as tourists availed themselves of the *Wilmington*. By World War I three generations of Wilmingtonians had been sailing with Captain Harper.[14]

To improve the navigability of the upper Cape Fear and promote trade between Wilmington and Fayetteville, Congress in the federal Rivers and Harbors Act of 1902 appropriated funds to construct three locks and dams above Wilmington to ensure an eight-foot channel at mean low water. After a survey, the Corps selected sites at King's Bluff, Brown's Landing, and Tolar's Landing, 39, 71, and 95 miles respectively beyond Wilmington. Opposition to the project developed within the Corps. District Engineer Joseph E. Kuhn contended that current traffic on the Cape Fear did not justify the effort, that increased traffic engendered by the project would be negligible, and that contrary to arguments Fayetteville would not become a major distribution center for interior trade. As a result Congress scaled down the project to two locks and dams—at King's Bluff and Brown's Landing. Work proceeded slowly. High water and poor foundation soil hampered efforts at King's Bluff. In 1915, after more than three years, Lock and Dam No. 1 became operational. Work on Lock and Dam No. 2 was finished in 1917. In lieu of a third lock and dam the Corps attempted to dredge a channel, but found that freshets rendered its efforts "utterly hopeless."[15]

World War I sharply curtailed Wilmington's trade and contributed to a reversal of the port's tradition of an excess of exports over imports. The loss of the German market for cotton, the threat of German submarine attacks, and insufficient cargo ships contributed to the decline. The value of imports and exports dropped by more than 50 percent in 1915, despite the fact that coastal arrivals and clearances rose significantly. Not only did Wilmington's trade falter, but in 1915, for the first time in its history, the tonnage in foreign trade of ships entering the port exceeded the tonnage of those clearing. However, rising prices offset declining tonnage. The value of Wilmington foreign exports rose 70 percent between 1914 and 1918, though shipping had dipped by 500,000 tons in the interim.[16]

The United States' declaration of war against Germany on April 6, 1917, found two German merchant ships, the *Kiel* and the *Nicaria*, anchored in the port of Wilmington. Having prepared for the eventuality, officers and sailors from the Coast Guard cutter *Seminole* quickly seized the vessels and imprisoned the captains and crews. However, the Germans had likewise anticipated hostilities and had greatly damaged the engines of the ships. Eventually the *Kiel* and the *Nicaria* were towed to Charleston, repaired, and fitted out for transatlantic service.[17]

Wilmington received a fillip from World War I in the revival of its shipbuilding industry. Marine construction languished at the turn of the century due to an increasing dependence upon rail traffic and the failure of shipbuilders to follow the trend from wooden-hulled to iron and steel vessels. Although a protected port with the advantages of a deep channel, rail connections, and available labor, which should have made it attractive to shipbuilding interests, Wilmington witnessed only an occasional small steamer or yacht leaving the ways.[18] However, when World War I began in 1914, several small shipyards lined the Wilmington waterfront, including the Wilmington Marine Railway, a subsidiary of the Wilmington Iron Works. The company constructed two marine railways on Eagles Island and employed approximately a hundred operatives. In 1916 it secured a contract from R. Lawrence Smith of New York to build two four-masted wooden schooners. The contract subsequently was given to the Naul Shipbuilding Company, which used the shipyard on Eagles Island to complete the vessels, after which the yard was returned to the Wilmington Iron Works.[19]

Upon the outbreak of World War I the United States, whose merchant marine had declined steadily since the Civil War to the point that it was transporting only 10 percent of the nation's commerce by 1914, had to enlarge its carrying fleet. In September 1916 Congress created the United States Shipping Board to supervise, coordinate, and expand the country's shipping. That agency initiated a shipbuilding program throughout the nation which created a boomlike atmosphere in eastern North Carolina and Wilmington.

In North Carolina a number of new companies, many representing out-of-state capital, sought shipbuilding contracts from the government. State politicians urged federal authorities to select North Carolina for shipbuilding sites, several cities sent delegations to Washington to lobby for their interests, and Wilmington retained an agent in the nation's capital to offer to donate waterfront property on behalf of the port for a shipbuilding facility. As a result nine new shipyards emerged in North Carolina in 1917–18.[20]

Two additional wooden-vessel shipyards, a yard for steel cargo vessels, and a yard for concrete steamers appeared in Wilmington. Joining the Wilmington Marine Railway in turning out wooden ships were the Wilmington Wooden Ship Construction Company and the Naul Shipbuilding Company. The former, headed by Philadelphia shipbuilding interests, bought land in July 1917 on the east side of the river between Queen and Wooster streets. The Wilmington Wooden Ship Company launched a 1500-ton schooner in the summer of 1918, followed by several wooden barges. The Naul Company obtained land on the Northeast Cape Fear River in September 1917 for its second shipyard and laid the keels for four small wooden craft, but never succeeded in obtaining a contract from the Shipping Board.[21]

By the fall of 1917 the Shipping Board began to curtail drastically its wooden-ship construction program in favor of steel- and concrete-hulled vessels. The George A. Fuller Company of New York, through a subsidiary called the Carolina Shipbuilding Company, secured a government contract in April 1918 to build prefabricated steel vessels in Wilmington. The shipyard, owned by the Shipping Board but built and operated by the Fuller Company, contained four shipways, a fabrication shop, and other buildings. The keel for the first of an expected twelve 9,600-ton steel cargo ships was laid on November 2, 1918, nine days before the signing of the armistice in Europe. Eight of the craft, measuring approximately 417 feet in length and 70 feet in the beam, were ultimately constructed. In addition, the Fuller Company apparently built two tankers for the Eagle Oil Company of London, England.[22]

The expense as well as a shortage of steel prompted the government to consider concrete construction. The Liberty Shipyard in Wilmington, established by the Liberty Shipbuilding Corporation of Boston, was one of three in North Carolina to produce concrete vessels. The government contract called for the construction of a shipyard with four shipways on land donated by the city of Wilmington and the building of six concrete-hulled cargo carriers and tankers ranging from 3,200 to 7,500 tons. Ship construction did not begin until October 1918, however, and orders for four of the vessels were later cancelled.[23]

The Liberty yard, employing about a thousand men at the peak of its operations, finished the *Cape Fear* and the *Old North State* in the summer of 1919, launching the concrete ships "sideways." Huge crowds gathered, and some of the onlookers were drenched when the *Cape Fear* crashed into the water, creating a veritable tidal wave. Unfortunately, the large concrete ships proved unwieldly. Both sank shortly after they entered the maritime service. The *Cape Fear* disappeared off Cape Cod; the *Old North State*, closer to home, in the vicinity of Cape Hatteras.[24]

The Warcrete Company, a subsidiary of West Coast Shipbuilding Company, also attempted to build concrete vessels in Wilmington during the war. After purchasing and modifying the Naul yard on the Northeast Cape Fear, the Warcrete Company received a government contract in July 1918 to build fourteen concrete river and harbor steamers, seven by a subsidiary in the state of Washington and seven in Wilmington. A protracted dispute between the Shipping Board and the War Department, followed by inadequate financial arrangements for construction by the West Coast Company, scuttled the contract for Wilmington, however, and none of the ships was built by Warcrete.

The shipyards in Wilmington encountered numerous difficulties in realizing their contractual arrangements. Among them were securing and retaining workers. Local labor, particularly skilled personnel, was soon exhausted. Mechanics, boilermakers, coppersmiths, and riveters were brought from neighboring and distant states. Turnover in the labor force was high, occasioned among other factors by Wilmington's isolated geographic position, relatively high cost of living, poor sanitary conditions, and lack of adequate housing. Prohibition, which obtained in North Carolina, and racial animosity proved additional deterrents.

Beyond personnel other problems added to the woes of the construction companies. The threat of strikes, though materializing during the war only in the walkout of the carpenters of the Naul Company in November 1917, was ever present. Obtaining materials, some from as far as Louisiana and the West Coast, proved vexatious. Epidemic disease, particularly influenza in late 1918, curtailed work. Finally, inexperienced management contributed to delays, poor workmanship, and high costs.[25]

The signing of the armistice in November 1918 brought immediate government retrenchment. The Shipping Board cancelled contracts with the Wilmington Wooden Ship Construction Company, which was auctioned in the summer of 1919. The board sold the Carolina Shipbuilding yard to the George A. Fuller construction company, which proceeded to complete ten of the twelve vessels originally under contract. After the Liberty Company launched the second of its concrete vessels, it tried to attract Japanese interest in concrete ships. Unsuccessful, it closed the shipyard in October 1919. The Shipping Board then sold the yard to the city of Wilmington.[26]

The city realized some success in an effort to perpetuate the shipbuilding industry by renting the Liberty yard to the Newport Shipbuilding Company. Having a government contract to build concrete river steamers, the Newport Company began operations in New Bern, then switched to Wilmington due to a lack of adequate housing in the Craven County city. Three vessels started in New Bern were towed to Wilmington and completed. Those undertaken in Wilmington were finished by 1922. The following year the assets of the Newport Company were offered at public auction; ownership of the shipyard reverted to the city of Wilmington.[27]

Wilmington emerged from World War I with expectations of a bright future. Its shipyards were busy. At the wharves of the port sixteen oceangoing vessels could load simultaneously. The city was the largest distribution point for the Standard Oil Company south of Baltimore. A booming fertilizer industry was accompanied by such enterprises as cotton mills, metal and wood works, and lumber factories. Pent-up consumer demand meant booming retail sales. And the Corps of Engineers immediately resumed efforts to improve the navigability of the Cape Fear River, still the lifeline of the city.

The wartime prosperity proved short-lived, however. The decline in shipbuilding undermined Wilmington's economy. The port, already laboring under a competitive shipping disadvantage vis-à-vis Norfolk and Charleston, gradually became an import distribution center. Unable to generate an export base, it saw its outward-bound shipments dwindle. Population declined as many of the war immigrants departed; others began to drift to newly-opened suburbs, and the port languished. The city gradually was transformed from a shipping entrepôt into a regional trade center serving southeastern North Carolina.[28]

Enlivening port life in the 20s, though not contributing to its licit commerce, was rum running, the smuggling of alcoholic beverages into the United States during the era of Prohibition. The Coast Guard cutter *Seminole* brought to port her first catch, the *Messenger of Peace*, in early January 1922. The owner, Arthur Coleman from the British West Indies, claimed innocence but spent five months in jail. The cargo of almost twelve thousand bottles of whisky and rum, valued at more than $95,000, was destroyed. With limited resources the Coast Guard found nature to be a valuable ally, for many apprehensions followed the grounding of vessels off the bar or shallow inlets. Still, the Coast Guard did catch the *George Slover* in 1928 as she tried to slip into Wilmington under cover of darkness with 1,009 cases of whisky.[29]

Meanwhile, Wilmington's port trade declined in the 20s in spite of marked improvements in land and water transportation facilities. During the first two decades of the twentieth century access to Wilmington by road had advanced little beyond the stage of development at the time of the Revolution. Ferries still spanned the Cape Fear River. Unpaved highways, ruts in dry weather and mud flats in wet, deterred travel and the transport of goods. The state created a highway commission in 1915 and began to assume responsibility for road construction, relieving the counties of a burden that they could never fully shoulder. Congress in 1916 proved willing to provide federal funds to the states on a matching basis for road construction. As a result, by 1930 a network of highways connected Wilmington with the rest of the state.[30]

Bridges replaced the cumbersome ferries across the Cape Fear and Northeast Cape Fear rivers at Wilmington, and facilitated overland travel to Wilmington and its markets. Spanning the Cape Fear were drawbridges at Wilmington and Navassa for highway and rail traffic respectively, and a steel highway bridge at Elizabethtown which had no draw but offered a twenty-foot clearance at high water. Just beyond the mouth of the Northeast Cape Fear a highway and a railroad bridge spanned the river; similar structures crossed the river at Castle Hayne, twenty-five miles beyond. Between Castle Hayne and Watha, fifty-six miles from the mouth, vessels encountered four more bridges.[31]

After World War I major changes occurred in the marking and lighting of the Cape Fear. The Bald Head lighthouse, fondly known as "Old Baldy," was deactivated in 1935, though it remained as a friendly landmark for fishermen and navigators of the area. The federal government not only deactivated but also demolished the lighthouse on Smith Island in 1958, replacing it with a light across the channel on Oak Island at the Coast Guard station. A light tower supplanted the lightship at Frying Pan Shoals in 1966.[32]

The Corps of Engineers continued to deepen the bar and channel of the Cape Fear River in order to allow larger ocean-going vessels to reach Wilmington. By 1932 the Corps had provided a channel thirty feet deep at mean low water and four hundred feet wide across the bar. Beyond the bar the width narrowed to three hundred feet, but the thirty-foot channel was maintained up the river to Hilton Bridge on the Northeast Cape Fear, about a mile and a quarter above the junction with the Northwest Cape Fear.[35]

Between the World Wars the improvement of the Cape Fear River from Wilmington to Fayetteville continued to occupy those interested in enhancing Wilmington's trade as well as those in the Cumberland County seat who sought the advancement of their town. Not only had the Corps failed to construct Lock and Dam No. 3 on the river, it had made no effort to maintain the mandated eight-foot channel. Corps representatives contended that barge traffic, which dominated upper Cape Fear commerce, would require more depth than that provided by an eight-foot channel. District Engineer J. C. Oakes claimed that "there is no possibility of developing a traffic on the stream commensurate with the additional cost of a third lock and dam." He was "positively convinced that the Government should not undertake the project." However, he failed to reckon with the anticipated completion of the Beaufort to Wilmington section of the Intracoastal Waterway.[34]

Despite the intransigence of the Corps, Lock and Dam No. 3 eventually materialized. Believing that barge traffic generated by the Intracoastal Waterway would justify the expense, the Corps in the early 30s reinstated the project of a lock and dam at Tolar's Landing. New Deal funds underwrote the project, which was completed in 1936. The first commercial cargo from Wilmington to Fayetteville consisted of a barge drawing slightly more than eight feet that carried gasoline and kerosene. The project to improve the navigability of the Northwest Cape Fear, finished in 1939, produced a channel twenty-five feet deep to Navassa, four miles above Wilmington, and eight feet deep thereafter to Fayetteville.[35]

Between the wars Wilmingtonians expected to benefit from a new artery of interior water commerce—the Atlantic Intracoastal Waterway. The idea of such a water passage had been broached by Secretary of the Treasury Albert Gallatin during the first decade of the nineteenth century. In 1837 Congress showed interest in a protected water route along the coast by authorizing a survey of North Carolina's coast for that purpose. Forty years later a similar government survey followed an effort by the state of North Carolina to promote the construction of a canal from the South Carolina line to Virginia to connect the Cape Fear River with Chesapeake Bay.[36]

The Intracoastal Waterway did not become a reality until the twentieth century, however. It was due in part to the enthusiasm for internal improvements generated by President Theodore Roosevelt and the creation of the Inland Waterways Commission in 1907. North Carolina figured prominently in the federal government's consideration of the project. The state's dangerous coast—capes Hatteras, Lookout, and Fear with their shoals—constituted a long-standing impediment to Atlantic shipping, particularly coastal traffic. Thus Wilmingtonians rejoiced at Congress's decision in the Rivers and Harbors Act of 1912 to create a continuous waterway from Boston to Galveston.[37]

Proponents of the waterway, including those in the Wilmington environs, advanced numerous arguments to justify funding the expensive project. They claimed that it would stimulate local commerce by opening areas to waterborne trade that previously had little or no access to transportation outlets or that found railroads prohibitively expensive. North of Wilmington some of the freight carried by rail from Jacksonville in Onslow County might more easily and cheaply be carried by water. The coastal area between New River and Cape Fear River, then virtually untapped, might well contribute to waterway commerce by some half-million dollars annually.[38]

Secondly, a protected inland watercourse would make local and ocean going traffic safer. Ships and barges sailing the coast above Wilmington at that time could not find a ready haven in the state's shallow inlets from northeasters or squalls unless the craft drew less than five or six feet of water. Vessels bound northward might wait two weeks in Southport for a favorable wind. Below Wilmington, on the other hand, the shorter distances from Southport to Little River (40 miles), from Little River to Georgetown (65 miles), and from Georgetown to Charleston (45 miles) offered the hope of reaching a safe harbor, even for slow-moving vessels like barges. Perhaps the most telling argument advanced for the waterway was its potential for lowering freight costs to the port. According to William Lord DeRosset, long-time Wilmington resident, in 1912 the loss at sea of several sailing vessels chartered to transport cement had raised transportation costs 60 to 75 percent. Such charters became difficult to obtain. And cement, along with lumber, coal, and fertilizer, were precisely those products best carried by barges which would use the waterway.[39]

Not only was canal transportation safe and inexpensive, but competition offered by barge traffic would have a salutary effort upon railroad charges. Most observers felt that competing water rates governed rail fares. And as William H. Bixby of the Corps of Engineers observed, "It is far more effective and probably better where possible to influence rail rates favorably by some natural competition than by arbitrary legislation," a sentiment with which no doubt, the Interstate Commerce Commission should have agreed.[40]

The Intracoastal Waterway in North Carolina materialized in segments. The first, completed in 1915, connected Norfolk and Beaufort. The second, from Beaufort to the Cape Fear, proceeded from the appropriation of the Rivers and Harbors Act of 1927. The Intracoastal Waterway approached Wilmington from the north via numerous small sounds below Beaufort. Ultimately it had to pass into the Cape Fear River. Wilmingtonians hoped that a crossing would be effected into the Northeast Cape Fear at Scotts Hill above the port or at Hewletts Creek just below the city, allowing the channel to pass close to Wilmington. The cost, however, was too great in comparison with a one-mile passage from the Myrtle Sound to the Cape Fear River at Carolina Beach, the site selected by the Corps of Engineers. With a twelve-foot channel and a ninety-ton bottom width, the Beaufort to Wilmington waterway opened in June 1932.[41]

Legislation in 1930 appropriated funds to extend the waterway from the Cape Fear River to Winyah Bay in South Carolina. It followed the Cape Fear River to Southport and thence up the Elizabeth River. At that juncture a series of cuts and locks took the canal to Little River, Davis Creek, Lockwoods Folly River, and Shallotte River. The waterway then moved to the Waccamaw River in South Carolina, from which it continued to Winyah Bay. Work began in 1931 and concluded three years later.[42]

The advent of the Intracoastal Waterway virtually eliminated coastal shipping at North Carolina's smaller ports, reduced railroad rates as predicted, and opened to water transport areas previously dependent upon railroads. Most of Wilmington's commerce along the waterway was carried via the North Carolina Line and the Norfolk, Baltimore & Carolina Line. The traffic involved bulky, slow-moving cargo that could be carried economically by way of the canal.[43]

In 1940, as the United States entered World War II, Wilmington reflected the impact of the Intracoastal Waterway. It boasted fifty-four wharves, piers, and docks. Thirty-nine were located along the city's waterfront, two below the city, nine on the west side of the river on Eagles Island, and four at Navassa. Several of the shipping facilities served the public. The city of Wilmington, ever conscious of the importance of the river traffic to the local economy, constructed a 101-foot dock between Orange and Dock streets. It also owned a municipal wharf at the foot of Greenfield Street. The United States Corps of Engineers and the Coast Guard maintained wharves of 525- and 330-feet frontage respectively. Private interests controlled the remaining piers and docks.[44]

Between the wars Wilmington's trade exhibited diverse trends, as may be seen by Table 18. Foreign import tonnage substantially exceeded export tonnage. Chemicals, mainly fertilizer products from Chile, constituted the bulk of imports, comprising some 80 percent of the incoming commerce. Foodstuffs (principally molasses and sugar), textiles (burlap), lumber,

Table 18
Wilmington Commerce, 1914–38, in Tons

	Foreign		Domestic	
Year	Imports	Exports	Imports	Exports
1924	255,985	25,573	322,643	25,375
1925	269,622	24,476	427,728	53,969
1926	191,125	29,157	451,283	44,900
1927	171,980	38,158	508,426	38,185
1928	290,820	29,737	524,683	42,829
1929	249,573	25,070	630,064	52,372
1930	290,279	13,953	631,709	54,144
1931	261,113	15,346	597,993	21,931
1932	94,007	14,374	527,286	20,341
1933	161,886	16,089	714,336	16,434
1934	133,052	31,534	831,811	24,780
1935	167,925	28,998	1,028,498	10,070
1936	164,675	40,275	1,212,844	19,123
1937	244,080	67,715	1,340,001	18,795
1938	217,508	57,244	1,423,163	12,996

Source: *The Ports of Charleston, S.C. and Wilmington, N. C.*, 183; *The Port of Wilmington, N.C.*, 66.

nonmetallic minerals (cement, gasoline, glass, gypsum), and inconsequential amounts of manufactures (barbed wire and nails) supplemented chemicals.[45] Imports showed considerable volatility, primarily due to slackened demand during the Depression. Shipping dipped to 94,007 tons in 1932 and only slowly recovered. Average foreign import tonnage in 1937–38 remained slightly below that for 1924–25.

Wilmington's foreign exports declined substantially during the Depression but rebounded by the late 30s to double the highs of the previous decade. Cotton was virtually the sole export from 1924 through 1926; it then steadily dropped from a peak of 35,723 tons in 1927 to 53 tons in 1938. Helping to fill the void was tobacco, which the port began to send abroad in some quantity in 1931. Fertilizer held its own in terms of tonnage. Italy (scrap metal), England (tobacco), the Netherlands (scrap metal), Germany (scrap metal), and China (fertilizer) in that order constituted Wilmington's best foreign markets.[46]

Several factors contributed to diminished cotton exports. The westward movement of cotton cultivation, reinforced by a European preference for

Texas cotton, added to Wilmington's woes. The boll weevil, the Depression, increasing government regulation, and in the long run simply the decline of the cotton fabric industry in the face of synthetic substitutes proved damaging. In any case, the heyday of the cotton commission merchant in the port, best exemplified by Alexander Sprunt & Son, had ended. The Sprunts' foreign exports dropped from 100,000 bales annually in the 1920s to 6,000 bales in 1938. After forging its way to the vanguard of Southern commercial endeavor, in the process making Wilmington a port of renown in European circles, the business succumbed to aging and divided management as well as to competition from newer firms in the Southwest, particularly the Oklahoma City–based firm of Anderson Clayton & Co.[47]

Domestic or coastal imports and exports evidenced polar trends. While imports rose dramatically, exports had dropped to less than 13,000 tons by 1938. Departing Wilmington for other coastal ports were lumber and timber, which usually made up more than half the outgoing tonnage, followed (in the order of their importance) by cross ties, cotton, fertilizer and fertilizer materials, and hardware. Fertilizer, fertilizer materials, sulphur, and groceries, including sugar and molasses, arrived in significant quantities. But most of the incoming commerce centered on petroleum products, principally gasoline and kerosene, which constituted some 70 percent of the port's trade, ranking Wilmington second among Atlantic ports handling petroleum products.[48]

The petroleum import industry gained a foothold in Wilmington in the latter years of the nineteenth century. Standard Oil Company had established an office in the port by 1889. Seven years later a company steamer, the *Maverick*, brought 6,000 gallons of kerosene to port, which was stored in Standard's seven-tank complex located at Front and Brunswick streets. At that time Wilmington was Standard's only distribution center along the South Atlantic and Gulf coasts. However, the spectacular increase in the demand for petroleum products in the twentieth century produced additional companies in Wilmington by World War I: Texaco, National, Universal Oil and Fertilizer.[49]

Wilmington's trade with the West Coast—California, Oregon, Washington—was mainly a one-way route. Imports far outweighed exports: 27,304 tons to 560 tons in 1938. In some years the port failed to ship any goods. Imports originated in San Francisco, Los Angeles, Astoria and Portland in Oregon, and several ports in Washington, mainly Seattle and Tacoma. Fruits and vegetables, lumber, animal products, fish, and dairy products in that order headed imports. Exports, mostly animal feed, went mainly to San Francisco. The import trade diminished greatly during the 30s, however, due to the near disappearance of petroleum products from Wilmington's Pacific commerce.[50]

Wilmington's internal shipping evidenced a rising trend during the decade of the 30s. Groceries, burlap bags, lumber and timber, metal cylinders, hardware, and various chemicals headed imports; tobacco, lumber, coal, chemicals, fertilizer materials, and petroleum products led exports. Most important in internal commerce by World War II was the shipment of gasoline. Although slightly over 200 tons of gasoline left the port in 1932, the amount rose steadily to 130,331 tons in 1938, or 52 percent of Wilmington's internal shipments during that year.[51]

Continental shipping service for Wilmington during the 20s and 30s proved irregular. The Clyde Line discontinued its runs after the war. Controlled by the Shipping Board during the conflict, the company was subsequently returned to private ownership. However, the condition of its ships had badly deteriorated, and it experienced difficulty competing with railroad-owned lines. A Clyde–Mallory Line reemerged in the 20s, but by 1938 ceased to call at Wilmington. Early in the decade of the 30s the Williams Steamship Corporation and the Bull Line, linking Wilmington to the Pacific and Gulf coasts respectively, provided bimonthly sailings. But in 1938 Wilmington's only regular steamer contact beyond the Atlantic coast was the American–Hawaiian Steamship Company, which offered an eastbound service from Pacific ports, discharging cargo at Wilmington every eleven days.[52]

Foreign service likewise declined. The South Atlantic Steamship Line and the Strachan Southern Shipping Company offered bimonthly service to the United Kingdom and the European continent in 1933. Five years later regular sailings ended. Foreign shipping thereafter consisted of irregular calls by vessels normally stopping at other South Atlantic ports and visiting Wilmington upon prior arrangements. Otherwise, only ships under charter called at the port.[53]

Most of Wilmington's commerce along the Intracoastal Waterway was carried by the North Carolina Line and the Norfolk, Baltimore & Carolina Line. The former operated a terminal on Eagles Island opposite the foot of Market Street in Wilmington; the latter, a terminal on the east side of the river between Parsley and Bradley Streets. The Southeastern Shipping Service, Champion Compress & Warehouse Co., and Wilmington Terminal Warehouse Co. also handled general cargo along the waterway.[54]

By the onset of World War II Wilmington had become essentially a local port, catering to a limited hinterland. Its internal tributary area—that in which Wilmington enjoyed a competitive advantage over other ports—extended from the Pamlico Sound northwestward through Wilson and Durham to Mount Airy, thence southwestward to the Tennessee border near Huntdale, and from there southeastward through Asheville, North Carolina, and Rock Hill, Lancaster, and Florence, South Carolina, to the Atlantic coast midway between Wilmington and Charleston. Exports originating from that area were locally manufactured goods. Most imports were used in the vicinity of Wilmington or, in the case of petroleum products, were transported to the Upper Cape Fear.[55]

Circumscribing Wilmington's hinterland market was the competition offered by Norfolk and Charleston. Both those ports actively sought to enlarge their rail capabilities at a time when rail traffic was still more important than trucking in supporting shipping activity. Railroad rates traditionally favored the Virginia and South Carolina ports; their trunk line connections and extensive railroad wharfage facilities appealed to shippers. Wilmington belatedly acquired a deepwater channel to accommodate modern heavy-draft ships; not until 1930 did Congress authorize the Army Corps of Engineers to dredge a 30-foot channel in the river. At midcentury Congress agreed to deepen the bar and channel to the Cape Fear to 35 and 34 feet respectively.[56] Still the port lagged behind Charleston and Norfolk in its ability to service larger ships.

Hampering Wilmington's port development was its inability to attract and handle general (usually packaged, containerized) cargo as opposed to bulk (non-packaged, such as coal) cargo. Most ships, except petroleum and other specialized carriers, transported both general and bulk cargoes, using the former as topping. Often the busiest ports attracted general cargo regardless of distance or cost. Shippers could afford higher overland transport costs because general cargo usually had a higher value per unit of weight. Handling general cargo, which was less adaptable to automated equipment, required more labor, and thus contributed more significantly to a port's economy. Although Wilmington could muster the labor, it lacked the necessary facilities, including heavy-lift equipment, to deal with general cargo. Moreover, the specialized petroleum vessels upon which Wilmington increasingly depended did not allow the transport of general cargo.[57]

Also hindering Wilmington's trade was its inordinate excess of imports over exports, a striking reversal of the shipping pattern that obtained in the eighteenth and nineteenth centuries. In 1915, for the first time, incoming tonnage exceeded that leaving the port. By 1925 foreign import tonnage was more than eight times greater than exports; domestic imports were four times greater than exports. Thus ships often left port in ballast—in 1930, for example, half the tonnage cleared in that fashion—which served to deter shippers who sought outward-bound cargoes to justify calling at the port.[58]

After the outbreak of World War II in Europe in 1939, a decision to construct ships for the merchant fleets of Great Britain and the United States forced the federal Maritime Commission to consider undertaking new shipyards. President Franklin D. Roosevelt, who had always viewed the South favorably, agreed that climate, available labor, and the need for economic stimulation made the region a prime candidate for shipbuilding sites.[59]

Large-scale shipbuilding in Wilmington had ceased in the early 20s, but interest in a shipyard revived quickly in 1939. Remembering the shipbuilding-induced prosperity of World War I, Wilmingtonians formed the Shipyard for Wilmington Committee in 1940 to lobby in Washington on behalf of the port. Meanwhile, the New Hanover County Defense Council organized to persuade the Newport News Shipbuilding and Dry Dock Company of Virginia to consider Wilmington as an additional site. After spirited competition between Wilmington and Morehead City for a government-supported shipbuilding facility, the Cape Fear port emerged victorious. By early November 1940 the Maritime Commission had selected Wilmington as one of several new sites for ship construction. It planned to work in conjunction with the North Carolina Shipbuilding Company, a subsidiary of the Newport News Shipbuilding and Dry Dock Company. The Maritime Commission agreed to purchase the shipyard, leasing it to the company and underwriting the cost of construction.[60]

Construction of the shipyard, located approximately three miles south of Wilmington on the east side of the Cape Fear River, began in February 1941. The North Carolina Shipbuilding Company laid the keels of its first vessels in May of that year and launched its last ship in April 1946. At its peak in 1943 the North Carolina Shipbuilding Company employed as many as 25,000 workers on an annual payroll of more than $50 million. With the V. P. Loftis Company's floating dry dock, the shipbuilding firm accounted for four-fifths of all manufacturing employees in New Hanover County. During its five years of operation in Wilmington the North Carolina Shipbuilding Company constructed 243 vessels. Of that number 126 were "Liberty ships," or the Maritime Commission's designated class EC2-S-C1. Built mainly for cargo purposes, the Liberty ships were 440 feet in length and 56 feet in the beam. They drew 27 feet of water and made 11 knots. The first off the ways, the *Zebulon B. Vance*, named for North Carolina's Civil War governor, was launched on December 6, 1941.[61]

Beginning in 1943 the company also turned out 117 C-2 design vessels known as "Victory ships." Though only slightly larger than the Liberty ships, improved propulsion pushed their potential speed to 17 knots. Unlike the Liberty vessels, the Victory ships were not built to standardized plan but constructed to suit the individual needs of potential owners—the Maritime Commission, the Navy, and private shipping concerns. Thus they proved more difficult and time-consuming to build. The first of the C-2's, the *S. S. Storm King*, was launched on September 17, 1943; the last, the *S. S. Santa Isabel*, in the fall of 1946.[62]

Following the war the Maritime Commission selected the Wilmington shipbuilding facility as a reserve yard, one of four in the country and the only one on the Atlantic coast, and designated the Brunswick River (across from Wilmington, connecting the Northwest Cape Fear and the Cape Fear rivers) as a reserve fleet basin. The first mothballed vessel arrived in August 1946, followed by row upon row of ships, including some Liberty and Victory vessels constructed in Wilmington during the war. Local and regional employment and income generated by the need for personnel to care for the ships proved to be a stimulus for the port's economy.[63]

Although the vessels began to be removed from time to time as early as 1948—for United States naval service, sale to foreign countries, or scrap—the reserve fleet continued to mount until 1958, when a peak number of 649 ships floated on the Brunswick River. Afterward they dwindled until the last, the *S. S. Dwight W. Morrow*, was removed in early 1970. Despite the abandonment of the reserve fleet basin, an occasional World War II vessel returned to the port. The *Vermilion*, built in Wilmington, decommissioned in 1949, and recommissioned for service in the Korean War, reappeared in Wilmington's harbor in 1988. She was destined to be scrapped and her hull sunk off Georgetown, South Carolina, as an artificial reef for the benefit of fisherman.[64]

During the war shipbuilding bolstered Wilmington's economy in the face of declining water traffic. The five-year annual average of tonnage passing through Wilmington from 1936 through 1940 was 2,134,664 tons. It dropped to 1,107,600 tons from 1941 through 1945, but recovered to 2,854,594 during the ensuing five years.[65] Subsequently familiar shipping patterns obtained. Imports still led exports by a wide margin, at least in the coastal trade, where gasoline and other petroleum products continued to dominate. As had been the case since the turn of the century, fertilizer comprised the bulk of foreign imports. The Inland Waterway assumed a significance during the war that its founders had not expected. By offering a protected avenue of commerce, it encouraged ever larger shipments of bulky, slow-moving freight, principally gasoline in the case of Wilmington.

At the end of World War II Wilmingtonians hoped to ease the transition to a peacetime economy by establishing a dry dock facility in the port and by creating a state ports authority to promote shipping. The shipyard, perhaps designed to refurbish Liberty and Victory ships for commercial purposes, might employ laborers of the North Carolina Shipbuilding Company if that business was terminated. The state ports authority would put returning veterans to work. To some extent both propositions were resurrections of schemes attempted unsuccessfully after World War I. Again the shipyard was doomed. Both the Newport News Shipbuilding and Dry Dock Company and the Todd Shipbuilding Company of Charleston opposed the potential competition from a Wilmington yard. Still the Maritime Commission and the navy in 1949 agreed to establish a dry dock at Wilmington if the state of North Carolina would maintain the facility. That dealt a death blow to Wilmington's hopes, for the state would not acquiesce in that proposal.[66]

However, the General Assembly did agree to the creation of the North Carolina State Ports Authority. Authorized by legislative enactment in 1945, the State Ports Authority culminated a twenty-year effort to secure state aid for port development. Back in 1924, during the gubernatorial administration of Cameron Morrison, a proposed state bond issue for $8,500,000 ($7 million to fund terminal facilities and $1.5 million to institute a steamship line) to improve the state's ports was defeated in a statewide referendum, largely because western voters failed to appreciate the positive impact of port development for the entire state.[67]

During the following decade, partially as a means of combatting the adverse effects of the Depression, the state legislature established the Morehead City Port Commission (1933) and the Wilmington Port Commission (1935). The lawmakers thereby instituted a "policy of the State of North Carolina to promote, encourage, and develop water transportation service and facilities in connection with the commerce of the United States and to foster and preserve in full vigor both rail and water transportation." Like Governor Morrison earlier, the legislators believed that port development was consonant with the interest of the entire state.[68]

The Wilmington Port Commission by law was directed to encourage the use of the port by shippers and industries within the distribution area of the port, to attempt to increase the tonnage and cargo moving through the port, and generally to promote the recognition of the advantages of shipping through the port. Limited to informational and promotional activity, the Wilmington Port Commission sought to improve the shipping facilities of the port by preparing plans for terminals and warehouses. Funding, however, was limited to a six-year property levy on New Hanover County residents. Thus the commission sought the aid of Governor R. Gregg Cherry to secure a state appropriation.[69]

A combination of factors in 1945, including the request of the Wilmington Port Commission, support from Governor Cherry and the State Planning Board, the prospect of extensive unemployment at the end of World War II, and relentless lobbying by Rinaldo B. Page, publisher of the Wilmington *Star* and *News*, convinced the state legislature to establish the North Carolina State Ports Authority. Perhaps most important was Page, who had spearheaded an effort in the 1930s to obtain deepwater shipping facilities for Wilmington and Morehead City, using his papers to promote his cause. He had also obtained a loan from the Works Progress Administration to finance studies of proposed terminals. Fittingly, Page became the first chairman of the State Ports Authority.[70]

The North Carolina State Ports Authority (SPA) emerged amid a flurry of similar efforts by neighboring states to improve their shipping capabilities. Georgia instituted its Ports Authority in 1945, supplementing the Savannah District Authority, created two decades earlier. The South Carolina State Ports Authority began in 1942; the Virginia State Ports Authority in 1952, four years after the inception of the Norfolk Port Authority. As the states realized, in the words of historian G. F. Mott, the port authority was a means of "achieving enlightened, coordinated, and planned harbor, port, and trade promotion and operation with protection to both public and private interests."[71]

After the initiation of the North Carolina State Ports Authority in 1945, the legislature struggled through several changes in the number and tenure of board members before settling upon nine (later eleven), appointed for six-year terms. The governor appointed members of the board, whose staggered terms were intended to remove the board from direct political influence. Board members supposedly reflected diverse economic interests—shipping, manufacturing, agricultural—from every geographic region of North Carolina.[72]

Extensive negotiations ensued between the SPA and the Maritime Commission to obtain the site of the shipyard used by the North Carolina Shipbuilding Company. The Maritime Commission held the Wilmington site as a reserve facility, fearing that ultimately the shipyard might find its way into private hands. By 1949 the federal agency relented sufficiently to lease the northern portion of the shipyard to the state. Seven years later the state bought 323 acres of land on the west bank of the Brunswick River, which it exchanged for the land under lease from the Maritime Commission. In 1961 the SPA leased another 115 acres from the Maritime Commission, which the state by agreement purchased ten years later from the federal government. Thus the SPA finally acquired full title to the entire facility.[73]

Although created in 1945, the SPA was "withering" in the estimation of Governor Kerr Scott when he assumed office in 1949. Funds were needed to construct port facilities in order to attract and service shipping. Scott led the effort that impelled the state legislature in 1949 to authorize the issuance of $7.5 million in bonds for the development of the SPA, two-thirds of which was earmarked for Wilmington. After the bonds had been marketed in 1950, construction began quickly. The state port at Morehead City—North Carolina Ocean Terminals—was dedicated in August 1952; that in Wilmington—North Carolina State Docks—in September 1952.[74]

Rivalry between Wilmington and Morehead City characterized SPA operations from the beginning. Morehead City interests objected to the establishment of the SPA executive office in Wilmington, and in the mid-50s claimed that the executive director of the SPA accorded Wilmington preferential treatment. Indeed, the executive director seemed to favor Wilmington, asserting, "The Port of Morehead City from its very beginning has been a failure," and noting that independent surveys showed Wilmington the superior port. Tiring of the squabbling, Governor Luther Hodges appointed new members to the board in 1957 under the mandate to maintain objectivity in dealing with the ports, to end the bickering, to increase shipping by an aggressive campaign of public relations, and to establish a long-range developmental program for the ports. The board proceeded to select a new executive director and to move the executive office of the SPA from Wilmington to Raleigh in an attempt to satisfy Morehead City. Nonetheless, the natural competitiveness and jealously between the ports proved impossible to eradicate over the years.[75]

From the opening of State Docks in 1952, Wilmington commerce increasingly flowed through the public facility. However, the tonnage was only a fraction of that conducted by private interests, as seen by Table 19. This imbalance was occasioned by an initial policy determination that State Docks should supplement private trade by encouraging commerce that private businesses were unable or ill-equipped to handle—relatively lightweight general cargo. In fact, State Docks controlled approximately nine-tenths of Wilmington's traffic other than petroleum products, fertilizer, and molasses and sugar.

Table 19
Tonnage, State Docks and the Port of Wilmington, 1952–63

Year	State Docks Tons	Other Facilities Tons	Total Tons
1952	23,498	3,405,000	3,428,498
1953	96,153	3,205,633	3,301,786
1954	104,837	3,321,727	3,426,564
1955	250,793	3,530,909	3,781,702
1956	278,583	3,534,001	3,812,584
1957	306,175	3,282,473	3,588,648
1958	184,457	3,674,954	3,859,411
1959	284,056	3,858,223	4,142,279
1960	352,271	3,827,480	4,179,751
1961	357,264	3,867,808	4,225,072
1962	317,782	4,502,417	4,820,199
1963	349,841	4,855,974	5,205,815

Randall, "Geographic Factors in the Growth and Economy of Wilmington, North Carolina," 91.

State Docks quickly attracted shipping, much of which began to call on regular schedules. In 1954 the Isthmian Steamship Company, bringing jute, jute products, and Egyptian cotton to the United States from Egypt, India, and Pakistan, decided to make Wilmington its first port of call. Four years later the company rescheduled Wilmington for outward-bound voyages to the Near East and India. Numerous other lines also stopped on a regular basis: South Atlantic Steamship Line, Inc. (Europe); Daido Line (Far East); Ozean-Stinner Line (northern Europe); Waterman Steamship Corporation (Far East); American Export Lines (southern Europe and Mediterranean); Splosna Plavba Line of Yugoslavia (Mediterranean).[76]

Bulk commodities constituted the mainstay (88 percent) of Wilmington's overall trade. Export tonnage in 1960 was devoted to petroleum products (39 percent), pulpwood and wood pulp (26 percent), and iron and steel scrap (23 percent). Internally petroleum products were distributed locally or regionally by barge, truck, and rail. Trucks moved about three-fourths of the shipments; barges, about 15 percent; railroads, less than a tenth. Pulpwood went to Georgetown, South Carolina; wood pulp went to South America, the Far East, and western Europe. Scrap metal found its way mostly to Japan, though some was exported to southern Europe.[77]

Imports, however, continued to dominate Wilmington's commerce, comprising approximately 85 percent of the tonnage passing through the port in 1961. Nine-tenths of that traffic involved petroleum products, most of which originated in Texas and Louisiana refineries; some 5 percent from Puerto Rico and Venezuela. In addition, shipments arrived via the Intracoastal Waterway.

The emergence of State Docks in Wilmington led to greatly improved terminal facilities in the port. After nine years State Docks offered a 2,510-foot wharf that could accommodate five 500-foot vessels simultaneously. Its operations also included three transit sheds, two storage warehouses, another 150,000-square-foot, five-bay shed with two overhead cranes, and a modern fumigation plant. A 240-freight-car holding yard, tracks, truck dock, weighing stations, two heavy-duty cranes, and two small cranes rounded out the facilities.[78]

Altogether in 1960 thirty-four piers, docks, and wharves lined Wilmington's waterfront along both banks of the Cape Fear and Northeast Cape Fear rivers. Reflecting the importance of petroleum products, oil companies owned eight handling and bunkering facilities. The SPA and five private firms operated thirteen warehouses that provided almost 700,000 square feet of storage. Port City Cold Storage, Inc., offered another 228,000 cubic feet of cold warehousing. In addition to the hoisting equipment owned by the SPA, five private concerns provided cranes and derricks ashore and afloat.[79]

Inadequate rail and road service handicapped Wilmington's shipping potential at the time. Only a branch track of the Seaboard Air Line ran to the port. And Wilmington remained an intermediate point on the Atlantic Coast Line route from the northern states to South Carolina and Georgia. Inasmuch as railroads preferred not to short-haul cargo, much of the north-south traffic on both lines bypassed Wilmington. Still, the number of railroad cars receiving or discharging goods at State Docks more than doubled from 2,888 in 1955 to 5,910 in 1961.[80]

In the second half of the twentieth century trucking, a burgeoning industry in the 30s, assumed paramount importance in transporting goods to the port. Four United States highways linked Wilmington to the interior of North Carolina and to surrounding states: 17, the Atlantic coast highway; 74, running west to Charlotte and beyond; 76, running west-southwest into South Carolina; 421, running northwest to Greensboro and Winston-Salem. But these were winding, twisting, usually two-lane roads that rendered extensive trucking activity onerous if not dangerous. Nevertheless, the number of trucks receiving or discharging cargo at State Docks rose steadily from 1,924 in 1955 to 6,327 in 1961.[81]

Throughout the ensuing quarter century traffic at State Docks steadily increased. Military traffic added to the commerce of State Docks, though such activity proved far more important at Ocean Terminals in Morehead City. After 1981, when separate figures were kept, as many as 40,000 tons of military goods flowed through the port. Assisting the port has been its designation as a primary embarkation point by the army and air force for their cargoes. State Docks also supports military training exercises. When the USNS Capella called in 1985 as part of a training program, the 946-foot vessel was the largest ship up until then to call at State Docks. Two and a half years later, as part of a training program, the army for the first time loaded a stern-ramped barge with equipment at State Docks.[82]

Over the years the number of steamship lines rose as the volume of shipping increased. Thirty-five regularly called at State Docks in 1963, connecting Wilmington with the Philippines and the Far East, Great Britain, northern Europe, southern Europe and the Mediterranean, the Near East, all parts of the African continent, and South America. By the mid-1980s, 111 lines serviced the port, 54 of which called regularly (29 weekly, 8 fortnightly, and 17 monthly).[83]

Still, from 1970 to 1986 the number of ships calling at State Docks rose slightly less than 30 percent, whereas the total tonnage flowing through the facility more than doubled. Explaining the discrepancy was the growing size of ships and the vastly increased number of barges that serviced State Docks, as seen in Table 20. When the Ming Prosperity docked in Wilmington in 1988, it was the latest of the "P" (Panamax) class vessels built for the Yang Ming Marine Line Transportation (Taiwan), and measured 885 feet in length and 106 feet in width.[84]

In constructing the Ming Prosperity for containerized cargo, the Yang Ming Line reflected a prevalent trend in world shipping. Since the 1960s containerization marked perhaps the most revolutionary change in the shipping industry. State Docks at Wilmington prepared accordingly for the advent of container traffic, which increased at an annual rate of about 8 percent in the mid-80s. In rendering shipping more efficient, containerization altered traditional market structures and traffic flow patterns. In its wake came larger ships, hence the need for deeper and wider harbor facilities, and complex computer systems to keep track of the cargo.[85]

The move to containerization heightened competition among ports. Rivalry transcended traditional regional boundaries. Final destination be-

Table 20
Shipping, State Docks, Wilmington

Year	Ships	Barges	Rail Cars	Trucks
1970	464	234	4,916	28,565
1972	567	397	7,216	36,675
1974	406	587	6,093	34,567
1976	484	506	7,442	45,530
1978	455	448	6,600	57,323
1980	529	426	6,292	69,629
1982	562	362	5,276	75,528
1984	594	393	6,546	73,957
1986	597	505	11,588	121,623

Figures supplied by William J. Stover, Jr., N.C. State Ports Authority.

came the ultimate consideration in traffic flow. The easy interchange of containers from ship to rail to truck opened new vistas in transportation opportunities as companies sought the fastest, most cost-effective means of transport.[86]

By the mid-80s, State Docks had greatly enlarged and improved its facilities, with the special intention of promoting containerization. Ten berths (580 to 780 feet) along 6,040 feet of continuous concrete wharf were serviced by eight pieces of hoisting equipment (five gantry cranes and three container-handling cranes). State Docks maintained 1.1 million square feet of dry warehousing space, four transit sheds containing 410,000 square feet, and some 90 acres of paved area, all accessed by rail and road. In an era of containerization adequate rail and road connections became mandatory. In the late 1980s the North Carolina State Ports Railroad Commission owned and operated over eighteen miles of track and considerable rolling stock within State Docks. That equipment interchanged with the CSX system, formerly Seaboard Coast Line (the result of a merger of Seaboard Air Line and Atlantic Coast Line). Double marginal tracks with crossovers served all ship berths. A rail holding yard stored approximately four hundred cars.[87]

As a result of containerization the trucking industry played an increasingly significant role in the development of the port, and highway access to Wilmington became the critical transportation linkage to Wilmington's hinterland. The number of truck trailers using State Docks in 1969 was almost quadruple the total at the beginning of the decade. The subsequent phenomenal increase of truck traffic at State Docks, reflecting the trend toward containerization and the growth of shipping activity, prompted State Docks to reorganize and expand its trucking facilities for handling containerized cargo.[88] Access to Wilmington by highway was enhanced by straightening and four-laning roads, improving bridges, and completing Interstate 40, which provides a direct link to Raleigh, the Piedmont, and indeed the nation's interstate system.

Financing the SPA program was a subject of dispute from the beginning. Some contended that the operation ought to be self-supporting. Others felt that the SPA was a public service, generating far-reaching returns on its investment that would benefit the entire state, and should not be sustained solely on a profit-making basis. It was hoped that revenues would cover operating and maintenance expenses and perhaps interest on bonded indebtedness; but the principal of such indebtedness, capital expenditures, and expansion would depend, directly or indirectly, upon the support of the state government. However, given the long-standing east-west antagonism in North Carolina and the understandable public perception that the ports and their environs mainly benefit from state appropriations, funding for the SPA received grudging approval and vigorous scrutiny. Voters defeated a bond referendum on a $13,500,000 issue in 1961 that would have modernized and expanded the terminals at Morehead City and Wilmington.[89]

Although the SPA continued to receive appropriations from the state legislature to supplement its own revenues, competition from neighboring ports and the need to upgrade Wilmington's containerization facilities led it to seek successfully a $35.9 million grant in fiscal 1987–88 for Wilmington and Morehead City. Wilmington stood to gain a 900-foot containerization berth ($13.7 million), two container cranes ($7 million), and a 100,000-square-foot warehouse ($3 million). Ironically, at the end of the fiscal year the Wilmington facility showed a loss of $515,000 on its operations. The deficit was ascribed mainly to the discontinuation of three container lines—Trans Freight, Sea-Land, and Atlantic Container—whose revenues were only partially offset by the addition of Senator Line of West Germany and Carolina Atlantic Transportation Service (a container barge service to Puerto Rico). Alarmed state legislators began to question the wisdom of funding the SPA.[90]

In its long-range master plan of 1986, the SPA acknowledged the need to rely more heavily on internally generated revenues. Yet it justified state financial assistance on the basis of shipping's contribution to the entire North Carolina economy as well as that of Wilmington and the Lower Cape Fear. State Docks employed some 260 state workers and 300 private personnel in 1988. Statewide, the SPA affected some 70,000 jobs directly, and every one-million-dollar increase in exports by North Carolina business created an estimated 2,400 jobs.[91]

A constant financial drain on the SPA was its Southport facility. In creating the SPA in 1945, the General Assembly mentioned the development of "harbors or seaports" at Wilmington, Morehead City, and Southport, an indication that early-nineteenth-century interest in Southport (Smithville) had not been totally abandoned. After approval of a bond issue in 1959 the SPA decided to construct a small marina in Southport, mainly as a pleasure boat facility but with the possibility of conversion into a commercial craft harbor. Dedicated in 1965, Southport Boat Harbor failed to show a profit. Leased in 1976, it continued to lose money, given the nature of the lease agreement, until 1987, when it earned $38,000.[92]

In the aftermath of the flap over the SPA's financial loss in 1987–88, investigations revealed some of the difficulties under which the agency operated. Among others was the rivalry between Morehead City and Wilmington, exacerbated by the removal of Morehead City's only container crane to Wilmington in the late 1970s. The politicization of the SPA posed another problem. Not only was the SPA a division of the state's Department of Commerce and thus subject to gubernatorial influence, but the governor also appointed seven of eleven members of the SPA board of directors. Some felt that greater autonomy in decision-making would enhance operations and perhaps alleviate a perceived low state of morale among SPA employees.[93]

Compounding the SPA's internal disarray was the competition offered by neighboring port authorities. During the decade ending in 1988, ports in Virginia, South Carolina, and Georgia had received almost $500 million in state appropriations; Morehead City and Wilmington, $56 million. As a result, in 1987 Norfolk, Charleston, and Savannah collectively boasted thirty container cranes; Wilmington, three. Consequently, as much as two-thirds of North Carolina exports left the state by way of Virginia, South Carolina, and Georgia.[94]

The SPA at Wilmington has made strenuous efforts to improve its attractiveness to shippers. In addition to enhancing its physical facilities officials have fostered a state intermodal network, a system of inland cargo transfer sites to cater to the increasing trend toward containerization. Federal deregulation in the 1980s and resulting consolidation of port calls by shipping lines mandated the move toward intermodalism. A truck-to-rail terminal in Charlotte opened in 1984, and later a rail-to-truck terminal in

Greensboro. As a result the SPA contended that it could save shippers from $150 to 200 per container in shipment costs.[95]

More aggressive marketing of the port and its advantages has been a principal thrust of SPA policy in light of the increasingly competitive atmosphere of the late twentieth century. The SPA signed a "sister port" agreement in 1988 with the Chinese city of Dandong on the Yalu River in hopes of promoting trade with the People's Republic of China. A "Declaration of Cooperation" with Le Havre in 1988 led to the regular exchange of marketing information with that French port. Overseas offices have been established in Asia, Great Britain, and West Germany, a positive result of which was the decision of the Senator Line of West Germany to select Wilmington as its mid-Atlantic gateway port.[96]

Among other advantages offered by the port is a Free Trade Zone (FTZ), No. 66, activated in August 1982. The four FTZ's in North Carolina (Charlotte, Durham, Morehead City, and Wilmington, the last two operated by the SPA) are among some 140 scattered throughout the United States. An FTZ is an isolated, self-contained area into which foreign and domestic imports may be placed without undergoing formal customs strictures. By storing or displaying for sale, by altering via a manufacturing process, or by simply reexporting the goods, the importer may reduce greatly customs duties.[97]

Wilmington's FTZ has been active since its inception. During the fiscal year of 1983–84 it received 4,044 tons of merchandise valued at $15.8 million. Goods stored in the zone have included cigarettes, heavy industrial equipment, automobiles, whiskey, and furniture. One of the principal users of the FTZ was L & L International, Inc., which imported Mercedes, BMWs, Porches, and Lamborghinis, and stored the cars while modifying them to meet U.S. environmental emission and safety standards. While a FTZ was restricted at first to an area of 510,206 square feet, by 1988 the entire SPA terminal complex at Wilmington had been designated a FTZ.[98]

As the twentieth century draws to a close, the port of Wilmington continues to be a vital force in the economy of the Lower Cape Fear and the state of North Carolina. Although the tonnage of general cargo that moved through the SPA rose steadily from the inception of the agency, it remained no more than a fifth of the total tonnage shipped through Wilmington until 1980, after which it assumed more significant proportions. Private shipping, which in the mid-eighties still comprised some fifty-five to sixty percent of the total tonnage passing through the port, rested on petroleum and chemical companies and Almont Shipping Company. Almont Shipping, located on the Northeast Cape Fear, annually handles some one and a half million tons of dry bulk cargo.

Internal traffic on the Cape Fear and local rivers still contributes to the commerce of Wilmington. Yet its impact diminished after World War II in light of competition from highway transport. Since 1960 the Army Corps of Engineers has deepened the channels of the Northeast Cape Fear and Black rivers and maintained the ocean inlets south of Wilmington; but Black River carried no appreciable traffic after 1949, and the Northeast Cape Fear averaged only 390,600 tons (mostly chemicals) from 1980 to 1984. Other than an annual average of 2,300 tons of logs and lumber on Smith Creek in the early 1980s, most of Wilmington's internal water traffic consists of chemicals and petroleum products that are carried from the port to Fayetteville.[99]

Supplementing private traffic and that of the SPA is the shipping of Military Ocean Terminal, Sunny Point (MOTSU). Located on the west bank of the Cape Fear about five miles above Southport and twenty-five miles below Wilmington and operated by the army, MOTSU is designed primarily to handle dangerous explosive cargoes. When activated in 1955, the facility was known as the Wilmington Ammunition Loading Terminal (WALT). After several name changes, the installation assumed its current designation, MOTSU—Sunny Point to most—in 1965. As the largest ammunition port in the free world and the only Department of Defense terminal specifically planned to deal with military explosives, Sunny Point serves as a transshipment site for United States and NATO forces throughout the world. Officials at Sunny Point also supervise the movement of Department of Defense cargo through the State Ports Authority at Wilmington and Morehead City.[100]

The presence of Sunny Point constitutes a continual reminder of the indispensability of the federal government to the development of the port of Wilmington. Following World War II the Army Corps of Engineers resumed its efforts to improve the navigability of the Cape Fear River. Eventually the Corps dredged the bar to a 40-foot depth and 500-foot width, and the channel to 38 and 400 feet respectively to the foot of Castle Street in Wilmington. From that point the depth and width decreased to 32 and 300 feet respectively to Hilton Bridge over the Northeast Cape Fear. The Corps also continued to enlarge the anchorage basin to the south of the city and the turning basin to the north.[101]

Despite support from state and federal governments the port of Wilmington still suffers from a competitive disadvantage with neighboring Atlantic coast ports. Containerization virtually destroyed the idea of a monopolized trade area, or a region controlled by a port, for the container itself became the carrier, moving by the least expensive means and route available. Thus a premium is placed on intermodal transportation. Yet Wilmington in the 1980s was served by only one railroad and only achieved an interstate highway connection in 1990.[102]

Partially as a result of containerization the shipping industry began to consolidate. Small lines merged into larger ones. Trying to cut costs, the major firms attempted to make as few port calls as possible, thus avoiding small ports to concentrate their business in such "Load Center Ports" as Norfolk and Charleston. Although the SPA made an effort to prepare for containerization, it lacked the public support provided by its competitors. The states of Virginia, South Carolina, and Georgia poured funds into the expansion and modernization of their port facilities.[103]

By the late 1980s Wilmington SPA officials apparently agreed that efforts to outstrip rival ports were futile. Rather than compete as a load center point, they felt that Wilmington ought to view itself as an intermediary point in a larger intermodal transportation network. Thus it should emphasize its ability to service smaller companies that might receive less personal attention in larger ports. All the while port authorities sought navigation improvements—a deeper channel and a passing lane for ships on the river—to make Wilmington more attractive to shipping lines.[104]

After two and a half centuries Wilmington remains North Carolina's only continuous port of commercial importance. Its future rests largely on the maintenance and enhancement of the navigability of the Cape Fear River, the success of the SPA, and the support of local authorities. The port continues to benefit from the long-standing presence of the federal government, particularly in the form of the Army Corps of Engineers, which evidences constant concern for the shipping potential of the river. Via the SPA the state of North Carolina has shown its recognition of the vital role played by the port in the economy of the entire state as well as in the Lower Cape Fear. And local officials, including the Chamber of Commerce and trade associations, remain vigilant in the protection and promotion of waterborne commerce. With continued governmental support, appropriate financing, and sufficient exertion on the part of local and regional interests, the port may look to a bright future as Wilmington moves toward the observance of its tricentennial.

Notes

Chapter 1. Origins of a Colonial Port

1. Journal of Susan D. Nye, May 6, 1815, Susan Davis Nye Hutchinson Papers, State Department of Archives and History, Raleigh; Janet Schaw, *Journal of a Lady of Quality*, ed. Evangeline W. Andrews and Charles M. Andrews (New Haven, 1921), 141.

2. For this and the following paragraph see Lawrence Lee, *The Lower Cape Fear in Colonial Days* (Chapel Hill, 1965), 3-4.

3. *South-Carolina Gazette* (Charles Town), Oct. 17, 1761; William L. Saunders, ed., *The Colonial Records of North Carolina*, 10 vols. (Raleigh, 1886-90), 6: 608; Adelaide L. Fries et al., eds., *Records of the Moravians in North Carolina*, 11 vols. (Raleigh, 1922-69) 1: 259.

4. David Beers Quinn, *North America from Earliest Discovery to First Settlements: The Norse Voyages to 1612* (New York, 1977), 155; Lee, *Lower Cape Fear*, 12-14.

5. Quinn, *North America from the Earliest Discovery*, 144-47.

6. For this and the following paragraph see Daniel W. Fagg, Jr., "Carolina, 1663-1683: The Founding of a Proprietary" (PhD diss., Emory University, 1970), ch. 2; Lee, *Lower Cape Fear*, ch. 4.

7. Lee, *Lower Cape Fear*, 98-100.

8. Lee, *Lower Cape Fear*, 101-02; "An Act for Regulating Vestrys in this Government and for the better Inspecting the Vestrymen and Church Wardens Accounts for Each and Every Parish within this Government," Colonial Office Papers 5/293, f. 147, Public Record Office, London, a copy of which was kindly supplied by Robert J. Cain, Division of Archives and History, Raleigh.

9. Alan D. Watson, "Wilmington: A Town Born of Conflict, Confusion, and Collusion," *Lower Cape Fear Historical Society Bulletin* 30 (Feb. 1988): 1, 3.

10. Hugh Meredith, *An Account of the Cape Fear Country, 1731*, ed. Earl Gregg Swem (Perth Amboy, NJ, 1912), 14-15, 27; Saunders, *Colonial Records*, 5: 158; Lord Adam Gordon, "Journal of an Officer's Travels in America and the West Indies, 1764-1765," in *Travels in the American Colonies*, ed. Newton D. Mereness (New York, 1916), 402; Schaw, *Journal of a Lady of Quality*, 145.

11. Watson, "Wilmington," 4–5; Donald R. Lennon and Ida B. Kellam, eds., *The Wilmington Town Book, 1743–1778* (Raleigh, 1973), xvi–xvii.

12. Lennon and Kellam, *Wilmington Town Book*, 2, nn2,3; 6, n12, 7, n17; Walter B. Edgar, ed., *The Letterbook of Robert Pringle*, 2 vols. (Columbia, SC, 1972), 1: 128–29, 135.

13. Nina M. Tiffany, ed., *Letters of James Murray, Loyalist* (Boston, 1901), 36; Saunders, *Colonial Records*, 4: 40, 43, 44–45, 186–87, 205, 216, 235–39, 241, 271, 277, 328, 333, 335, 342, 441; Walter Clark, ed., *The State Records of North Carolina*, 16 vols. [numbered 11–26] (Winston and Goldsboro, NC, 1895–1907), 23: 215–19.

14. Clark, *State Records*, 23: 133–35; Watson, "Wilmington, Part 2," *Lower Cape Fear Historical Society Bulletin* 30 (May 1988): 4–5; Saunders, *Colonial Records*, 4: 18.

15. Clark, *State Records*, 23: 146–49; Alan D. Watson, "The Founding Fathers of Wilmington, 1743–1775," *Lower Cape Fear Historical Society Bulletin* 24 (Oct. 1980).

16. Schaw, *Journal of a Lady of Quality*, 279; Meredith, *Account of the Cape Fear Country*, 16; Johann David Schoepf, *Travels in the Confederation, 1783–1784*, ed. and trans. by Alfred J. Morrison, 2 vols. (Philadelphia, 1911), 2: 145; "A New Voyage to Georgia by a Young Gentleman, London, 1737," *Collections of the Georgia Historical Society*, 2: 56; *South-Carolina Gazette*, June 7, 1740; David Leroy Corbitt, ed., *The Formation of the North Carolina Counties, 1663–1943* (Raleigh, 1950), 34.

17. *Virginia Gazette* (Purdie) (Williamsburg), Apr. 5, 1776; Lawrence Lee, *The History of Brunswick County, North Carolina* (Charlotte, 1980), 74–81.

18. Schaw, *Journal of a Lady of Quality*, 281; William S. Powell, ed., "Tryon's 'Book' on North Carolina," *North Carolina Historical Review* 24 (1957): 411; William K. Boyd, ed., *Some Eighteenth Century Tracts Concerning North Carolina* (Chapel Hill, 1927), 440, 443; Mark A. DeWolfe Howe, ed., "The Southern Journal of Josiah Quincy, Jr.," *Massachusetts Historical Society Proceedings* 59 (1915–16): 462; H. Roy Merrens, *Colonial North Carolina in the Eighteenth Century: A Study in Historical Geography* (Chapel Hill, 1964), 153.

19. Clark, *State Records*, 25: 259; Lennon and Kellam, *Wilmington Town Book*, xxii, 57, 59, 207.

20. Lennon and Kellam, *Wilmington Town Book*, 57, 72, 79, 88, 107, 109, 177, 180, 181, 197, 199, 237.

21. Alan D. Watson "Port Brunswick in the Colonial Era," *Lower Cape Fear Historical Society Journal*, 31 (1989); 23–32. See also Thomas C. Barrow, *Trade and Empire: The British Customs Service in Colonial America, 1660–1775* (Cambridge, MA, 1967).

22. Saunders, *Colonial Records*, 3: 259; 4: 6.

23. Lee, *Lower Cape Fear*, 166.

24. Charles C. Crittenden, *The Commerce of North Carolina, 1763–1789* (New Haven, 1936), 77–83; Lee, *Lower Cape Fear*, 162.

25. Saunders, *Colonial Records*, 6: 969; Crittenden, *Commerce of North Carolina*, 80–81; Lee, *Lower Cape Fear*, 162–63.

26. Byron Eugene Logan, "An Historical Geographic Survey of North Carolina Ports" (PhD diss., University of North Carolina, 1956), 62; Crittenden, *Commerce of North Carolina*, 79, 79 n5.

27. Crittenden, *Commerce of North Carolina*, 69–70; Lee, *Lower Cape Fear*, 164.

28. Merrens, *Colonial North Carolina*, 127; Crittenden, *Commerce of North Carolina*, 75–76, 84.

29. *South-Carolina & American General Gazette* (Charles Town), Aug. 5, 1768; Merrens, *Colonial North Carolina*, 131–32.

30. Lee, *Lower Cape Fear*, 155.

31. Merrens, *Colonial North Carolina*, 93–101.
32. Ibid., 109.
33. Ibid., 120–24; Saunders, *Colonial Records*, 9: 539; Schoepf, *Travels in the Confederation*, 2: 129–30; Donald Jackson and Dorthy Twohig, eds., *The Diaries of George Washington*, 6 vols. (Charlottesville, VA, 1976–79), 6: 119.
34. Meredith, *Account of the Cape Fear Country*, 20; Saunders, *Colonial Records*, 5: 316; 6: 1029; 9: 270, 364; Tiffany, *Letters of James Murray*, 78n; Merrens, *Colonial North Carolina*, 125–28.
35. Tiffany, *Letters of James Murray*, 64; Schaw, *Journal of a Lady of Quality*, 177; Charles C. Crittenden, "Inland Navigation in North Carolina, 1763–1789," *North Carolina Historical Review* 8 (1931): 145–50.
36. Benjamin F. Hall, Autobiography, Hall Papers, State Archives, Raleigh; Schaw, *Journal of a Lady of Quality*, 185.
37. Hall, Autobiography; Crittenden, "Inland Navigation," 151.
38. Boyd, *Some Eighteenth Century Tracts*, 440; Hall, Autobiography; Grimes, North Carolina Wills and Inventories, 153; James H. Brewer, "An Account of Negro Slavery in the Cape Fear Region Prior to 1860" (PhD diss., University of Pittsburgh, 1949), 126–27.
39. Watson, "Port Brunswick in the Colonial Era," 23–32.
40. Clark, *State Records*, 23: 239–43; Lee, *Lower Cape Fear*, 231, 238, 240.
41. Fries, *Records of the Moravians*, 1: 262; Tiffany, *Letters of James Murray*, 27; Clark, *State Records*, 23: 610.
42. Clark, *State Records*, 23: 355–58, 381, 383.
43. Ibid., 357; Fries, *Records of the Moravians*, I: 335; New Hanover Court Minutes, Oct. 1768.
44. Clark, *State Records*, 23: 650–52.
45. Ibid., 653, 683.
46. Ibid., 652–53, 682; 24: 896; *Wilmington Gazette*, Mar. 2, 1797.
47. Clark, *State Records*, 23: 462, 728; 25: 263; New Hanover Court Minutes, Apr. 1768.
48. Clark, *State Records*, 23: 639–49, 790–801; 25: 313–19, 378–87.
49. Saunders, *Colonial Records*, 4: 5–6, 16; 8: 186–89.
50. Saunders, *Colonial Records*, 4: 6; 5: 293, 316–17, 573–74, 714; 6: 449, 1030; 8: 38, 66; Clark, *State Records*, 23: 613–14, 646, 649, 797–98; Schaw, *Journal of a Lady of Quality*, 195; Lee, *Lower Cape Fear*, 159–60.
51. Philip M. Hamer and George C. Rogers, Jr., eds., *The Papers of Henry Laurens*, 11 vols. to date (Columbia, SC, 1968—), 3: 95, 357, 374; 4: 39–43, 208–09.
52. Lee, *Lower Cape Fear*, 172–80.
53. "A New Voyage to Georgia," 54–56, 59; Hugh Finlay, *Journal Kept by Hugh Finlay, Surveyor of the Post Roads on the Continent of North America* (Brooklyn, 1867), 67; Schaw, *Journal of a Lady of Quality*, 202, 280.
54. Saunders, *Colonial Records*, 9: 659; Clark, *State Records*, 23: 753–54, 870–71, 908–09, 918–20.
55. Clark, *State Records*, 15: 786; 23: 791, 920–22, 974; 25: 268–70, 786.
56. Saunders, *Colonial Records*, 4: 449, 1030; Clark, *State Records*, 24: 513–17; 25: 470–72; Merrens, *Colonial North Carolina*, 157–60.
57. Boyd, *Some Eighteenth Century Tracts*, 448–49; Merrens, *Eighteenth Century North Carolina*, 159–60.
58. "A New Voyage to Georgia," 55, 56; Saunders, *Colonial Records*, 5: 321–24; 9: 844–45; Lee, *Lower Cape Fear*, 167.

59. Schaw, *Journal of a Lady of Quality*, 155; Saunders, *Colonial Records*, 10: 48, 236; Merrens, *Colonial North Carolina*, 152–53.

60. Schaw, *Journal of a Lady of Quality*, 323–25; Merrens, *Colonial North Carolina*, 153.

61. Schaw, *Journal of a Lady of Quality*, 281; Joseph A. Ernst, *Money and Politics in America: A Study in the Currency Act of 1764 and the Political Economy of Revolution* (Chapel Hill, 1973), 203, 296; Boyd, *Some Eighteenth Century Tracts*, 448–49.

Chapter 2. Revolution and Independence: A Burgeoning Commerce

1. Alan D. Watson, *Money and Monetary Problems in Early North Carolina* (Raleigh, 1980), 29–36, quotation on 29. See also Robert M. Weir, "North Carolina's Reaction to the Currency Act of 1764," *North Carolina Historical Review* 40 (1963): 183–99.

2. Lawrence Lee, *The Lower Cape Fear in Colonial Days* (Chapel Hill, 1965), 244–46.

3. Donna J. Spindel, "Law and Disorder: The North Carolina Stamp Act Crisis," *North Carolina Historical Review* 57 (1980): 8; Jesse Lemisch, "Jack Tar in the Streets: Merchant Seamen in the Politics of Revolutionary America," *William and Mary Quarterly* 3rd series 25 (1968): 371–407.

4. D. L. Corbitt, ed., "Historical Notes," *North Carolina Historical Review* 5 (1928): 329–30; Lee, *Lower Cape Fear*, 247–50.

5. Arthur M. Schlesinger, *The Colonial Merchants and the American Revolution, 1763–1776* (New York, 1964), 148–49; *South-Carolina Gazette and Country Journal* (Charles Town), Dec. 8, 1769.

6. *Cape Fear Mercury* (Wilmington), July 11, 1770; *South-Carolina Gazette* (Charles Town), Aug. 9, 1770; Schlesinger, *Colonial Merchants and the American Revolution*, 208–09; William L. Saunders, ed., *The Colonial Records of North Carolina*, 10 vols. (Raleigh, 1886–90), 8: 496.

7. Leora H. McEachern and Isabel M. Williams, eds., *Wilmington–New Hanover Safety Committee Minutes, 1774–1776* (Wilmington, 1976), 28.

8. Ibid., 4–5, 7. Significantly, the chairman of the safety committee, Cornelius Harnett, was allowed to keep a slave that he had purchased but had not imported before the deadline imposed by the Association (ibid., 25).

9. Ibid., 56–57, 65, 74; Kemp P. Battle, ed., *Letters and Documents Relating to the Early History of the Lower Cape Fear*, James Sprunt Historical Monograph 4 (Chapel Hill, 1903), 26.

10. McEachern and Williams, *Minutes*, 6, 12–13, 16. Occasionally residents in the county, styled "regulators," took it upon themselves to intimidate merchants into lowering prices (Battle, *Letters and Documents*, 27–28).

11. McEachern and Williams, *Minutes*, 70, 72.

12. Saunders, *Colonial Records*, 10: 93, 102–03, 113–14; McEachern and Williams, *Minutes*, 44.

13. Charles C. Crittenden, *The Commerce of North Carolina, 1763–1789* (New Haven, 1936), 125–26; Walter Clark, ed., *The State Records of North Carolina*, 16 vols. (numbered 11–26) (Winston and Goldsboro, 1895–1907), 13: 84–85.

14. William N. Still, Jr., *North Carolina's Revolutionary War Navy* (Raleigh, 1976), 3, 14; Lee, *Lower Cape Fear*, 275; Adelaide L. Fries et al., eds., *Records of the Moravians in North Carolina*, 11 vols. (Raleigh, 1922–69), 3: 1323.

15. Still, *North Carolina's Revolutionary War Navy*, 19, 22.

16. Gregory L. Massey, "The British Expedition to Wilmington, January–November 1781," *North Carolina Historical Review*, 46 (1989): 388–96, 410.

17. Francisco de Miranda, *The New Democracy in America: Travels of Francisco de Miranda in the United States, 1783–1784*, trans. Judson P. Wood, ed. John S. Ezell (Norman, OK, 1963), 14; Lawrence Lee, *The History of Brunswick County, North Carolina* (Charlotte, 1980), 86–87.

18. Lee, *Brunswick County*, 88–94.

19. *Heads of Families at the First Census of the United States Taken in the Year 1790: North Carolina* (Baltimore, 1966), 9; Alonzo T. Dill, Jr., "Eighteenth Century New Bern: A History of the Town and Craven County, 1700–1800: Part VIII," *North Carolina Historical Review* 23 (1946): 515; *Wilmington Centinel*, July 23, 1788; Clark, *State Records*, 18: 597–98.

20. Miranda, *New Democracy*, 14; Robert Hunter, Jr., *Quebec to Carolina in 1785–1786*, ed. Louis B. Wright and Marion Tinling (San Marino, CA, 1943), 286–87; Donald Jackson and Dorothy Twohig, eds., *The Diaries of George Washington*, 6 vols. (Charlottesville, VA, 1976–79), 6: 119–22; Clark, *State Records*, 15: 995, 1000; Alice Barnwell Keith, William H. Masterson, and David T. Morgan, eds., *The John Gray Blount Papers*, 4 vols. (Raleigh, 1952–82), 1: 163; Fries, *Records of the Moravians*, 5: 2270, 2287; Dill, "Eighteenth Century New Bern," 515.

21. John L. Cheney, Jr., comp., *North Carolina Government, 1585–1974: A Narrative and Statistical History* (Raleigh, 1975), 768, 770; Griffeth J. McRee, ed., *Life and Correspondence of James Iredell*, 2 vols. (New York, 1857), 2: 225, 243–44.

22. John J. McCusker and Russell R. Menard, *The Economy of British America, 1607–1789* (Chapel Hill, 1985), 367, 373–75; Fries, *Records of the Moravians*, 4: 1921.

23. McRee, *Life of James Iredell*, 2: 70, 115; Clark, *State Records*, 14: 553; 16: 995; Crittenden, *Commerce of North Carolina*, 158.

24. *Wilmington Gazette*, Feb. 5, 1805; *The New American State Papers, Commerce and Navigation*, Vols. 1–47 (Wilmington, DE, 1973), 2: 88; 3: 13–14.

25. Crittenden, *Commerce of North Carolina*, 158; *State Gazette of North Carolina* (Edenton), Oct. 27, 1788.

26. Crittenden, *Commerce of North Carolina*, 160–61.

27. Ibid., 161; Jackson and Twohig, *Diaries of George Washington*, 6: 119.

28. *Wilmington Gazette*, Mar. 24, 1807.

29. Ibid., May 12, 1812; Jan. 20, Feb. 24, 1803.

30. Crittenden, *Commerce of North Carolina*, 121; Clark, *State Records*, 24: 686–88, 850–51.

31. Clark, *State Records*, 24: 124–28, 167–68, 218–19.

32. Ibid., 502, 506–07.

33. Ibid., 25: 57; *Laws and Resolutions of the State of North Carolina, 1802*, ch. 46.

34. *Laws*, 1792, ch. 22; *Wilmington Centinel*, July 9, 1788.

35. *Laws*, 1805, ch. 23; 1815, ch. 15; 1812, ch. 91, 92.

36. *Laws*, 1792, ch. 22.

37. *Laws*, 1796, ch. 21; 1811, ch. 24; 1815, ch. 14; Russell B. Hartzer, *To Great and Useful Purpose: A History of the Wilmington District U.S. Army Corp of Engineers* (n.p., n.d.), 11.

38. *Laws*, 1811, ch. 24.

39. Clark, *State Records*, 24: 7; Alan D. Watson, "Benjamin Smith: The Early Years of a North Carolina Governor," *Lower Cape Fear Historical Society Bulletin* 25 (Feb. 1982).

40. *Wilmington Gazette*, Aug. 24, 1800; Dec. 10, 1801; *Laws*, 1802, ch. 44.

41. Delbert H. Gilpatrick, *Jeffersonian Democracy in North Carolina, 1789–1815* (New York, 1967), 236; *Wilmington Gazette*, Feb. 5, 1805; *Laws, 1810*, ch. 5; William S. Powell, "Beginning of Banking in North Carolina, 1804–1860," *Tarheel Banker* 41 (July 1962): 59–60; William K. Boyd, "Currency and Banking in North Carolina, 1790–1836," *Trinity College Historical Society Papers* 10 (1914): 52–86.

42. Alan D. Watson, *Richard Dobbs Spaight* (New Bern, NC, 1986), 18; *North Carolina Gazette* (New Bern), Oct. 19, 1793; *Laws, 1795*, ch. 20.

43. *Hall's Wilmington Gazette*, Feb. 16, Mar. 2, 1797; *Wilmington Gazette*, Apr. 1, 1802. Legislation in 1802 reinforced and enhanced existing quarantine provisions for the state's ports (*Laws, 1802*, ch. 24).

44. Clark, *State Records*, 15: 56–57; *Laws, 1792*, ch. 12.

45. *Laws, 1794*, ch. 50; *1804*, ch. 20; *1806*, ch. 60.

46. *State Gazette of North Carolina* (Edenton), Mar. 26, 1789.

47. David Stick, *Bald Head: A History of Smith Island and Cape Fear* (Wendell, NC, 1985), 30–33; *Laws, 1792*, ch. 23; *Wilmington Chronicle*, July 24, Aug. 7, 1795.

48. Florence Kern, *William Cooke's U.S. Revenue Cutter Diligence, 1792–1798* (Washington, ca. 1979), 5–6, 12.

49. Ibid., 1, 20.

50. Ibid., 33–35.

51. This and the following three paragraphs are based on Watson, *Richard Dobbs Spaight*, 15–17; Kern, *Diligence*, 22–28; "A Statement of Facts Relative to the Sloop Providence L'Aimee Marguerite," Treasurer's and Comptroller's Papers, Ports, Box 11, North Carolina State Archives.

52. *Wilmington Chronicle*, July 17, 31, 1795; *Wilmington Gazette*, May 28, Aug. 6, 1801; Lee, *History of Brunswick County*, 94–95.

53. *Wilmington Gazette*, July 14, 21, 1807.

54. Ibid., June 28, 1808; Mar. 14, 1809.

55. Sarah M. Lemmon, *Frustrated Patriots: North Carolina and the War of 1812* (Chapel Hill, 1973), 41–42.

56. Ibid., 135.

57. Ibid., 130; *Raleigh Register*, June 3, 1814.

58. Lemmon, *Frustrated Patriots*, 124, 138.

59. Ibid., 154–55.

60. Ibid., 155, 156 n23; *Raleigh Register*, July 15, 1814.

61. Lemmon, *Frustrated Patriots*, 156.

62. Byron Eugene Logan, "An Historical Geographic Survey of North Carolina Ports" (PhD diss., University of North Carolina, 1956), 70–71.

63. Lemmon, *Frustrated Patriots*, 11; Annals of Congress, 19th Congress, 1st Session, 1825–1826, 1234.

64. Logan, "Historical Geographic Survey of North Carolina Ports," 74.

Chapter 3. Antebellum Wilmington: North Carolina's Maritime Entrepôt

1. James Sprunt, *Chronicles of the Cape Fear River, 1660–1916*, 2nd ed. (Raleigh, 1916), 139; Sarah Woodall Turlington, "Steam Navigation in North Carolina Prior to 1860," (MA Thesis, University of North Carolina, 1933), 40; *Wilmington Chronicle*, Mar. 31, 1841; Aug. 3, Sept. 28, 1842.

2. William H. Hoyt, ed., *The Papers of Archibald D. Murphey*, 2 vols. (Raleigh, 1914), 2: 160.

3. *Cape Fear Recorder* (Wilmington), Apr. 11, 1827; *People's Press and Wilmington Advertiser*, Aug. 7, 1833; Roger B. Starling, "The Plank Road Movement in North Carolina, Parts I and II," *North Carolina Historical Review*, 16, (1939): 169; *Wilmington Chronicle*, Mar. 31, 1841.

4. *Cape Fear Recorder*, Nov. 4, 1820; Sprunt, *Chronicles of the Cape Fear River*, 140–44; *Wilmington Chronicle*, Dec. 6, 1843.

5. Fredrick Law Olmsted, *A Journey in the Seaboard Slave States, with Remarks on Their Economy* (1856; New York, 1969), 374; *Laws and Resolutions of the State of North Carolina, 1858–1859*, Private, ch. 257; *People's Press and Wilmington Advertiser*, Oct. 1, 1834; *Wilmington Journal*, June 18, 1847; Dec. 22, 1848; Feb. 21, 1851; Mar. 12, 1852; Mar. 2, 1855; June 24, 1859; T. Tuther, comp., *Kelley's Wilmington Directory, to Which Is Added a Business Directory for 1860–61* (Wilmington, 1860), 13.

6. *Wilmington Advertiser*, Aug. 31, Sept. 14, 1838; *Wilmington Journal* (weekly), Mar. 20, 1846; Jan. 21, 1859; Jan. 12, 1860; Sprunt, *Chronicles of the Cape Fear River*, 140; *Kelley's Wilmington Directory*, 13.

7. *Wilmington Journal*, Feb. 13, 1846; *People's Press* (Wilmington), Mar. 27, 1833.

8. *People's Press and Wilmington Advertiser*, Apr. 22, May 13, Oct. 30, 1835; *Laws, 1835*, ch. 145; *1856–57*, Public, ch. 31; *1858–59*, Public, ch. 59; Deed from Edward B. Dudley to the Wilmington Marine Hospital Association, Mar. 3, 1836, Seamen's Friend Society Papers, Perkins Library, Duke University; "Expenditures upon the new marine hospital at Wilmington, July 12, 1858 to September 1, 1859," Miscellaneous, Samuel A'Court Ashe Papers, State Department of Archives and History, Raleigh.

9. *Wilmington Journal*, Feb. 11, 1853; Articles of Agreement, June 14, 1853, Seamen's Friend Society Papers; J. S. Reilly, *Wilmington Past Present, and Future* (Wilmington, 1884), 37–38.

10. *Cape Fear Recorder*, Dec. 20, 1816; *Wilmington Advertiser*, Mar. 16, 1838.

11. Starling, "Plank Road Movement," 2–5.

12. *Laws, 1848–1849*, chs. 213, 214; *1850–1851*, ch. 138; *Wilmington Journal*, Nov. 26, 1852; Apr. 15, 1853; Jan. 1858; Starling, "Plank Road Movement," 153.

13. Cecil K. Brown, *A State Movement in Railroad Development* (Chapel Hill, 1928), 17; *People's Press*, May 1, June 5, 26, 1833.

14. Brown, *State Movement in Railroad Development*, 19, 27–32; *Laws, 1833–1834*, ch. 78; *1835*, ch. 30.

15. *Wilmington Advertiser*, Oct. 4, Nov. 1, 1839.

16. *Wilmington Journal*, May 22, June 12, 1846.

17. Ibid., July 2, 1847; Feb. 21, 1851; Dec. 24, 1852.

18. Lawrence Lee, *The History of Brunswick County, North Carolina* (Charlotte, 1980), 124–25; *Wilmington Journal*, Aug. 5, 1853; Nov. 25, 1859.

19. *Wilmington Journal*, June 2, 1854; *Laws, 1854–1855*, Private, ch. 226.

20. *Wilmington Journal*, Mar. 23, 1855; Dec. 2, 1859; Mar. 2, 1860; *Tri-Weekly Commercial* (Wilmington), Feb. 17, 1857; *Laws, 1860–1861*, Private, ch. 142.

21. *Laws, 1812*, ch. 93; *Raleigh Register*, May 28, 1813.

22. Turlington, "Steam Navigation," 21–25; *Laws, 1822*, ch. 140; *Raleigh Minerva*, Apr. 27, 1818; *Hillsborough Recorder*, Apr. 27, 1823; Sept. 7, 1825; *Carolina Observer* (New Bern), Oct. 23, 1823.

23. *Laws, 1827–1828,* ch. 52; *1838–1839,* ch. 16; *1848–1849,* Private, ch. 223, *1850–1851,* ch. 276; *1852,* Private, ch. 160; *1854–1855,* Private, chs. 176, 177; *1858–1859,* Private, ch. 154.

24. *Laws, 1846–1847,* Private, ch. 125; *Wilmington Commercial,* Aug. 25, 1848; *Wilmington Journal,* Apr. 12, 1850; Apr. 30, 1852.

25. *Wilmington Journal,* Apr. 14, 1848; F. Roy Johnson, *Riverboating in Lower Carolina* (Murfreesboro, NC, 1977), 45.

26. Olmsted, *Journey in the Seaboard Slave States,* 369–71.

27. Johnson, *Riverboating,* 46–47, 49, 51; *People's Press and Wilmington Advertiser,* Dec. 3, 1834; *Wilmington Journal,* May 20, 1853; June 25, Dec. 22, 1854; *New Bern Journal,* Jan. 23, 1856; *Laws, 1858–1859,* Private, ch. 154.

28. Turlington, "Steam Navigation," 26; *Hillsborough Recorder,* Apr. 2, 1823.

29. Turlington, "Steam Navigation," 37–38; *Carolina Observer,* Oct. 7, 1824.

30. *Wilmington Journal,* Apr. 7, 1848; Apr. 28, May 26, June 2, 1854.

31. *Wilmington Advertiser,* Aug. 24, 1838; Sept. 27, 1839.

32. Olmsted, *Journey in the Seaboard Slave States,* 374–75.

33. *Wilmington Advertiser,* May 10, 1839; Sprunt, *Chronicles of the Cape Fear River,* 195; *Wilmington Journal,* Jan. 22, 1847.

34. *Wilmington Journal,* Aug. 31, 1849; Oct. 10, 1850; Aug. 1, 1851; Mar. 12. 1852.

35. Lee, *Brunswick County,* 119; *Laws, 1854–1855,* Public, ch. 17. A triweekly line of steamers from Wilmington to Charleston, including the *Calhoun, Nina,* and *Carolina,* was started as an experiment to determine if sufficient demand existed to support such a venture (*Wilmington Journal,* May 26, June, 1854).

36. *Wilmington Journal,* Sept. 3, 1852; Mar. 10, 1854; May 21, 1858; Mar. 22, 1860; Percival Perry, "The Naval Stores Industry in the Antebellum South, 1789–1861" (PhD dissertation, Duke University, 1947), 131.

37. Olmsted, *Journey in the Seaboard Slave States,* 374.

38. *Wilmington Advertiser,* July 7, 28, 1837; Johnson, *Riverboating,* 16–17.

39. Olmsted, *Journey in the Seaboard Slave States,* 368; *Wilmington Advertiser,* Aug. 9, 1839.

40. Joshua Potts, "On the Trade of Wilmington, N. C., May 1st, 1815," *Our Living and Our Dead* 1 (Sept. 1874–Feb. 1875): 51; Robert W. Brown, "On the Trade of Wilmington, N. C., August 1st, 1843," ibid., 56; John F. Burgwin to "Sir," Jan. 1819, manuscript, New Hanover County Library, Wilmington.

41. John F. Burgwin to "Sir"; Potts, "On the Trade of Wilmington," 53.

42. *Laws, 1831–1832,* ch. 91; *1840–1841,* ch. 47; *1842–1843,* Public, ch. 51; *1858–1859,* Public, ch. 23.

43. *Wilmington Journal,* Mar. 5, June 4, 1847; Apr. 27, Dec. 21, 1849; May 16, 1851.

44. *Revised Code of North Carolina, Enacted by the General Assembly at the Session of 1854* (Boston, 1855), 460–63, 490–93; *Laws, 1858–1859,* Public, ch. 23.

45. *Wilmington Journal,* May 12, 1848; May 16, 1851; May 13, 1859; May 17, 1860; *Laws, 1854–1855,* Private, ch. 131.

46. *People's Press and Wilmington Advertiser,* May 27, 1835; *Laws, 1850–1851,* Public, ch. 27.

47. Hoyt, *Papers of Archibald Murphey,* 2: 139, 193.

48. Turlington, "Steam Navigation," 11–12; Ronald B. Hartzer, *To Great and Useful Purpose: A History of the Wilmington District U.S. Army Corps of Engineers* (n. p., n. d.), 11.

49. *People's Press*, Feb. 27, 1833; Hartzer, *Great and Useful Purpose*, 11.

50. *Wilmington Journal*, Apr. 20, 1849; July 4, 1851; Wade H. Hadley, Jr., *The Story of the Cape Fear and Deep River Navigation Company, 1849–1873* (Siler City, NC, 1980), 25. The company was probably organized as early as 1845, but not chartered until 1849 (*Wilmington Journal*, Nov. 21, 1845).

51. *North Carolina Standard* (Raleigh), Feb. 24, 1855; *Wilmington Journal*, Mar. 28, 1856; Hadley, *Cape Fear and Deep River Navigation Company*, 29–30, 36–37, 59.

52. *Laws, 1852*, Public, ch. 83; *Wilmington Journal*, Apr. 20, 1849; Aug. 9, 1850; Dec. 3, 1852; Mar. 12, 1856.

53. *Wilmington Journal*, Dec. 3, 1858; *Laws, 1860–1861*, Public, ch. 122; Hadley, *Cape Fear and Deep River Navigation Company*, 53–54, 56–58.

54. Hoyt, *Papers of Archibald Murphey*, 2: 124–25.

55. Hartzer, *Great and Useful Purpose*, 13–14.

56. *Wilmington Advertiser*, Sept. 14, Nov. 1, 1838.

57. *Wilmington Journal*, June 3, 1853; July 6, 1859.

58. Ibid., Mar. 12, 1852.

59. Ibid., Feb. 11, Mar. 11, 1853.

60. Ibid., Apr. 1, 1853.

61. Report of the Chief Topographical Engineer, Accompanying the Annual Report of the Secretary of War, 1857, Samuel A'Court Papers.

62. *Wilmington Journal*, Apr. 8, May 13, 1853.

63. Ibid., May 26, June 2, July 28, 1854.

64. Hartzer, *Great and Useful Purpose*, 19.

65. David Stick, *Bald Head: A History of Smith Island and Cape Fear* (Wendell, NC, 1985), 34–38; *Cape Fear Recorder*, June 17, 1816.

66. David Stick, *North Carolina Lighthouses* (Raleigh, 1981), 23; *Wilmington Advertiser*, May 19, 1837.

67. Stick, *North Carolina Lighthouses*, 38–41; *Wilmington Commercial*, Sept. 1, Dec. 22, 1848.

68. Potts, "On the Trade of Wilmington," 51–53, 56; Brown, "On the Trade of Wilmington," 56; John F. Burgwin to "Sir"; Perry, "Naval Stores Industry," 136–37.

69. John F. Burgwin to "Sir"; Charles Livingston to William C. Lord, Sept. 28, 1822, Livingston Papers, Perkins Library, Duke University.

70. *People's Press and Wilmington Advertiser*, May 28, 1834; *Wilmington Advertiser*, Oct. 4, 1839; *Wilmington Journal*, Sept. 4, 1857; Perry, "Naval Stores Industry," 129.

71. *Wilmington Journal*, May 12, 1854; May 15, 1857; May 7, 1858.

72. See *Raleigh Register*, Sept. 30, 1828; *People's Press and Wilmington Advertiser*, Apr. 10, 1833; July 29, 1835; *Wilmington Journal*, Dec. 7, 1849; Sept. 24, 1852; Apr. 14, May 19, 1854; May 15, 1861; *Wilmington Daily Journal*, Dec. 7, 1857. Figures compiled from information kindly supplied by Professor William N. Still, Jr., East Carolina University.

73. *Wilmington Journal*, May 12, 1854; May 15, 1857; May 7, 1858.

74. Ibid., June 6, Nov. 21, 1845; *The New American State Papers: Commerce and Navigation*, 47 vols. (Wilmington, DE, 1977), 22: 286; 32: 4; 44: 652; *Wilmington Advertiser*, July 20, 1838.

75. *Wilmington Journal*, Jan. 2, 1857; Jan. 8, 1858; Jan. 7, 1859; Jan. 5, 1860; Jan. 3, 1861.

76. *Wilmington Journal*, Feb. 9, Mar. 22, 1860; Sales account of J. J. Philips, Feb. 3, 1855, James J. Phillips Papers, State Archives, Raleigh.

77. Sprunt, *Chronicles of the Cape Fear River*, 203–05; *Laws, 1850–1851*, Public, ch. 116; *Revised Code, 1854*, 464.
78. *Wilmington Advertiser*, June 14, 1839; *Wilmington Journal*, Mar. 25, 1853; Mar. 10, 1854.

Chapter 4. The Civil War: Lifeline of the Confederacy

1. *Daily Herald* (Wilmington), Nov. 7, 8, 9, 1860; *Wilmington Daily Journal*, Nov. 7, 10, 15, 1860.
2. *Daily Herald*, Nov. 16, 1860.
3. *Daily Herald*, Dec. 6, 1860; *Wilmington Daily Journal*, Dec. 20, 1860.
4. *War of the Rebellion: A Compilation of the Official Records of the Union and Confederate Armies*, 70 vols. in 127 (Washington, 1880–1901), Series I, Vol. 1, 447, 486–87, hereafter cited as ORA; *Wilmington Daily Journal*, May 20, 1861; Richard Everett Wood, "Port Town at War; Wilmington, North Carolina, 1860–1865" (PhD diss., Florida State University, 1976), 58–60.
5. ORA, I, 4: 639, 648; 9, 446–47; 18, 848–49; Wood, "Port Town at War," 66–67, 74, 77.
6. Henry Judson Beeker, "Wilmington during the Civil War" (MA thesis, Duke University, 1941), 116–19; *Official Records of the Union and Confederate Navies in the War of the Rebellion*, 28 vols. (Washington, 1894–1922), Series I, Vol. 11, 436, hereafter cited as ORN.
7. ORN, I, 8; 859–961; James W. Albright Diary, Jan. 22, 1864, Albright Papers, Southern Historical Collection, University of North Carolina; Beeker, "Wilmington during the Civil War," 114–16; James Randall to Katie, Feb. 26, Apr. 8, 1864, Randall Papers, Southern Historical Collection, University of North Carolina; John G. Barrett, *The Civil War in North Carolina* (Chapel Hill, 1963), 246; Lawrence Lee, The *History of Brunswick County, North Carolina* (Charlotte, NC, 1980), 96, 150–52.
8. Lee, *History of Brunswick County*, 95–97, 150–52; Barrett, *Civil War in North Carolina*, 246–247; Beeker, "Wilmington during the Civil War," 115–16.
9. Wood, "Port Town at War," 85–87; Diane Dolan, "A Yankee View of the Fall of Wilmington, 1865," *Lower Cape Fear Historical Society Bulletin* 20 (Feb. 1977).
10. Joseph T. Durkin, *Stephen R. Mallory: Confederate Navy Chief* (Chapel Hill, 1954), 166; Captain Roberts [C. Augustus Hobart-Hampden], *Never Caught: Personal Adventures Connected with Twelve Successful Trips in Blockade-Running during the American Civil War, 1863–1864* (1867; Carolina Beach, NC, 1967), 35; *Wilmington Journal*, July 16, 1863; Thomas E. Taylor, *Running the Blockade: A Personal Narrative of Adventures, Risks, and Escapes during the American Civil War* (1896; New York, 1971), 64; Royce Gordon Singleton, *John Taylor Wood: Sea Ghost of the Confederacy* (Atlanta, 1979), 70.
11. *Wilmington Daily Journal*, Apr. 16, 1861; Wood, "Port Town at War," 60–63.
12. Addie to Sister, June 11, 1861, W. T. Trotter Collection, North Carolina State Archives, Raleigh; Mrs. Armand J. DeRosset to Kate Meares, Oct. 29, 1861, DeRosset Family Papers, Southern Historical Collection, University of North Carolina; Friend to Kate McGeachy, Jan. 18, 1862, Catherine (McGeachy) Buie Papers, Perkins Library, Duke University.
13. Alexander McRae to Don, Jan. 13, 1863, Hugh MacRae Papers, Perkins Library, Duke University; Barrett, *Civil War in North Carolina*, 150n.
14. ORA, I, 18: 773, 809, 849; I, 19, pt. 2: 887–89.

15. Barrett, *Civil War in North Carolina*, 150n; J. G. deRoulhac Hamilton, ed., *The Letters of Jonathan Worth*, 2 vols. (Raleigh, 1909), 1: 226–28; James Green to Sister, Jan. 29, 1862, Wright and Green Family Papers, Southern Historical Collection, University of North Carolina.

16. *Wilmington Journal* (weekly), Jan. 23, 1862.

17. Wood, "Port Town at War," 97–98; *Wilmington Daily Journal*, Mar. 12, 27, 1862.

18. Wood, "Port Town at War," 102–03; William N. Still, Jr., *Iron Afloat: The Story of the Confederate Armorclads* (Nashville, TN, 1971), 166.

19. Wood, "Port Town at War," 103; Charles S. Peek to Sis, May 7, July 6, 24, 1863, Charles S. Peek Papers, privately owned, from notes in the possession of William N. Still, East Carolina University; Still, *Iron Afloat*, 166.

20. Wood, "Port Town at War," 104; Still, *Iron Afloat*, 156; ORA, I, 18: 823, 829–30; ORN, I, 9: 798, 809–10; Still, *Iron Afloat*, 166; William Calder to Robert Calder, Apr. 18, 1864, Calder Papers, Southern Historical Collection, University of North Carolina.

21. Wood, "Port Town at War," 105–07; ORN, I, 10: 19–21; *Wilmington Journal*, May 12, 1864; Still, *Iron Afloat*, 166–67.

22. James Randall to Katie, June 3, 1864, Randall Papers; ORN, I, 10: 24–25; Charles S. Peek to Sis, May 9, 1864, Peek Papers; W. Calder to Mother, June 7, 1864, Calder Papers; Still, *Iron Afloat*, 167.

23. Still, *Iron Afloat*, 99; Charles S. Peek to Bro., June 4, 1864, Peek Papers.

24. Wood, "Port Town at War," 112; Walter Clark, comp., *Histories of the Several Regiments and Battalions from North Carolina in the Great War, 1861–65*, 5 vols. (Raleigh, 1901), 5: 289.

25. ORN, I, 5: 663; Wood, "Port Town at War," 113.

26. ORN, II, 1: 250, 252, 272; Clark, *Regiments*, 5: 289.

27. William Calder to Mother, May 2, 1864, Calder Papers; Wood, "Port Town at War," 115 n57; Charles S. Peek to Bro., Dec. 30, 1863, Peek Papers.

28. Charles S. Peek to Sis, July 1, Dec. 25, 1863; Jan. 16, 1864; Charles S. Peek to Bro., Jan. 21, 1864, Peek Papers; *Wilmington Journal*, June 16, 1864.

29. *Wilmington Daily Journal*, Oct. 25, 1861; June 28, 1864; Macon Bonner to Wife, Apr. 21, May 7, 1864, Bonner Papers, Southern Historical Collection, University of North Carolina; John Johns, "Wilmington During the Blockade," *Harper's New Monthly Magazine*, 73 (Sept. 1886), 497.

30. *Wilmington Daily Journal*, Oct. 25, 1861; Aug. 10, 1864; Wood, "Port Town at War," 96.

31. William Morrison Robinson, *The Confederate Privateers* (New Haven, 1928), 105–06.

32. Ibid., 291–93; *Wilmington Journal*, Apr. 9, 1863.

33. J. Thomas Scharf, *History of the Confederate Navy*, 2 vols. (1886; Freeport, NY, 1969), 2: 806–07; Singleton, *John Taylor Wood*, 140–41. See also David M. Sullivan, "The Confederate States Marines at Wilmington, 1864–1865," *Lower Cape Fear Historical Society Bulletin* 30 (Oct. 1986): 6.

34. Scharf, *History of the Confederate Navy*, 2: 806–07. For a slightly different assessment see Sullivan, "Confederate States Marines," 6.

35. Scharf, *History of the Confederate Navy*, 2: 808–09; Charles S. Peek to Sister, Sept. 16, Nov. 20, 1864; Charles S. Peek to Bro., Sept. 18, 1864, Peek Papers.

36. George W. Gift to Wife, Oct. 18, 1864, Gift Letters, Southern Historical Collection, University of North Carolina, Chapel Hill; *Wilmington Daily Journal*, Sept. 20, Nov. 25,

1864; ORN, I, 10: 747; ORA, I, 42, pt. 2: 1294, 1296–97; Durkin, Stephen R. Mallory, 315–16.

37. Charles S. Peek to Sis, Sept. 25, 1864, Peek Papers; ORA, I, 42, pt. 3: 1148–49; Durkin, Stephen R. Mallory, 315–16, 315 n79; Clark, Regiments, 5: 337–39. Stephen R. Wise, however, contends that Vance's accusation was unfounded (Wise, Lifeline of the Confederacy: Blockade Running during the Civil War [Columbia, 1988], 201).

38. ORA, I, 42, pt. 3: 1273–75; Robert R. Daly, ed., Aboard the USS Florida, 1863–65: The Letters of Paymaster William Frederick Keeler, U.S. Navy to his Wife, Anna (Annapolis, MD, 1968), 190–91. For an opposing point of view, which belittles the effectiveness of the cruisers, see Wise, Blockade Running, 199. See also Sullivan, Confederate States Marines, 6.

39. ORA, I, 42, pt. 3: 1274–75; Durkin, Stephen R. Mallory, 317; Harold and Margaret Sprout, The Rise of American Naval Power, 1776–1918 (Princeton, NJ, 1946), 159–60.

40. ORA, I, 42, pt. 3: 1146–48.

41. ORA, I, 42, pt. 2: 1295–96; pt. 3: 1160.

42. Scharf, History of the Confederate Navy, 2: 422–26; Charles S. Peek to Georgie, Dec. 25, 1864, Peek Papers; David M. Sullivan, "The Confederate States Marines at Wilmington, 1864–1865," Lower Cape Fear Historical Society Bulletin 30 (Feb. 1987), 3–4; Dolan, "Yankee View of the Fall of Wilmington."

43. Johns, "Wilmington during the Blockade," 497.

44. Wilmington Journal, Nov. 14, 1861; Barrett, Civil War in North Carolina, 27; Daily North Carolinian, Jan. 13, 1865; Wilmington Daily Journal, May 14, 1862; Mrs. J. C. Wood to John Judge, Apr. 8, 1863; Lizzie Milligan to John Judge, July 22, 1864; Judge Papers, Southern Historical Collection, University of North Carolina.

45. Morning Star (Wilmington), Apr. 23, 1917; Hamilton Cochran, Blockade Runners of the Confederacy (Indianapolis, 1958), 179. However, at least one individual thought that Wilmington ship repair facilities were "limited" (Taylor, Running the Blockade, 127).

46. W. Buck Yearns and John G. Barrett, eds., North Carolina Civil War Documentary (Chapel Hill, 1980), 204.

47. Ibid., 210.

48. Wilmington Journal, Nov. 27, 1862; June 11, 1863; F. Roy Johnson, Riverboating in Lower Carolina (Murfreesboro, NC, 1977), 54.

49. J. Wilkinson, The Narrative of a Blockade Runner (New York, 1877), 199–200; Johns, "Wilmington during the Blockade," 497.

50. D. MacRae to Dix, May 15, 1861, MacRae Papers; Wood, "Port Town at War," 163.

51. Cochran, Blockade Runners of the Confederacy, 171; Wilmington Journal, Aug. 15, 1861; Addie to Sister, July [?], 1861, W. T. Trotter Collection, State Archives, Raleigh; W. G. Curtis, Reminiscences of Wilmington and Smithville-Southport, 1848–1900 (Southport, NC, 1900), 15–18.

52. Wilmington Journal, Apr. 9, Dec. 30, 1863; Charles S. Peek to Bro., Dec. 30, 1863, Peek Papers; Johns, "Wilmington during the Blockade," 498–99; Aubrey Harrison Stark, Sidney Lanier: A Biographical and Critical Study (Chapel Hill, 1933), 64–65. See also Roberts, Never Caught and Taylor, Running the Blockade.

53. Wilmington Journal, June 18, Aug. 6, 1863.

54. Wilkinson, Narrative, 199–200; Roberts, Never Caught, 32; John D. Bellamy, Memoirs of an Octogenarian (Charlotte, 1942), 26.

55. Uriah T. Vinson to "Dear Father," Jan. 27, 1863, "The Vinson Confederate Letters," ed. Hugh Buckner Johnston, North Carolina Historical Review, 25 (1948), 104; Wilmington Journal, Jan. 29, Mar. 10, 1863.

56. Scharf, *History of the Confederate Navy*, 2: 464; *Wilmington Journal*, Feb. 4, 1864.

57. Mrs. Armand J. DeRosset to ?, 1862, DeRosset Family Papers; *Wilmington Daily Journal*, May 28, 1862; *Wilmington Journal*, Sept. 4, 1862; James Randall to Katie, Nov. 3, 1863, Randall Papers; J. C. Settle to C. M. Wallace, Oct. 29, 1864, John Clopton Papers, Perkins Library, Duke University.

58. Johns, "Wilmington during the Blockade," 498.

59. Ibid., 498; Wood, "Port Town at War," 174–75.

60. James Randall to Katie, Feb. 26, 1864, Randall Papers; Roberts, *Never Caught*, 8, 10.

61. Taylor, *Running the Blockade*, 65.

62. Johns, "Wilmington during the Blockade," 498–99; Roberts, *Never Caught*, 10.

63. Johns, "Wilmington during the Blockade," 499; Dix to Don, July 9, 1862, MacRae Papers; *Wilmington Daily Journal*, Aug. 12, 1863.

64. *Wilmington Daily Journal*, Sept. 3, Nov. 17, 1862; *Wilmington Journal*, Nov. 20, 1862.

65. Wood, "Port Town at War," 177–78.

66. *Wilmington Journal*, May 21, 1863; Aug. 25, Oct. 20, 1864; Clark, *Regiments*, 5: 326–27.

67. Barrett, *Civil War in North Carolina*, 254–55; Cochran, *Blockade Runners*, 172–73.

68. Clement Dowd, *Life of Zebulon B. Vance* (Charlotte, 1897), 454, 489–90.

69. Ibid., 89.

70. Barrett, *Civil War in North Carolina*, 255n.

71. Cochran, *Blockade Runners*, 173–74; Curtis, *Reminiscences*, 24; Diary of James W. Albright, Jan. 22, 1864, Albright Papers; Wise, *Blockade Running*, 157–58.

72. Richard D. Goff, *Confederate Supply* (Durham, 1969), 141; Cochran, *Blockade Runners*, 49; Wise, *Blockade Running*, 46, 96–100, 128, 136–42.

73. John B. Jones, *A Rebel War Clerk's Diary at the Confederate States Capital* (New York, 1935), 226, 230; *Wilmington Journal*, June 23, 1864.

74. *Wilmington Journal*, June 18, 1863; Wood, "Port Town at War," 164; Barrett, *Civil War in North Carolina*, 245; Cochran, *Blockade Runners*, 46; Wise, *Blockade Running*, 132–35.

75. Emma Maffitt, *The Life of John Newland Maffitt* (New York and Washington, 1906), 341; Johns, "Wilmington during the Blockade," 500; *Wilmington Journal*, Oct. 13, 1864; Wise, *Blockade Running*, 196–98; Sullivan, "Confederate States Marines," 6. Utilizing Halifax, however, allowed the steamers to avoid quarantine. Moreover, the port was one of the few where iron-hulled vessels could obtain extensive repairs (Wise, *Blockade Running*, 191–92).

76. Diary of James Albright, Jan. 21, 1864, Albright Papers; Daly, *Aboard the USS Florida*, 189.

77. Scharf, *History of the Confederate Navy*, 2: 468 n1; Cochran, *Blockade Runners*, 93; James Sprunt, *Chronicles of the Cape Fear River*, 2nd ed. (Raleigh, 1916), 427–29.

78. Roberts, *Never Caught*, 14; *Wilmington Journal*, Dec. 5, 1861; Daly, *Aboard the USS Florida*, 127.

79. Johns, "Wilmington during the Blockade," 498–500; Scharf, *History of the Confederate Navy* 2: 465; Clark, *Regiments*, 5: 365–70; Wilkinson, *Narrative*, 202–03. The slave on the *Banshee* received his freedom in Nassau but cost the owners of the blockade runner $4,000, the value of the slave, which had to be paid to his owner in Wilmington (Taylor, *Running the Blockade*, 80).

80. *Wilmington Journal*, Oct. 3, 1861; Roberts, *Never Caught*, 20.

81. Taylor, *Running the Blockade*, 117; James Randall to Katie, Feb. 7, 1864, Randall Papers.

82. *Wilmington Journal*, Feb. 11, 1864. Supercargo Thomas E. Taylor placed the blame squarely on the captain (Taylor, *Running the Blockade*, 113–14).

83. Wilkinson, *Narrative*, 197–99; Durkin, *Stephen R. Mallory*, 139–40; Wise, *Blockade Running*, 155.

84. Barrett, *Civil War in North Carolina*, 249; Roberts, *Never Caught*, 5, 15; Taylor, *Running the Blockade*, 167–68.

85. Wilkinson, *Narrative*, 149–56; Roberts, *Never Caught*, 8; Taylor, *Running the Blockade*, 72.

86. Wilkinson, *Narrative*, 149–56, 197–99; Scharf, *History of the Confederate Navy*, 2: 465; Diary of James W. Albright, Apr. 11, 1864, Albright Papers.

87. Clark, *Regiments*, 5: 633–34; Roberts, *Never Caught*, 8; Taylor, *Running the Blockade*, 52–53.

88. Daly, *Aboard the USS Florida*, 16, 187; Taylor, *Running the Blockade*, 55–56; Clark, *Regiments*, 5: 351–52; Barrett, *Civil War in North Carolina*, 250–51; Roberts, *Never Caught*, 34–35.

89. ORA, I, 29: 671; Clark, *Regiments*, 5: 351–52; *Wilmington Journal*, Aug. 27, 1863; Taylor, *Running the Blockade*, 56.

90. Scharf, *History of the Confederate Navy*, 2: 471; Daly, *Aboard the USS Florida*, 42.

91. Sprunt, *Chronicles of the Cape Fear River*, 427–29.

92. *Wilmington Journal*, Nov. 27, 1863.

93. Roberts, *Never Caught*, 13; Cochran, *Blockade Runners*, 63; *Wilmington Journal*, July 9, 1863.

94. *Wilmington Journal*, July 9, Dec. 3, 1863.

95. Johns, "Wilmington during the Blockade," 498; Scharf, *History of the Confederate Navy*, 2: 471; *Wilmington Daily Journal*, Mar. 9, 1863.

96. Taylor, *Running the Blockade*, 97–99; James Randall to Katie, Oct. 17, 1863, Randall Papers.

97. Taylor, *Running the Blockade*, 97–99.

98. *Wilmington Journal*, Oct. 10, 1861; Wood, "Port Town at War," 179.

99. James Randall to Katie, Feb. 6, 1864, Randall Papers; George W. Gift to Wife, Oct. 18, 1864, Gift Letters; *Wilmington Journal*, June 11, 1863.

100. *Wilmington Journal*, Sept. 3, 1863.

101. Wood, "Port Town at War," 118–20.

102. Ibid., 179; Scharf, *History of the Confederate Navy*, 2: 467; Wise, *Blockade Running*, 155.

103. James M. Matthews, comp., *Public Laws of the Confederate States of America*. (Richmond, 1864), 179, 181; Cochran, *Blockade Runners*, 50; Oscar G. Parsley, Jr., to John Judge, Mar. 8, 1864, Judge Papers; James Randall to Katie, Apr. 3, 1864, Randall Papers; *Wilmington Journal*, May 19, 1864.

104. Taylor, *Running the Blockade*, 69, 85; James Randall to Katie, Sept. 15, Nov. 2, 1863, Randall Papers.

105. Roberts, *Never Caught*, 13, 20; Barrett, *Civil War in North Carolina*, 252; Cochran, *Blockade Runners*, 64.

106. Roberts, *Never Caught*, 4–5; *Wilmington Journal*, July 18, Aug. 15, 1861; Barrett, *Civil War in North Carolina*, 245.

107. Virginia Jeans Laas, " 'Sleepless Sentinels': The North Atlantic Blocking Squadron, 1862–1864," *Civil War History* 31 (1985), 24, 26, 28–29; Daly, *Aboard the USS Florida*, 20–23.

108. Laas, "Sleepless Sentinels," 30–31; Roberts, *Never Caught*, 4–5, 15, 17–18; Taylor, *Running the Blockade*, 46–47.

109. Laas, "Sleepless Sentinels," 30–31; Roberts, *Never Caught*, 1; Daly, *Aboard the USS Florida*.

110. Wood, "Port Town at War," 183; Daly, *Aboard the USS Florida*, 88.

111. Laas, "Sleepless Sentinels," 29; Daly, *Aboard the USS Florida*, 189.

112. See Daly, *Aboard the USS Florida*, 39–40 and passim.

113. Barrett, *Civil War in North Carolina*, 252; Daly, *Aboard the USS Florida*, 53–54.

114. David Stick, *Bald Head: A History of Smith Island and Cape Fear* (Wendell, NC, 1985), 53.

115. Barrett, *Civil War in North Carolina*, 251–52; Johns, "Wilmington during the Blockade," 501.

116. *Wilmington Journal*, June 30, 1864.

117. Daly, *Aboard the USS Florida*, 136, 190; Diary of James W. Albright, Jan. 24, 1864, Albright Papers; Clark, *Regiments*, 2: 754–56; *Wilmington Journal*, Mar. 24, 1864.

118. *Wilmington Journal*, Jan. 22, 1863.

119. Laas, "Sleepless Sentinels," 32–33.

120. Beeker, "Wilmington during the Civil War," 82; Sprunt, *Chronicles of the Cape Fear River*, 372; J. S. Reilly, *Wilmington Past, Present, and Future* (Wilmington, 1884), 21; Wood, "Port Town at War," 184.

121. Wise, *Blockade Running*, 233–50.

122. *Wilmington Journal*, Aug. 4, 1864.

123. Ibid.; Daly, *Aboard the USS Florida*, xvii; Wise, *Blockade Running*, 3, 7–8, 164–65, 226.

124. Lawrence Lee, *The History of Brunswick County, North Carolina* (Charlotte, 1980), 159–62; Barrett, *Civil War in North Carolina*, 276–79; Wood, "Port Town at War," 207–08, 215–16.

125. Lee, *Brunswick County*, 162–63; Wise, *Blockade Running*, 209.

126. Cochran, *Blockade Runners*, 332–33; Wise, *Blockade Running*, 209.

127. Wise, *Blockade Running*, 3, 7–8, 164–65, 226.

128. Barrett, *Civil War in North Carolina*, 282; Dolan, "Yankee View of the Fall of Wilmington."

129. Wood, "Port Town at War," 255–56.

130. Beeker, "Wilmington during the Civil War," 133.

Chapter 5. The Postwar Transition: A Struggle for Recognition

1. Frank D. Smaw, Jr., comp., *Smaw's Wilmington Directory Comprising a General and City Business Directory, and a Directory of Colored Persons to Which Is Added a Complete Historical and Commercial Sketch of the City* (Wilmington, [1867]), 46.

2. Byron Eugene Logan, "An Historical Geographic Survey of North Carolina Ports" (PhD diss., University of North Carolina, 1956), 102–06.

3. W. McKee Evans, *Ballots and Fence Rails: Reconstruction on the Lower Cape Fear* (New York, 1974), 198–200; *Wilmington Journal*, Mar. 29, 1872; J. S. Reilly, *Wilmington Past, Present, and Future* (Wilmington, 1884), 72.

4. *Wilmington Journal* (weekly), Jan. 19, 1873; Jan. 7, 1876.

5. Reilly, *Wilmington Past, Present, and Future*, 67; *Wilmington Journal*, Apr. 12, 1872. The policies of Union military occupation authorities at the end of the war greatly encouraged the resumption of the naval stores industry; see Evans, *Ballots and Fence Rails*, 59–60.

6. Quoted in Evans, *Ballots and Fence Rails*, 198–99.

7. Reilly, *Wilmington Past, Present, and Future*, 51–52; *Weekly Star* (Wilmington), Feb. 11, 1876.

8. Reilly, *Wilmington Past, Present, and Future*, 76.

9. *Weekly Star*, Apr. 21, 1882; Sept. 21, 1883.

10. Reilly, *Wilmington Past, Present, and Future*, 65.

11. *Weekly Star*, Sept. 13, 27, 1889; Sept. 19, 1890; Julius A. Bonitz, comp., *Directory of the City of Wilmington, North Carolina, 1889* (Wilmington, 1889).

12. *Weekly Star*, Jan. 7, 1881; Bonitz, *Directory of Wilmington, 1889*.

13. J. R. Killick, "The Transformation of Cotton Marketing in the Late Nineteenth Century: Alexander Sprunt and Son of Wilmington, N. C., 1884–1956," *Business History Review*, 55 (1981): 145.

14. Ibid., 146–47.

15. James Sprunt, *Information and Statistics Respecting Wilmington, North Carolina, Being a Report by the President of the Produce Exchange.* (Wilmington, 1883), 143–45; *James Sprunt: A Tribute from the City of Wilmington* (Raleigh, 1925), 39; Killick, "Transformation of Cotton Marketing," 147–49; Lewis Philip Hall, *Land of the Golden River* (Wilmington, 1980), 131–37.

16. *Weekly Star*, Sept. 30, 1881.

17. *James Sprunt: A Tribute*, 35–36; Killick, "Transformation of Cotton Marketing," 153–54; *Weekly Star*,, Jan. 6, 1893; *Sheriff's Wilmington, N. C. Directory and General Advertiser for 1877–8* (Wilmington, 1877), 175; Bonitz, *Directory of the City of Wilmington, 1889*, 163; H. Gerken, comp., *Directory and General Advertiser of the City for 1894–'95* (Wilmington), 165; *Wilmington Star*, June 21, 1895.

18. Killick, "Transformation of Cotton Marketing," 155.

19. *Wilmington Journal*, Sept. 10, 1869; Killick, "Transformation of Cotton Marketing," 156; *Report on the Internal Commerce of the United States, by Joseph Nimmo, Jr., Chief of the Bureau of Statistics, Treasury Department, Submitted May 6, 1885* (Washington, 1885), 359.

20. Reilly, *Wilmington Past, Present, and Future*, 73; *Weekly Star*, Sept. 29, 1882.

21. Quoted in Evans, *Ballots and Fence Rails*, 206. See also *Wilmington Journal*, May 21, 1875.

22. *Wilmington Journal*, Dec. 3, 1875; *Weekly Star*, Feb. 12, 1881; Sprunt, *Information and Statistics*, 208–10; Evans, *Ballots and Fence Rails*, 208.

23. Sprunt, *Information and Statistics*, 148, 208–10.

24. *Weekly Star*, Sept. 23, 1887; Oct. 20, 1893; Aug. 13, 1897.

25. *Laws and Resolutions of the State of North Carolina, 1873–1874*, Private, ch. 105; *Wilmington Journal*, Nov. 19, 1875; *Wilmington Post*, Apr. 12, 1878; Evans, *Ballots and Fence Rails*, 204; Hall, *Land of the Golden River*, 162–63.

26. Sprunt, *Information and Statistics*, 145–46; James Sprunt, *Tales and Traditions of the Lower Cape Fear, 1661–1896* (Wilmington, 1896) XXIII, XXIV; *J. L. Hill Printing Co.'s Directory of Wilmington, N. C. 1900* (Richmond, 1900), 230; Hall, *Land of the Golden River*, 162–64.

27. *Wilmington Journal*, Aug. 23, 1867; Mar. 29, 1872; Evans, *Ballots and Fence Rails*, 198–200; Reilly, *Wilmington Past, Present, and Future*, 73; Sprunt, *Information and Statistics*, 146–54.

28. Evans, *Ballots and Fence Rails*, 201.
29. Ibid., 202; *Wilmington Review*, June 6, 1887.
30. Evans, *Ballots and Fence Rails*, 202.
31. *Wilmington Journal*, July 19, 1867; quotation from May 21, 1875; *Laws, 1870–1871*, Private, ch. 60; Evans, *Ballots and Fence Rails*, 203.
32. *Weekly Star*, Jan. 15, 1897. *Hill's Directory* listed five fertilizer companies in 1900: Navassa, Acme, Powers-Gibbs, Calder Bros., and Smith & Gilchrist.
33. *Weekly Star*, Mar. 22, 1895; notes compiled from information supplied by Professor William N. Still, Jr., East Carolina University; *Weekly Star*, Apr. 30, 1886; *Morning Star* (Wilmington), July 29, 1886; *Hill's Directory*, 247.
34. *Weekly Star*, Aug. 16, 1889; Mar. 18, 1890; Sept. 29, 1893; *Abstract of the Twelfth Census of the United States, 1900* (Washington, 1904), 381.
35. Richard E. Prince, *Seaboard Air Line Railway: Steam Boats, Locomotives, and History* (Green River, WY, [1969]), 9; Evans, *Ballots and Fence Rails*, 186.
36. Reilly, *Wilmington Past, Present, and Future*, 48–49; Evans, *Ballots and Fence Rails*, 186; *Wilmington Journal*, Jan. 12, 1872. Because of financial trouble the Wilmington, Columbia, and Augusta was sold under foreclosure in 1879 and reorganized in 1880.
37. *Wilmington Journal*, Jan. 10, Feb. 8, 1868; Dec. 20, 1872; May 2, 1873; Mar. 5, Dec. 1, 1875; Reilly, *Wilmington Past, Present, and Future*, 49; Prince, *Seaboard Air Line Railway*, 23.
38. *Laws, 1879*, Public, ch. 67; *1881*, Public, ch. 374; Reilly, *Wilmington Past, Present, and Future*, 50–51; *Weekly Star*, Aug. 31, 1888; Jan. 3 [10], 1890.
39. *Wilmington Journal*, July 1, 1870; *Laws, 1869–1870*, Public, ch. 207; *1885*, Public, ch. 233; *Weekly Star*, Feb. 6, 1891; Sept. 22, 1895; Prince, *Seaboard Air Line Railway*, 15.
40. *Directory and General Advertiser for the City of Wilmington for 1894–'95*, 204–06; Prince, *Seaboard Air Line Railway*, 23; Hall, *Land of the Golden River*, 248–49; *Wilmington, the Port City of North Carolina* (Wilmington, 1937).
41. *Wilmington Journal*, Sept. 2, 1870.
42. Ibid., Sept. 20, 1866; *Weekly Star*, Feb. 11, 1898; *Laws, 1868–1869*, Public, ch. 256; *1873–1874*, Public, ch. 79; *1891*, Public, ch. 105; *1893*, Public, ch. 291; *1895*, Private, ch. 45; *1899*, Public, ch. 256.
43. Evans, *Ballots and Fence Rails*, 183; *Weekly Star*, Jan. 21, 1881; Feb. 2, 1883.
44. F. Roy Johnson, *Riverboating in Lower Carolina* (Murfreesboro, NC, 1977), 57–58; *Laws, 1872–1873*, Private, ch. 14; *Weekly Star*, Apr. 15, 1881; Aug. 2, 9, 1895; Evans, *Ballots and Fence Rails*, 185. For ice blockage on the Northwest Cape Fear and Black rivers see *Weekly Star*, Jan. 27, 1893.
45. *Weekly Star*, Nov. 4, 1881; Ronald B. Hartzer, *To Great and Useful Purpose: A History of the Wilmington District U. S. Army Corps of Engineers* (n. p., n. d.), 48–49; *Wilmington Post*, Mar. 12, 1882.
46. Sprunt, *Information and Statistics*, 114–19; *Weekly Star*, Nov. 2, 1883; Hartzer, *Great and Useful Purpose*, 49.
47. Sprunt, *Information and Statistics*, 113–14, 119; *Wilmington Messenger*, July 12, 1894.
48. *Weekly Star*, Feb. 14, 1890; Jan. 25, Mar. 1, 1895; *Wilmington Messenger*, July 12, 1894.
49. Johnson, *Riverboating*, 71–74.
50. Ibid., 74–75; *Laws, 1876–1877*, Private, ch. 37.
51. Johnson, *Riverboating*, 75–77; *Laws, 1883*, Public, ch. 119.
52. Johnson, *Riverboating*, 78–83; *Weekly Star*, Aug. 12, 1887.
53. Johnson, *Riverboating*, 81–82; *Weekly Star*, Jan. 24, 1896.

54. Sprunt, *Information and Statistics*, 132–33; *Wilmington Post*, Feb. 8, 1878; *Weekly Star*, Mar. 17, 1882; *Laws, 1876–1877*, Public, ch. 232.

55. Johnson, *Riverboating*, 75; *Weekly Star*, Dec. 30, 1881.

56. *Weekly Star*, Dec. 21, 1888; Jan. 16, May 1, Oct. 23, 1891; Dec. 7, 1894.

57. Lawrence Lee, *The History of Brunswick County, North Carolina* (Charlotte, 1980), 189–92.

58. *Wilmington Journal*, Apr. 12, 1872; Bill Reaves, *Southport (Smithville): A Chronology, Vol. I, 1520–1887* (Wilmington, 1978), 57, 62, 65, 80–81; *Weekly Star*, Apr. 21, 1882; Feb. 3, 1883; June 1, 1888; Sept. 9, 1892; Sprunt, *Information and Statistics*, 114; *Hill's Directory*, 247.

59. Lee, *Brunswick County*, 195–97; *Hill's Directory*, 247.

60. Frank D. Smaw, Jr., comp., *Wilmington Directory, Including a General and City Business Directory, for 1865–66* (Wilmington, 1865), 95–96; *Laws, 1870–1871*, Private, ch. 103; *1871–1872*, Private, ch. 21; *Weekly Star*, Sept. 17, 1883; *Report on the Internal Commerce of the United States, May 6, 1885*, 359.

61. Sprunt, *Information and Statistics*, 113; Reilly, *Wilmington Past, Present, and Future*, 94; *Weekly Star*, Sept. 20, Oct. 28, 1887; Apr. 12, 1889; Sprunt, *Tales and Traditions*, XXIII.

62. *Wilmington Journal*, Feb. 8, 1867; *Laws, 1893*, Private, ch. 176; *Weekly Star*, Apr. 14, 1893; *The Foreign Commerce and Navigation of the United States for the Year Ending June 30, 1895*, Pt. I, Vol. 1 (Washington, 1896), 680–83.

63. *Foreign Commerce and Navigation*, Pt. I, Vol. 2, 27, 223, 680–83; Vol. 2, 816, 885.

64. *Wilmington Daily Journal*, Dec. 12, 1869.

65. Hartzer, *Great and Useful Purpose*, 32–33; *Wilmington Journal*, Aug. 19, 1870; Sprunt, *Information and Statistics*, 108.

66. Hartzer, *Great and Useful Purpose*, 33–34; *Wilmington Journal*, Mar. 5, 1875.

67. Evans, *Ballots and Fence Rails*, 181–82.

68. *Wilmington Journal*, June 2, 1876; *Wilmington Post*, June 1, 1879.

69. Lee, *Brunswick County*, 188; Hartzer, *Great and Useful Purpose*, 36–37.

70. Hartzer, *Great and Useful Purpose*, 37–38.

71. Ibid., 46; *Weekly Star*, Aug. 12, 1887; Nov. 1, 1889.

72. *Weekly Star*, May 1, 1891; Hartzer, *Great and Useful Purpose*, 48; Richard H. Rayburn, "One of the Finest Rivers in the South: Corps of Engineers Improvements on the Cape Fear River below Wilmington, 1881–1919," *Lower Cape Fear Historical Society Bulletin*, 28 (Feb. 1985): 3–4.

73. *Weekly Star*, Dec. 19, 1888; Feb. 27, 1891; Jan. 6, 1893; Aug. 17, 1894.

74. *Weekly Star*, Sept. 15, 1893; Oct. 16, 1896; Sprunt, *Chronicles of the Cape Fear River*, 532.

75. *Wilmington Journal*, Oct. 8, Nov. 12, 1869. For a very different account see Sprunt, *Chronicles of the Cape Fear River*, 514–15.

76. *Weekly Star*, Sept. 28, 1895; Stephen H. Halkiotis, "Guns for Cuba Libre: An 1895 Filibustering Expedition from Wilmington, North Carolina," *North Carolina Historical Review*, 55 (1978): 60–61.

77. *Weekly Star*, Oct. 11, 1895.

78. Ibid., Oct. 11, Oct. 18, Nov. 1, 1895; Feb. 21, July 31, 1896.

79. Ibid., May 22, July 17, Dec. 18, 1896; Aug. 6, Dec. 24, 1897.

80. Ibid., Feb. 11, 1898; Ethel Herring and Carolee Williams, *Fort Caswell in War and Peace* (Wendell, NC, 1983), 59–75.

81. *Weekly Star*, Apr. 29, July 30, 1898.

82. Ibid., May 20, 1898.

83. David Stick, *North Carolina Lighthouses* (Raleigh, 1981) 61; Stick, *Bald Head: A History of Smith Island and the Cape Fear* (Wendell, NC, 1985), 71.

84. Stick, *Bald Head*, 75, 78.

85. Stick, *North Carolina Lighthouses*, 72–73; *Weekly Star*, Sept. 21, 1883; Dec. 7, 1888; Feb. 7, 1890.

86. Sprunt, *Information and Statistics*, 99; *Wilmington Journal*, Feb. 2, 1872; *Weekly Star*, Dec. 14, 1888; Mar 14, 1890; Jan. 12, Feb. 16, 1894. See the account of the farewell testimonial dinner given to Captain Eric Gabrielson of the Colfax in 1883 (*Weekly Star*, June 29, 1883).

87. Stick, *Bald Head*, 58–60. For later activity see Sprunt, *Chronicles of the Cape Fear River*, 525, 527–29; Stick, *Bald Head*, 61–62, 65, 68; *Weekly Star*, Sept. 14, 1891.

88. *Historical Sketch of the Signal Corps, 1860–1941* (Fort Monmouth, NJ, 1942), 1–22; *Wilmington Journal*, Apr. 2, 1875; Reaves, *Southport*, 74.

89. *Weekly Star*, Mar. 13, 1891; Jan. 12, May 11, 1894.

90. Sprunt, *Information and Statistics*, 82.

91. Reilly, *Wilmington Past, Present, and Future*, 53–57; *Revised Code of North Carolina, Enacted by the General Assembly of 1854* (Boston, 1855), 460–63, 490–93; *Laws, 1869–1870*, Public, ch. 235; *1876–1877*, Public, ch. 238; *1883*, Public, ch. 183; *Weekly Star*, Mar. 25, 1898.

92. *Wilmington Journal*, Dec. 3, 1875; *Weekly Star*, Jan. 7, 1881; Jan. 5, 1883.

93. *Weekly Star*, Dec. 15, 1882; Oct. 26, 1894.

94. Sprunt, *Information and Statistics*, 175.

95. *Wilmington Journal*, July 7, 14, 1876; *Weekly Star*, May 24, 1895.

96. Sprunt, *Information and Statistics*, 176–79.

97. *Wilmington Journal*, Nov. 1, 1866; *Wilmington Post*, Mar. 29, June 23, 1878; May 7, 1897.

98. *Wilmington Journal*, May 1, 1891; *Wilmington Post*, Aug. 6, 1879. See also *Weekly Star*, Oct. 31, 1890.

99. *Weekly Star*, Apr. 14, May 12, 1883; May 7, 1897; Sprunt, *Tales and Traditions*, 120; Richard H. Lewis to Thomas J. Jarvis, June 27, 189[3], Lewis Papers, State Archives, Raleigh.

100. *Weekly Star*, Apr. 5, 1889; Feb. 4, 1898; Sprunt, *Tales and Traditions*, 37; *Wilmington Morning Star*, Mar. 28, 1988; Hall, *Land of the Golden River*, 138–40.

101. Reilly, *Wilmington Past, Present, and Future*, 37–38; *Laws, 1899*, Private, ch. 355; *Wilmington Post*, Feb. 16, 1879; *Weekly Star*, Oct. 28, 1887; Feb. 4, 1898.

102. *Weekly Star*, Sept. 21, 1883; Apr. 8, Dec. 9, 1887; Sept. 15, 1893.

103. Reilly, *Wilmington Past, Present, and Future*, 53; *Weekly Star*, June 21, 1895; *Hill's Directory*, 230; *James Sprunt: A Tribute*, 41–42.

104. Reilly, *Wilmington Past, Present, and Future*, 37–38; *Wilmington Post*, Feb. 16, 1879; *Weekly Star*, Oct. 28, 1887; Feb. 4, 1898; *Laws, 1899*, ch. 355.

105. Sprunt, *Information and Statistics*, 95–97.

106. Reilly, *Wilmington Past, Present, and Future*, 52.

107. Evans, *Ballots and Fence Rails*, 204.

Chapter 6. Revival and Modernization in the Twentieth Century

1. "Cape Fear," *Sunday Star–News* (Wilmington), supplement, May 9, 1976, 8.

2. *Laws and Resolutions of the State of North Carolina*, *1905*, ch. 104; *1907*, ch. 625; *1908*, ch. 104; *1921*, ch. 114.

3. *North Carolina General Statutes, 1985*, ch. 76A.
4. James Sprunt, *Chronicles of the Cape Fear River, 1660–1916*, 2nd ed. (Raleigh, 1916), 516–21.
5. Ibid., 522–29.
6. *The Port of Wilmington, N. C.* (Washington, 1940), 76; *Morning Star,* Jan. 27, Oct. 20, 1988.
7. Richard H. Rayburn, "One of the Finest Rivers in the South: Corps of Engineers Improvements on the Cape Fear River below Wilmington, 1881–1919," *Lower Cape Fear Historical Society Bulletin,* 28 (Feb. 1985): 4–5; Byron Eugene Logan, "An Historical Geographic Survey of North Carolina Ports" (PhD diss., University of North Carolina, 1956), 117, 121.
8. Rayburn, "One of the Finest Rivers in the South," 4–5.
9. Logan, "Historical Geographic Survey of North Carolina Ports," 117, 121.
10. W. McKee Evans, *Ballots and Fence Rails: Reconstruction on the Lower Cape Fear* (New York, 1974), 194, 210.
11. J. R. Killick, "The Transformation of Cotton Marketing in the Late Nineteenth Century: Alexander Sprunt and Son of Wilmington, N. C.," *Business History Review* 55 (1981), 156–60, 164.
12. Logan, "Historical Geographic Survey of North Carolina Ports," 113–14; I. J. Isaacs, comp., *The City of Wilmington, the Metropolis and Port of North Carolina: Its Advantages and Interests* (Wilmington, 1912), 32, 45, 89, 99.
13. *Intracoastal Waterway, Beaufort, N. C., to Key West, Fla., Section* (Washington, 1913), 46.
14. Isaacs, *City of Wilmington,* 103.
15. Ronald B. Hartzer, *To Great and Useful Purpose: A History of the Wilmington District U. S. Army Corps of Engineers* (n.p., n. d.), 49–52.
16. Rayburn, "One of the Finest Rivers in the South," 5; Logan, "Historical Geographic Survey of North Carolina Ports," 119, 121.
17. "Cape Fear," 13.
18. William N. Still, Jr., "Shipbuilding in North Carolina: The World War I Experience," *American Neptune,* 41 (1981): 188–89; *Weekly Star* (Wilmington), Feb. 6, 1903; *Morning Star,* Apr. 29, 1906; Isaacs, *City of Wilmington,* 41.
19. Lewis Philip Hall, *Land of the Golden River* (Wilmington, 1980), 341–42; W. W. Storm to Louis [T. Moore], Feb. 11, 1948, "Shipbuilding" [folder containing various documents], Louis T. Moore Collection, New Hanover County Library, Wilmington; Isaacs, *City of Wilmington,* 41.
20. This paragraph and the following discussion of shipbuilding in Wilmington during World War I depend greatly upon William N. Still, Jr., "Shipbuilding in Wilmington," address to the Lower Cape Fear Historical Society, Wilmington, May 17, 1979; Still, "Shipbuilding in North Carolina"; and notes kindly supplied by William N. Still, Jr., East Carolina University.
21. Still, "Shipbuilding in North Carolina," 190–91.
22. *Morning Star,* Aug. 31; Sept. 3, 5; Nov. 9, 1919; Still, "Shipbuilding in North Carolina," 194–95.
23. Ibid., Oct. 19, Nov. 9, 1919; Still, "Shipbuilding in North Carolina," 197.
24. Louis T. Moore, "Concrete Ships Built at Wilmington During World War I" and "Shipbuilding" [folders containing various documents], Moore Collection, New Hanover County Library.
25. *Morning Star,* Jan. 13, 1919; Still, "Shipbuilding in North Carolina," 198–205.

26. Ibid., Feb. 1, 4, Apr. 16, Oct. 19, 1919.

27. Still, "Shipbuilding in North Carolina," 205–06.

28. Duncan Peter Randall, "Geographic Factors in the Growth and Economy of Wilmington, North Carolina" (PhD diss., University of North Carolina, 1965), 45.

29. Hall, *Land of the Golden River*, 354–56, 358–59.

30. Randall, "Geographic Factors," 44–45; William L. DeRosset, *Wilmington, the Port City of North Carolina* (Wilmington, 1937).

31. *The Ports of Charleston, S. C. and Wilmington, N. C.* (Washington, 1935), 117–19.

32. David Stick, *North Carolina Lighthouses* (Raleigh, 1981), 73; David Stick, *Bald Head: A History of Smith Island and the Cape Fear* (Wendell, NC, 1985), 78.

33. *Port of Wilmington*, 9.

34. Hartzer, *Great and Useful Purpose*, 53–54.

35. Ibid; *Port of Wilmington*, 3.

36. Hartzer, *Great and Useful Purpose*, 56–57; James Sprunt, *Information and Statistics Respecting Wilmington, North Carolina, Being a Report by the President of the Produce Exchange* (Wilmington, 1883), 139–40.

37. Hartzer, *Great and Useful Purpose*, 57; Logan, "Historical Geographic Survey of North Carolina Ports," 118.

38. *Intracoastal Waterway*, 45.

39. Ibid., 10, 58, 60–61.

40. Ibid., 65.

41. Hartzer, *Great and Useful Purpose*, 62; *Intracoastal Waterway*, 25–26.

42. Hartzer, *Great and Useful Purpose*, 62–63; *Intracoastal Waterway*, 26–27.

43. Logan, "Historical Geographic Survey of North Carolina Ports," 119; *Port of Wilmington*, 61; DeRosset, *Wilmington*.

44. *Port of Wilmington*, 7–8, 11, 71, 80–81.

45. Ibid., 112, 114; DeRosset, *Wilmington*.

46. *Port of Wilmington*, 113, 115.

47. Killick, "Transformation of Cotton Marketing," 59–68; DeRosset, *Wilmington*.

48. *Ports of Charleston and Wilmington*, 171–72; DeRosset, *Wilmington*.

49. *Wilmington Messenger*, Apr. 25, 1896; *Wilmington Star*, Jan. 19, 1931, references kindly supplied by Bill Reaves of Wilmington; *Directory of the City of Wilmington, North Carolina, 1889* (Wilmington, 1889); *Wilmington, N. C., Directory, 1917* (Wilmington and Richmond, 1917), 74.

50. *Port of Wilmington*, 116–17.

51. Ibid., 64–66.

52. Ibid., 99; *Ports of Charleston and Wilmington*, 167.

53. *Ports of Charleston and Wilmington*, 167; *Port of Wilmington*, 99.

54. *Port of Wilmington*, 11.

55. Randall, "Geographic Factors," 93–94.

56. Ibid., 78, 92–93; *City of Wilmington, North Carolina, New Hanover County* (Wilmington, 1946), 11.

57. Randall, "Geographic Factors," 84–85.

58. Logan, "Historical Geographic Survey of North Carolina Ports," 123–24, 126.

59. Ralph Lee Scott, "Welding the Sinews of History: A History of the North Carolinian Shipbuilding Corporation," (MA thesis, East Carolina University, 1979), 2–3.

60. Ibid., 15–16, 18–26, 30–31.

61. Ibid., 28–29, 57, 138, 148; *Five Years of North Carolina Shipbuilding* (Wilmington, 1946), 8–10.
62. Ibid., 10–14; Scott, "North Carolina Shipbuilding Corporation," 138–43.
63. Scott, "North Carolina Shipbuilding Corporation," 143, 151–52; Frederic C. Lane, *Ships for Victory* (Baltimore, 1951), 116–17; Hall, *Land of the Golden River,* 445–46.
64. Hall, *Land of the Golden River,* 446–47; *Morning Star,* Mar. 14, 1988; *Sunday Star–News,* Mar. 20, 1988.
65. Charles E. Landon, *The North Carolina State Ports Authority* (Durham, 1963), 3.
66. Scott, "North Carolina Shipbuilding Corporation," 149–59.
67. Landon, *North Carolina State Ports Authority,* 3; *Ports of Charleston and Wilmington,* 190.
68. *Laws, 1935,* Public-Local and Private, ch. 390; Landon, *North Carolina State Ports Authority,* 4.
69. Landon, *North Carolina State Ports Authority,* 5–6; *Port of Wilmington,* 81.
70. Landon, *North Carolina State Ports Authority,* 6–7; "SPA: Dream Come True," *Carolina Cargo* (Summer 1976): 16–17.
71. Landon, *North Carolina State Ports Authority,* 8; G. F. Mott, *A Survey of United States Ports* (New York, 1951), 30.
72. Landon, *North Carolina State Ports Authority,* 8–10.
73. Scott, "North Carolina Shipbuilding Corporation," 163–73.
74. Landon, *North Carolina State Ports Authority,* 19–21.
75. Ibid., 11–13.
76. Ibid., 47–49.
77. Randall, "Geographic Factors," 87–89.
78. Al Smith, "Wilmington," *North Carolina State Ports,* 7 (June 1961): 8.
79. *The Port of Wilmington, N. C.,* Part 2 (Washington, 1961), 7–22.
80. Landon, *North Carolina State Ports Authority,* 43–44.
81. See Table 20.
82. "Big, Bigger, Biggest Ever," *Carolina Cargo* (June 1985): 7; "The Deep-Water Port at Wilmington," (June/July 1986): 20; "Military First," *North Carolina Cargo,* 13 (Jan./Feb. 1988): 10.
83. "Steamship Lines Serving Wilmington and Morehead City," *Carolina Cargo* (Dec./Jan. 1985/86): 31–32.
84. "*Ming Prosperity* Makes First Call at Wilmington," *North Carolina Cargo* 13 (Mar./Apr. 1988): 16.
85. *Sunday Star–News,* Nov. 15, 1987.
86. *North Carolina State Ports Authority; Master Development Plan, 1986–1990,* 94–95.
87. "The Deep-Water Port at Wilmington," *Carolina Cargo* (June/July 1986): 21.
88. "New Developments: Port of Wilmington," *Carolina Cargo* (June/July 1987): 18–20.
89. Landon, *North Carolina State Ports Authority,* 23–24.
90. "Expansion News," *Carolina Cargo* (Aug./Sept. 1987): 6; *Sunday Star–News,* Sept. 4, 1988; *Morning Star,* Sept. 7, 1988.
91. *Morning Star,* Aug. 1, 1988; *North Carolina State Ports Authority; Master Development Plan,* 46; "State of the Ports," *North Carolina Cargo,* 13 (Mar./Apr. 1988): 18; "Expansion News," *Carolina Cargo* (Aug./Sept. 1987): 6; Randall, "Geographic Factors," 94.
92. "Southport Grows," *North Carolina State Ports,* 13 (1967): 7; "Ports Authority Leases Southport Boat Harbor," *Carolina Cargo* (Summer 1976): 7; *Morning Star,* Sept. 7, 1988; *North Carolina State Ports Authority; Master Development Plan,* 18, 215–20.

93. *Morning Star,* Sept. 7, 1988.

94. *Sunday Star–News,* July 1, 1987; *Morning Star,* Sept. 30, 1988.

95. "North Carolina's Industries Find Convenience and Profit in State's Intermodal Network," *Carolina Cargo* (Apr./May 1987): 4; *Sunday Star–News,* Sept. 4, 1988.

96. *Morning Star,* Feb. 8, Dec. 6, 1988, Aug. 9, 1990; "N. C. Ports Begin China Trade Mission," *Carolina Cargo* (Aug./Sept. 1986): 6–7; "Wilmington, North Carolina and Dandong, China Sign Sister City Agreement," *Carolina Cargo* (Apr./May 1987): 10–11; "State of the Ports," *North Carolina Cargo,* 13 (Mar./Apr. 1988): 18, 20.

97. "Foreign Trade Zones Possible for North Carolina," *Carolina Cargo* (Summer 1976): 6–7; "The Trade Zone," *Carolina Cargo* (June/July 1986): 8–9.

98. Ibid. (June/July 1986), 9; *Sunday Star–News,* May 22, 1988; "Entire Port of Wilmington Designated Foreign Trade Zone," *North Carolina Cargo,* 13 (May/June 1988): 28.

99. *Water Resources Development by the U. S. Army Corps of Engineers,* Jan. 1, 1987, 11, 18, 20–22, 60, 62, 65.

100. "Military Ocean Terminal, Sunny Point," an information circular supplied by MOTSU; "Sunny Point Terminal," *North Carolina State Ports,* 1 (May 1955): 8–9; Hartzer, *Great and Useful Purpose,* 75, 77.

101. *Water Resources Development,* 63–64.

102. *North Carolina State Ports Authority; Master Development Plan,* 56–58, 66, 94–95; *Sunday Star–News,* Sept. 4, 1988.

103. *North Carolina State Ports Authority; Master Development Plan,* 100; *Sunday Star–News,* Sept. 4, 1988; Feb. 5, 1989.

104. *North Carolina State Ports Authority; Master Development Plan,* 101; *Sunday Star–News,* Sept. 4, 1988.

Bibliography

Manuscript Collections

North Carolina State Archives, Raleigh, N.C.

Samuel A'Court Ashe Papers
Benjamin F. Hall Papers
Hayes Collection
Susan Davis Nye Hutchinson Papers
Richard H. Lewis Papers
A. G. Owen Collection
James J. Phillips Papers
W. T. Trotter Collection
Dr. Thomas Fanning Wood Papers

Southern Historical Collection,
University of North Carolina at Chapel Hill, Chapel Hill, N. C.

James W. Albright Papers
Macon Bonner Papers
William Calder Papers
DeRosset Family Papers
George W. Gift Papers
John Judge Papers
James R. Randall Papers
Wright and Green Family Papers

William R. Perkins Library
Duke University, Durham, N.C.

Catherine (McGeachy) Buie Papers
John Clopton Papers

Charles Livingston Papers
Hugh McRae Papers
Minutes of the Board of Commissioners of Navigation and Pilotage for the Cape Fear River and Bar, Volume of Records
William A. B. Richardson and John H. Richardson Papers
Seamen's Friend Society Papers
Alexander Sprunt & Son, Inc. Papers
William H. Turlington Papers

New Hanover County Library, Wilmington, N. C.

John Burgwin to "Sir" Paper, January 1819
Louis T. Moore Collection

Charles S. Peek Papers

Typescript copies in the possession of William N. Still, Jr., East Carolina University, Greenville, N. C.

Newspapers

Cape Fear Mercury (Wilmington)
Cape Fear Recorder (Wilmington)
Carolina Observer (New Bern)
Daily Herald (Wilmington)
Daily North Carolinian (Wilmington)
Fayetteville Observer
Federal Republican (New Bern)
Hall's Wilmington Gazette
Hillsborough Recorder
Morning Star (Wilmington)
New Bern Journal
North Carolina Gazette (New Bern)
North Carolina Standard (Raleigh)
People's Press (Wilmington)
People's Press and Wilmington Advertiser
Raleigh Minerva
Raleigh Register
South-Carolina & American General Gazette (Charles Town)
South-Carolina Gazette (Charles Town)
South-Carolina Gazette and Country Journal (Charles Town)
State Gazette of North Carolina (Edenton)
Sunday Star-News (Wilmington)
Tri-Weekly Commercial (Wilmington)

Bibliography || 193

Virginia Gazette, Purdie (Williamsburg)
Weekly Star (Wilmington)
Wilmington Advertiser
Wilmington Centinel, and General Advertiser
Wilmington Chronicle
Wilmington Commercial
Wilmington Daily Journal
Wilmington Gazette
Wilmington Herald
Wilmington Journal
Wilmington Messenger
Wilmington Post

Public and Official Records

Abstract of the Twelfth Census of the United States. Washington, D.C., 1904.

An Account of Duties Collected and the Fines and Forfeitures recovered in the several ports now under the American Commission, Oct. 10, 1766 to Oct. 10, 1767. Treasury Papers, Class 1/452, Public Record Office, London, Photostat, Library of Congress, Washington, D.C.

An Act for Regulating Vestrys in this Government and for the better Inspecting the Vestrymen and Church Wardens Accounts of Each and Every Parish within this Government. Colonial Office Papers, Class 5/293, Public Record Office, London. Photostat, North Carolina State Archives, Raleigh.

Cheney, John L., Jr., comp. *North Carolina Government, 1585–1974. A Narrative and Statistical History.* Raleigh, 1975.

The Foreign Commerce and Navigation of the United States for the Year Ending June 30, 1895. Part I. Volume I. Washington, D.C., 1896.

General Statutes of the State of North Carolina. Raleigh, 1975–1985.

Governors Letter Books, 1792–1795. North Carolina State Archives, Raleigh.

Grimes, J. Bryan, ed. *North Carolina Wills and Inventories.* Raleigh, 1912.

Heads of Families at the First Census of the United States Taken in the Year 1790. Baltimore, 1966.

Intracostal Waterway, Beaufort, N. C. to Key West, Fla., Station. Washington, D.C., 1913.

Laws and Resolutions of the State of North Carolina. Raleigh, 1791–1935.

Lennon, Donald R., and Kellam, Ida B., eds. *The Wilmington Town Book, 1743–1778.* Raleigh, 1973.

Mathews, James M., comp. *Public Laws of the Confederate States of America.* . . . Richmond, 1864.

McEachern, Leora, and Williams, Isabel, eds. *Wilmington-New Hanover Safety Committee Minutes, 1774–1776.* Wilmington, 1976.

"Military Ocean Terminal, Sunny Point." Information Circular. N. p., n. d.
Minutes of the New Hanover County Court of Pleas and Quarter Sessions. North Carolina State Archives, Raleigh.
The New American State Papers. Commerce and Navigation. 47 vols. Wilmington, Del., 1977.
North Carolina State Ports Authority. Master Development Plan, 1986–1990. N. p., n. d.
Official Records of the Union and Confederate Navies in the War of Rebellion. 28 vols. Washington, D.C., 1894–1922.
The Port of Wilmington, N. C. Washington, D.C. 1940.
The Port of Wilmington, N. C. Part 2. Washington, D.C., 1961.
The Ports of Charleston, S. C. and Wilmington, N. C. Washington, D.C., 1935.
Report on the Internal Commerce of the United States, by Joseph Nimmo, Jr., Chief of the Bureau of Statistics. Treasury Department. Submitted May 6, 1885. Washington, D.C., 1885.
Revised Code of North Carolina, Enacted by the General Assembly at the Session of 1854. . . . Boston, 1855.
State-Wide Navigation Inventory. Part 1. Wilmington, N.C., n. d.
Treasurers' and Comptrollers' Papers. North Carolina State Archives, Raleigh.
Walker, Francis A., comp. *A Compendium of the Ninth Census.* Washington, D.C., 1904.
War of the Rebellion: A Compilation of the Official Records of the Union and Confederate Armies. 70 vols. Washington, D.C., 1880–1881.
Water Resources Development by the U. S. Army Corps of Engineers, Jan. 1, 1987. N. p., n. d.
Waterborne Commerce of the United States. Calendar Year, 1970. Part 1; Calendar Year, 1975. Part 1; Calendar Year 1980, Part 1; Calendar Year 1986, Part 1 N. p., n. d.

Letters, Memoirs, Directories, Compilations, and Miscellaneous Published Primary Sources

Battle, Kemp P., ed. *Letters and Documents Relating to the Early History of the Lower Cape Fear.* James Sprunt Historical Monograph No. 4. Chapel Hill, 1903.
Bellamy, John D. *Memoirs of an Octogenarian.* Charlotte, 1942.
Bonitz, Julius A., comp. *Directory of the City of Wilmington, North Carolina, 1890.* Wilmington, 1889.
Boyd, William K., ed. *Some Eighteenth Century Tracts Concerning North Carolina.* Chapel Hill, 1927.
Brown, Robert W. "On the Trade of Wilmington, August 1st 1843." *Our Living and Our Dead,* 1 (September 1874–February 1875), 56–59.
Clark, Walter, comp. *Histories of the Several Regiments and Battalions from North Carolina in the Great War, 1861–'65.* 5 vols. Raleigh, 1901.

———, ed. *The State Records of North Carolina*. 16 vols. Numbered XI-XXVI. Winston and Goldsboro, N.C., 1895–1907.
Corbitt, David Leroy, ed. *The Formation of the North Carolina Counties, 1663–1943*. Raleigh, 1950.
———, ed. "Historical Notes." *North Carolina Historical Review*, 5 (1928), 97–118, 224–44, 329–44, 447–57.
Curtis, W. G. *Reminiscences of Wilmington and Smithville-Southport. 1848–1900*. Southport, N.C., 1900.
Daly, Robert R., ed. *Aboard the USS Florida, 1863–65. The Letters of Paymaster William Frederick Keeler, U. S. Navy, to his Wife, Anne*. Annapolis, 1968.
Edgar, Walter B., ed. *The Letterbook of Robert Pringle*. 2 vols. Columbia, S.C., 1972.
Fries, Adelaide et al., eds. *Records of the Moravians in North Carolina*. 11 vols. Raleigh, 1922–1969.
Finlay, Hugh, *Journal kept by Hugh Finlay, Surveyor of the Post Roads on the Continent of North America. . . .* Brooklyn, 1867.
Gerken, H., comp. *Directory and General Advertiser of the City of Wilmington for 1894–'95*. Wilmington, n. d.
Gordon, Lord Adam. "Journal of an Officer's Travels in America and the West Indies," *Travels in the American Colonies*. Ed. Newton D. Mereness. New York, 1916.
Hamer, Philip M. et al., eds. *The Papers of Henry Laurens*. 12 vols. to date. Columbia, S.C., 1968–.
Hamilton, J. G. de R., ed. *The Letters of Jonathan Worth*. 2 vols. Raleigh, 1909.
Heide, R. E. *Report on the Resources, Trade and Commerce of North Carolina*. Wilmington, 1875.
J. L. Hill Printing Co.'s Directory of Wilmington, N. C. 1900. Richmond, 1900.
Hoyt, William H., ed. *The Papers of Archibald D. Murphey*. 2 vols. Raleigh, 1914.
Hunter, Robert, Jr. *Quebec to Carolina in 1785–1786*. Ed. Louis B. Wright and Marion Tinling. San Marino, Calif., 1943.
Isaacs, I. J., comp. *The City of Wilmington. The Metropolis and Port of North Carolina. Its Advantages and Interests*. Wilmington, 1912.
Jackson, Donald, and Twohig, Dorothy, eds. *The Diaries of George Washington*. 6 vols. Charlottesville, 1976–1979.
Johns, John. "Wilmington During the Blockade." *Harper's New Monthly Magazine*, 73 (Sept. 1886): 497–503.
Johnston, Hugh B., ed. "The Vinson Confederate Letters." *North Carolina Historical Review*, 25 (1948): 100–110.
Jones, John B. *A Rebel War Clerk's Diary at the Confederate States Capital*. New York, 1935.
Keith, Alice Barnwell; Masterson, William H.; and Morgan, David T., eds. *The John Gray Blount Papers*. 4 vols. Raleigh, 1952–1982.

Tuther T. Kelley's Wilmington Directory to Which Is Added a Business Directory for 1860–'61. Wilmington, 1860.

McRee, Griffth J., ed. *Life and Correspondence of James Iredell.* 2 vols. New York, 1857.

Meredith, Hugh. *An Account of the Cape Fear Country, 1731.* Ed. Earl Gregg Swemm. Perth Amboy, N.J., 1912.

Miranda, Francisco de. *The New Democracy in America. Travels of Francisco de Miranda in the United States, 1783–1784.* Trans. Judson P. Wood, ed. John S. Ezell. Norman, Okla., 1963.

"A New Voyage to Georgia. By a Young Gentleman, London, 1737." *Collections of the Georgia Historical Society,* 9 vols. Savannah, 1840–1916.

Olmsted, Frederick Law. *A Journey in the Seaboard Slave States, With Remarks on Their Economy.* 1856; rpt. New York, 1969.

Potts, Joshua. "On the Trade of Wilmington, May 1st, 1815." *Our Living and Our Dead,* 1 (September 1874-February 1875): 51–56.

Powell, William S., ed. "Tryon's 'Book' on North Carolina." *North Carolina Historical Review,* 34 (1957): 406–15.

Quincy, Josiah, Jr. "The Southern Journal of Josiah Quincy, Jr." *Massachusetts Historical Society Proceedings.* 49 (1915–1916), 424–81.

Reaves, Bill. *Southport (Smithville): A Chronology.* Vol. 1. (1520–1887). Wilmington, 1978.

Reilly, J. S. *Wilmington Past, Present, and Future.* Wilmington, 1884.

Roberts, Captain [C. Augustus Hobart-Hampden]. *Never Caught: Personal Adventures Connected with Twelve Successful Trips in Blockade-running During the American Civil War, 1863–1864.* 1867; rpt. Carolina Beach, N.C., 1967.

Saunders, William L., ed. *The Colonial Records of North Carolina.* 10 vols. Raleigh, 1886–1890.

Schaw, Janet. *Journal of a Lady of Quality.* . . . Ed. Evangeline and Charles M. Andrews. New Haven, 1921.

Schoepf, Johann David. *Travels in the Confederation, 1783–1784.* 2 vols. Trans. and ed. Alfred J. Morrison. Philadelphia, 1911.

Sheriff's Wilmington, N.C. Directory, and General Advertiser for 1877–8. Wilmington, 1877.

Smaw, Frank D., Jr., comp. *Smaw's Wilmington Directory Comprising a General and City Business Directory and a Directory of Colored Persons to Which Is Added a Complete Historical and Commercial Sketch of the City.* Wilmington, 1867.

———, comp. *Wilmington Directory, Including a General and City Business Directory for 1865–66.* Wilmington, 1866.

Sprunt, James, *Information and Statistics Respecting Wilmington, North Carolina, Being a Report By the President of the Produce Exchange. Presented to Its Members, April, 1883.* Wilmington, 1883.

St. Mary, Moreau de. *Moreau de St. Mary's Journey, 1793–1798.* Ed. Kenneth Roberts and Anna Roberts. Garden City, N.Y., 1947.

Taylor, Thomas E. *Running the Blockade. A Personal Narrative of Adventures, Risks and Escapes during the American Civil War.* 1896; rpt. New York, 1971.

Tiffany, Nina M., ed. *Letters of James Murray, Loyalist.* Boston, 1901.

Waddell, Alfred Moore. *Some Memories of My Life.* Raleigh, 1908.

Wilkinson, J. *The Narrative of a Blockade Runner.* New York, 1877.

Yearns, W. Buck, and Barrett, John G., eds. *North Carolina Civil War Documentary.* Chapel Hill, 1980.

Published Secondary Sources

Barrett, John G. *The Civil War in North Carolina.* Chapel Hill, 1963.

Barrow, Thomas C. *Trade and Empire. The British Customs Service in Colonial America, 1660–1775.* Cambridge, Mass., 1967.

"Big, Bigger, Biggest Ever." *Carolina Cargo* (June 1985): 6–7.

Black, Robert C. *Railroads of the Confederacy.* Chapel Hill, 1952.

Boyd, William K. "Currency and Banking in North Carolina, 1790–1836." *Trinity College Historical Society Papers,* 10 (1914): 52–86.

Brown, Cecil K. *A State Movement in Railroad Development.* Chapel Hill, 1928.

Cochran, Hamilton. *Blockade Runners of the Confederacy.* Indianapolis, 1958.

Crittenden, Charles C. *The Commerce of North Carolina, 1763–1789.* New Haven, 1936.

———. "Inland Navigation in North Carolina, 1763–1789." *North Carolina Historical Review,* 8 (1931): 145–54.

"The Deep-Water Port at Wilmington." *Carolina Cargo* (June/July 1986): 20–21.

Dill, Alonzo T., Jr. "Eighteenth Century New Bern: A History of the Town and Craven County, 1700–1800. Part VIII." *North Carolina Historical Review,* 23 (1946): 495–535.

Dolan, Diane. "A Yankee View of the Fall of Wilmington, 1865." *Lower Cape Fear Historical Society Bulletin,* 20 (February 1977).

Dowd, Clement. *Life of Zebulon Vance.* Charlotte, 1897.

Durkin, Joseph T. *Stephen R. Mallory: Confederate Navy Chief.* 1954; rpt. Columbia, S.C., 1987.

"Entire Port of Wilmington Designated Foreign Trade Zone." *North Carolina Cargo,* 13 (May/June 1988): 28.

Ernal, Marc, and Ernst, Joseph Albert. "An Economic Interpretation of the American Revolution." *William and Mary Quarterly,* 3rd Series, 29 (1972): 3–32.

Ernst, Joseph A. *Money and Politics in America. A Study in the Currency Act of 1764 and the Political Economy of Revolution.* Chapel Hill, 1973.

———, and Merrens, H. Roy. " 'Camden's turrets pierce the skies!': The Urban Process in the Southern Colonies during the Eighteenth Century." *William and Mary Quarterly*, 3rd Series, 30 (1973): 549–74.

Evans, W. McKee. *Ballots and Fence Rails: Reconstruction on the Lower Cape Fear.* New York, 1974.

"Expansion News." *Carolina Cargo* (August/September 1987): 6.

Five Years of North Carolina Shipbuilding. Wilmington, 1946.

"Foreign Trade Zones Possible for North Carolina." *Carolina Cargo* (Summer 1976), 6–7.

Gilpatrick, Delbert H. *Jeffersonian Democracy in North Carolina, 1789–1815.* 1931; rpt. New York, 1967.

Goff, Richard D. *Confederate Supply.* Durham, N.C., 1969.

Hadley, Wade H. *The Story of the Cape Fear and Deep River Navigation Company.* Siler City, N.C., 1980.

Halkiotis, Stephen H. "Guns for Cuba Libre: An 1895 Filibustering Expedition from Wilmington, North Carolina." *North Carolina Historical Review*, 55 (1978): 60–75.

Hall, Lewis Philip, *Land of the Golden River.* Wilmington, 1980.

Hartzger, Ronald B. *To Great and Useful Purpose. A History of the Wilmington District U. S. Army Corps of Engineers.* N. p., n. d.

Herring, Ethel, and Williams, Carolee. *Fort Caswell in War and Peace.* Wendell, N.C., 1983.

Historical Sketch of the Signal Corps (1860–1941). Fort Monmouth, N.J., 1942.

James Sprunt: A Tribute from the City of Wilmington. Raleigh, 1925.

Johnson, F. Roy. *Riverboating in Lower Carolina.* Murfreesboro, N.C., 1977.

Johnson, Ludwell H. "Commerce Between Northeastern Ports and the Confederacy." *Journal of Southern History*, 54 (1967): 30–42.

Jones, Virgil. *The Civil War at Sea.* 3 vols. New York, 1960–1962.

Kern, Florence. *William Cooke's U.S. Revenue Cutter Diligence, 1792–1798.* Washington, D.C., 1979.

Killick, J. R. "The Transformation of Cotton Marketing in the Late Nineteenth Century: Alexander Sprunt and Son of Wilmington, N.C., 1884–1956." *Business History Review*, 55 (1981): 143–69.

Laas, Virginia Jeans. " 'Sleepless Sentinels': The North Atlantic Blockading Squadron, 1862–1864." *Civil War History*, 31 (1988): 24–38.

Landon, Charles E. *The North Carolina State Ports Authority.* Durham, N.C., 1963.

Lane, Frederic C. *Ships for Victory.* Baltimore, 1951.

Lee, Lawrence. *The History of Brunswick County, North Carolina.* Charlotte, 1980.

———. *The Lower Cape Fear in Colonial Days.* Chapel Hill, 1965.

Lemisch, Jesse, "Jack Tar in the Streets: Merchant Seamen in the Politics of Revolutionary America." *William and Mary Quarterly.* 3rd Series, 25 (1968): 371–407.

Lemmon, Sarah M. *Frustrated Patriots: North Carolina and the War of 1812.* Chapel Hill, 1972.
Maffitt, Emma. *The Life of John Newland Maffitt.* New York and Washington, D.C., 1906.
Massey, Gregory L. "The British Expedition to Wilmington, January–November 1781." *North Carolina Historical Review,* 66 (1989): 387–411.
McCusker, John J. and Menard, Russell R. *The Economy of British America, 1607–1789.* Chapel Hill, 1985.
McEachern, Leora, and Williams, Isabel. "The Prevailing Epidemic—1862." *Lower Cape Fear Historical Society Bulletin,* 11 (1967).
Merrens, H. Roy. *Colonial North Carolina in the Eighteenth Century: A Study in Historical Geography.* Chapel Hill, 1964.
"Military First." *North Carolina Cargo,* 13 (January/February 1988): 10.
"Ming Prosperity Makes First Call at Wilmington." *North Carolina Cargo,* 13 (March/April 1988): 16–17.
Mott, G. F. *A Survey of the United States Ports.* New York, 1951.
"New Developments: Port of Wilmington." *Carolina Cargo* (June/July 1987): 18–23.
"N. C. Ports Begin China Trade Mission." *Carolina Cargo* (August/September 1986): 6–7.
"North Carolina's Industries Find Convenience and Profit in State's Intermodal Network." *Carolina Cargo* (April/May 1987): 4–5.
"Ports Authority Leases Southport Boat Harbor." *Carolina Cargo* (Summer 1976): 7.
Powell, William S. "Beginning of Banking in North Carolina, 1804–1860." *Tarheel Banker,* 41 (1962): 59–60.
Price, Marcus W. "Ships that Tested the Blockade of the Carolina Ports, 1861–1865." *American Neptune,* 8 (1948): 196–241.
Prince, Richard E. *Seaboard Air Line Railways. Steam Boats, Locomotives, and History.* Green River, Wyo., 1969.
Quinn, David Beers. *North America from Earliest Discovery to First Settlements. The Norse Voyages to 1612.* New York, 1977.
Rayburn, Richard. "One of the Finest Rivers in the South: Corps of Engineers Improvements on the Cape Fear River Below Wilmington, 1881–1919." *Lower Cape Fear Historical Society Bulletin,* 28 (February 1985).
Robinson, William Morrison. *The Confederate Privateers.* 1928; rpt. Columbia, S.C., 1990.
Scharf, J. Thomas, *History of the Confederate Navy.* 2 vols. 1886; rpt. Freeport, N.Y., 1969.
Schlesinger, Arthur M. *The Colonial Merchants and the American Revolution, 1763–1776.* 1919; rpt. New York, 1964.
"Shipbuilding in Wilmington." *The State.* 12 (September 1944): 10–11, 16.
Singleton, Royce Gordon. *John Taylor Wood: Sea Ghost of the Confederacy.* Atlanta, 1979.

Smith, Al. "Wilmington." *North Carolina State Ports*, 7 (June 1961): 8.
"Southport Grows." *North Carolina State Ports*, 13 (1967): 7.
"SPA: Dream Come True." *Carolina Cargo* (Summer 1976): 16–17.
Spindel, Donna. "Law and Disorder: The North Carolina Stamp Act Crisis." *North Carolina Historical Review*, 57 (1980): 1–16.
Sprout, Harold and Margaret. *The Rise of American Naval Power, 1776–1918*. Princeton, 1946.
Sprunt, James. *Chronicles of the Cape Fear River*. 2nd ed. Raleigh, 1916.
―――. *Tales and Traditions of the Lower Cape Fear, 1661–1896*. Wilmington, 1896.
Starling, Roger B. "The Plank Road Movement in North Carolina. Parts I and II." *North Carolina Historical Review*, 16 (1939): 1–22, 147–73.
Stark, Aubrey Harrison. *Sidney Lanier: A Biographical and Critical Study*. Chapel Hill, 1933.
"State of the Ports." *North Carolina Cargo*, 13 (March/April 1988): 18–20.
"Steamship Lines Serving Wilmington and Morehead City." *Carolina Cargo* (December/January 1985–1986): 31–39.
Stick, David. *Bald Head: A History of Smith Island and the Cape Fear*. Wendell, N.C., 1985.
―――. *North Carolina Lighthouses*. Raleigh, 1981.
Still, William N., Jr. *Confederate Shipbuilding*. 1969; rpt. Columbia, S.C., 1987.
―――. *Iron Afloat: The Story of the Confederate Armonclads*. 1971; rpt. Columbia, S.C., 1985.
―――. *North Carolina's Revolutionary War Navy*. Raleigh, 1976.
―――. "Shipbuilding in North Carolina: The World War I Experience." *American Neptune*, 41 (1981): 188–207.
Sullivan, David M. "The Confederate States Marines at Wilmington, 1864–1865." *Lower Cape Fear Historical Society Bulletin*, 30 (October 1986).
"The Trade Zone." *Carolina Cargo* (June/July 1986): 8–9.
Weir, Robert. "North Carolina's Reaction to the Currency Act of 1764." *North Carolina Historical Review*, 40 (1963): 183–99.
"Wilmington, North Carolina and Dandong, China Sign Sister City Agreement." *Carolina Cargo* (April/May 1987): 10–11, 44.
Watson, Alan D. "Benjamin Smith: The Early Years of a North Carolina Governor." *Lower Cape Fear Historical Society Bulletin*, 25 (February 1982).
―――. "Benjamin Smith: The General and Governor." *Lower Cape Fear Historical Society Bulletin*, 25 (May 1982).
―――. "The Founding Fathers of Wilmington, 1743–1775." *Lower Cape Fear Historical Society Bulletin*, 24 (October 1980).
―――. *Money and Monetary Problems in Early North Carolina*. Raleigh, 1980.

———. "Port Brunswick in the Colonial Era." *Lower Cape Fear Historical Society Journal*, 30 (1989): 23–32.
———. *Richard Dobbs Spaight*. New Bern, N.C., 1986.
———. "Wilmington: A Town Born of Conflict, Confusion, and Collusion." *Lower Cape Fear Historical Society Bulletin*, 30 (February, May 1988).
Wise, Stephen R. *Lifeline of the Confederacy: Blockading Running during the Civil War.* Columbia, S.C., 1988.

Theses and Dissertations

Beeker, Henry Judson. "Wilmington During the Civil War." M.A. thesis, Duke University, 1941.

Brewer, James F. "An Account of Negro Slavery in the Cape Fear Region Prior to 1860." Ph.D. dissertation, University of Pittsburgh, 1949.

Browning, Robert M. "The Blockade of Wilmington, 1861–1865." M.A. thesis, East Carolina University, 1980.

Fagg, Daniel W., Jr. "Carolina, 1663–1683: The Founding of a Proprietary." Ph.D. dissertation, Emory University, 1970.

Fonvielle, Chris E. "To Forge a Thunderbolt: The Wilmington Campaign, February, 1865." M.A. thesis, East Carolina University, 1987.

Logan, Byron Eugene. "An Historical Geographic Survey of North Carolina Ports." Ph.D. dissertation, University of North Carolina, 1956.

Perry, Percival. "The Naval Stores Industry in the Ante-Bellum South, 1789–1861." Ph.D. dissertation, Duke University, 1947.

Randall, Duncan Peter. "Geographic Factors in the Growth and Economy of Wilmington, North Carolina." Ph.D. dissertation, University of North Carolina, 1965.

Scott, Ralph Lee. "Welding the Sinews of History: A History of the North Carolina Shipbuilding Corporation." M.A. thesis, East Carolina University, 1979.

Turlington, Sarah Woodhall. "Steam Navigation in North Carolina Prior to 1860." M.A. thesis, University of North Carolina, 1933.

Wood, Richard Everett, "Port Town at War: Wilmington, North Carolina, 1860–1865." Ph.D. dissertation, Florida State University, 1976.

Index

Abbot, Joseph C., 124; mills of, 106
Acme Fertilizer Company, 114
Adrian, Aldrich, 119
Adrian & Volles (Co.), 119
Advance, 78, 80, 87, 88; *See also Lord Clyde*
Albion Trading Company, 83
Alexander Collie and Company, 87
Alexander Sprunt & Son, 109–11, 134, 139–40, 151
Allyon, Lucas Vasquez de: attempted settlement by, 4
Almont Shipping Company, 165–66
Amerian Agricultural Company, 140
American Export Lines, 159
American-Hawaiian Steamship Company, 152
American Naval Stores (Co.), 140
American Pine Fibre Company, 115
American Revolution, 1, 3, 8, 28–30; consequences of, 31; origin of in N.C., 23–28
American Seamen's Aid Society, 48
Ames, J. W., 103
Anderson, Joseph R., 72
Anderson Clayton & Co., 151
Army Corps of Engineers. *See* United States, Army Corps of Engineers
Army Signal Corps. *See* United States, Army Signal Corps
Articles of Confederation, 31
Ashe, William S., 63
Atalanta, 79. *See also Tallahassee*

Atlantic Coast Line Railroad, 116–17, 160, 162
Atlantic Container (Co.), 163
Atlantic Intracoastal Waterway, 140, 147–49, 152, 155
Autry, W. T., 118
Aycock, Charles B., 127

Bache, A. D., 63, 64
Bache, Hartman, 62
Bacon, 47, 50, 56, 69, 87, 95
Badger, George, 63
Bald Head Island, 37, 65, 92, 97, 99, 114, 125, 129, 137
Bald Head Lighthouse, 39, 65, 129, 146
Bald Head Point, 64
Ballast, 11, 124, 154
Baltimore, 33, 66, 106, 122, 145, 134
Banking, 37–38, 47
Banks Line, 53
Banshee, 85, 93, 97, 101
Banshee No. 2, 95
Barnesmore, 110
Bastille, 40
Batchelor, Capt., 27
Beaufort, N.C., 16, 43, 50, 98, 111, 112, 147, 148
Beatty, Thomas, 34
Beery, Benjamin W., 78; shipyard of, 72, 76, 78, 82. *See also* Confederate Naval Yard
Bermuda, 78, 87, 88, 89, 90, 94, 98

202

Bixby, W. H., 120, 121, 148
Blackmore, Harold, 27
Black River, 56, 119–20, 166
Black River Navigation Company, 119
Bladen Company, 119
Bladen County, 8, 21, 36, 64, 118, 120
Bladen Steamboat Company, 53
Blockade, 76, 79, 80, 83, 89; description of, 97–101; difficulties of, 97–98; effectiveness of, 99–102
Blockade runners: cargoes of, 94–95; description of, 90; egress of, 90; factors for success of, 93; ingress of, 92; regularity of runs of, 93; salvaging of, 100; signals for, 92; stowaways on, 90–91
Blockade running, 83–103; auctions from, 86; Confederate States of America regulation of, 95, 96; Confederate States of America role in, 87–89; criticism of, 95; description of, 85–86; disease brought to Wilmington by, 86–87; effectiveness of, 101–2; end of, 102; English role in, 89; North Carolina regulation of, 95; North Carolina role in, 87–88; rewards of, 84, 96; Wilmingtonians engaged in, 83–84
Bloodworth, John, 41
Board of Health. *See* Wilmington, Board of Health in
Board of Internal Improvements. *See* North Carolina, Board of Internal Improvements of
Board of Trade. *See* Wilmington, Board of Trade in
Boston, 26, 33, 66, 106, 112, 122, 143, 148
Bragg, Braxton, 80, 81, 103
Bremen, 107, 109, 126, 139, 140
Bridges, 21, 117, 146
Brown, Roert W., 48, 63
Brunswick County, 30, 36, 51, 57, 116, 122, 137; creation of, 8
Brunswick River, 4, 51, 117, 118, 155, 158
Brunswick River Ferry, 51
Brunswick Town, 5, 7, 9, 16, 18, 21, 35, 36, 41; demise of, 6, 29–30; description of, 6; founding of, 6; port of, 8; shipping of, 10; Spanish invasion of, 6, 17
Bull Line, 152
Bunting, Robert H., 127
Burgwin, John F., 30, 57
Burns, Otway, 52
Burrington, George, 6, 7, 9
Burris, James, 91
Butterfield, Capt., 27

Calder, William, 76
Calder & Bros., 110
Calhoun, John C., 71
Camden, 39, 65; port of, 32
Camden and Gadsden Railroad, 51
Campbellton, 21, 22
Canadian Bank of Commerce, 110
Canal, 36, 120; proposal for, 147
C & P Pelham (Co.), 34
Cape Fear, 147; exploration and settlement of, 5–6; trade of, 31–32. *See also* Lower Cape Fear
Cape Fear and Deep River Navigation Company, 60–61, 70
Cape Fear and Deep River Steam Boat Company, 52
Cape Fear and People's Steamboat Company, 119
,Cape Fear and Western Steam Boat Company, 52
Cape Fear and Yadkin Valley Railroad, 116, 117, 119
Cape-Fear Canal Company, 36
Cape Fear Guano Company, 114
Cape Fear Lifesaving Service, 130
Cape Fear Lifesaving Station, 137
Cape Fear Line, 53
Cape Fear Minute Men, 71
Cape-Fear Navigation Company, 36, 59, 118
The Cape-Fear Pilot, or Commerce & Navigation of Wilmington, North-Carolina, 37
Cape Fear River, 1, 3–4, 5, 7, 9, 14, 22, 35, 40, 59, 77, 89, 112, 126, 135, 136, 146, 147, 148, 149, 154, 155; improvement of navigability of, 17–18, 36, 37, 61–65, 70, 108–9, 124–26, 137, 138, 145, 146; mining of, 74, 128–29; navigational aids for, 129, 137, 146. *See also* Northeast Cape Fear River; Northwest Cape Fear River
Cape Fear Steam Boat Company, 52
Cape Fear Transportation Company, 119
Cape Fear Tobacco Works, 113
Cape François, 33
Cape Hatteras, 130, 135, 137, 144, 147
Cape Lookout, 147
Carolina Atlantic Transportation Service, 163
Carolina Beach, 121, 140, 149
Carolina Central Railway Company, 116, 117. *See also* Wilmington, Charlotte and Rutherford Railroad; Carolina Central Railroad Company

Carolina Oil and Creosote Company, 113
Carolina Rice Mills, 112, 113
Carolina Shipbuilding Company, 143, 144
Cartagena, 127
Cassidey, James, 55, 68
Cassidey Ship Yard, 82
Castle Hayne, 21, 146
Central Railroad Company, 116. *See also* Carolina Central Railway Company; Wilmington, Charlotte and Rutherford Railroad
Chamber of Commerce. *See* Wilmington, Chamber of Commerce
Champion Compress & Warehouse Co., 152
Champion Cotton Compress Company, 110
Charleston, S.C., 1, 2, 11, 12, 20, 22, 29, 33, 40, 54, 55, 56, 59, 66, 74, 89, 97, 101, 102, 107, 110, 111, 115, 116, 130, 135, 137, 142, 148, 153, 156, 164, 167
Charles Town, N. C., 5
Charlotte, 21, 22, 160, 164; railroad interest in, 51
Charlotte Ocean Steamship Company, 122
Chatham County, 3, 21, 54, 60, 64, 70
Chemicals, 149, 150, 152, 166
Cheraw and Darlington Railroad, 51
Cherry, R. Gregg, 157
Chesapeake Affair, 41, 42
Chickamauga, 79, 80, 81. *See also Edith*
Civil War, 1, 70–104 passim
Clarendon Company, 52
Clark, Henry T., 95
Clingman, Thomas, 63
Clinton, N.C., 120
Clinton, Sir Henry, 28
Clyde Line, 152; imports and exports of, 122. *See also* New York and Wilmington Steamship Company
Clyde-Mallory Line, 152
Coal, 60, 70, 80, 83, 88, 121, 135, 148. *See also* Egypt coal mines
Coast Guard. *See* United States, Coast Guard
Coast Survey. *See* United States, Coast Survey
Coleman, Arthur, 145
Colfax, 129, 130, 134
Collet, John, 28
Columbia, 100. *See also Tuscarora*
Commissioners of Navigation and Pilotage, 34–38, 57–58, 86, 131–32, 136–37.

Committee of Safety. *See* Wilmington, Committee of Safety of
Committee of Thirteen. *See* Wilmington, Committee of Thirteen of
Commodities inspection system, 19
Commodore, 127, 128
Compton, Spencer, Earl of Wilmington, 7
Confederate Naval Yard, 82. *See also* Beery, Benjamin W., shipyard of
Confederate Point, 72, 73. *See also* Federal Point
Confederate States of America, 71, 124; army of, 72, 88; cruisers of, 80; exports of, 93–94; navy of, 75–80, 91, 96; privateers of, 78–80; trade of, 1; war department of, 96
Congress. *See* United States, Congress
Containerized cargo, 153, 161–63, 166–67
Continental Association, 27
Continental Congress, 26, 27
Corn, 22, 47, 56, 60, 64, 68, 69, 140
Cornwallis, Lord Charles, 28, 29
Corps of Engineers. *See* United States, Army Corps of Engineers
Cotton, 1, 2, 19, 20, 33, 46, 50, 60, 66, 70, 82, 89, 93, 94, 95, 96, 97, 104, 107–12, 115, 116, 117, 118, 120, 122, 124, 135, 138–39, 140, 150–51, 159
Cotton mills, 115, 145
Cotton Plant Steamboat Company, 52
Cowan, R. H., 51
Craig, Maj. James H., 29
Creosoting works, 115
Crossan, Thomas M., 87
Cross Creek (town), 21, 22, 25, 36
CSX, 162
Cuba, 33; independence of, 126–29; insurrectionaries, 127–28
Cuba, 127
Cubbins, Thomas, 91
Cumberland County, 21, 36, 64
Currency Act (1764): effects on N.C., 25
Curtis, Dr. W. G., 132
Cushing, William B., 102
Customs Service. *See* United States, Customs Service

Dandong, People's Republic of China, 165
Davis, Jefferson, 72, 80, 94–95
Dawson, John, 63, 64, 74, 103
Deep and Haw River Company, 36
Deep River, 3, 36, 59, 60, 61, 83; improvement of navigability of, 70

Delacy, John D., 52
Delgado Cotton Mills, 113
Department of Defense. *See* United States, Department of Defense
Department of Justice. *See* United States, Department of Justice
DeRosset, Armand J., 75
DeRosset, Mrs. Armand J., 74, 84–85
DeRosset, William Lord, 148
Dickerson, Platt F., 48
Diligence, 39, 41
Diligence II, 40
Diligence III, 40
Diligence IV, 40
Dillon, John G., 127, 128
Disease, 18, 35, 38, 47, 132. *See also* Smallpox; Yellow fever
Dobbs, Arthur, 9, 10, 19
Dram Tree, 85
DuBois, John, 15
Dudley, Edward B., 48
Dunbibin, Daniel, 7
Dunbibin, Jonathan, 28
Duplin Canal Company, 120
Duplin County, 21, 114
Duplin Road, 20

Eagle Oil Company, 143
Eagles Island, 3–4, 51, 68, 82, 94, 116, 117, 142, 149
Edenton, 9, 24, 28, 32, 39, 65; privateering from, 28
Edgecombe County, 50, 70, 114
Edith, 79, 88. *See also Chickamauga*
Egypt coal mines, 61, 70
E. J. Lilly (Co.), 110
Elizabeth River, 36, 62, 140, 149
Elizabethtown, 21, 53, 56, 118, 146
Ellis, John W., 72
Embargo (1807), 42
England, 10, 33, 139, 150; colonial port districts of, 11; regulation of colonial trade by, 9. *See also* Great Britain; United Kingdom
Evans, Oliver, 52
Evans, William T., 53
Express Company, 119
Express Line, 53
Express Steamboat Company, 118

Fayetteville, 14, 21, 33, 36, 37, 49–50, 52, 53, 54, 56, 59, 60, 70, 82, 114, 116, 118, 119, 141, 147, 166; population of, 30; trade of, 46–47. *See also* Campbellton; Cross Creek
Fayetteville and Yadkin Railroad, 49
Fayetteville Convention (1789), 31
Federal Constitution: N.C. reaction to, 31
Federal Point, 43, 58, 65, 72–73. *See also* Confederate Point
Federal Point Lighthouse, 129
Ferries, 21, 51, 117, 146
Fertilizer, 2, 117, 135, 139, 140, 145, 148, 149, 150, 151, 152, 155; manufacture of, 114
Flanner, Andrew, 112
Flatboats, 15, 56, 61, 68, 118, 120
The Flats (sandbar), 7, 9, 36, 61
Flour, 22, 42, 47, 50, 60
Foodstuffs, 10, 20, 33, 56, 69, 122, 149, 151
Fort Anderson, 73, 87, 103
Fort Campbell, 89
Fort Caswell, 72, 73, 89, 103, 137; strengthening of, 128
Fort Fisher, 72, 74, 75, 76, 78, 79, 81, 89, 92, 93, 98, 124; assault on, 102; fall of, 77, 102
Fort Hatteras, 72, 91
Fort Holmes, 89, 99, 100, 103
Fort Johnston, 17, 18, 28, 40, 41, 42, 43–44, 72, 73, 74, 103
Fort Malakoff, 73
Fort Sumter, 72
Frank and Jerry Line, 53
Free Trade Zone, 165
French, Samuel R., 72
Frying Pan Lightship, 129
Frying Pan Shoals, 4, 64, 89, 97, 124, 125, 130, 131, 137, 146
Fulton, Hamilton, 62
Fulton, Robert, 52
Fumigation, 58, 90
F. W. Kerchner (Co.), 110

Gabourel, Amice, 22
Gallatin, Albert, 147
Galveston, 111, 139, 148
Gasoline, 147
Gautier, Thomas N., 42, 43
General Assembly. *See* North Carolina, General Assembly of
General cargo, 153, 165
General Washington, 29
George A. Fuller Company, 143, 144
Georgetown, S. C., 122, 130, 148, 155, 159

Georgia, 14, 29, 52, 67, 101, 114, 160, 164, 167; State Ports Authority of, 157
Germany, 124, 134, 139, 141, 150
Giles, Norwood, 112
Gilmer, J. F., 82
Giraffe, 90. *See also Robert E. Lee*
Glasgow, 27, 90, 107
Gordon, Lord Adam, 6
Graham, Edward, 49
Gray, William, 6
Great Britain, 10, 19, 33, 69, 89, 134, 161, 163; attacks of on N. C. coast, 43; commercial policies of, 23–24; naval operations of, 29. *See also* England; United Kingdom
Green, James, 75
Greenhow, Rose O'Neal, 89
Greenock, 28, 33
Guano, 114, 117, 134
Guilford County, 54, 59, 64
Gunboat Committee. *See* Wilmington, Gunboat Committee of

Halifax, Nova Scotia, 89
Hall & Pearsall (Co.), 110
Hamburg, 107, 109
Hamilton, Alexander, 39
Hansen, Ludwig, 113
Harbor master, 35, 58, 101, 131, 136, 138; fee of, 135
Harnett, Cornelius, 24
Harper, John W., 121, 140, 141
Harper, T. J., 132
Harper's Line Steamers, 140
Harriss, George, 115
Hattridge, Alexander, 34
Havana, 44, 56
Haw River, 3, 36, 59
Heide, Rudolph E., 110
Henrietta, 52, 53
Henrietta Steam Boat Company, 52
Henry Lowe & Company, 81
Hervieux, François Henri, 40
Hillsborough, 22, 36, 54. *See also* Orange Court House
Hillsborough Convention (1788), 31
Hilton, William, 5
Hilton Bridge, 146, 166
Hodges, Luther, 158
Hogg, James, 22
Hogg, Samuel, 22
Hogg and Campbell (Co.), 22
Hooper, George, 39

Hope (blockade runner), 99
Hope (brig), 34
Houston, William, 25
Howe, Charles, 119
Hull, England, 16, 33
Hydrographic Office. *See* United States, Hydrographic Office

Immigration and Naturalization. *See* United States, Immigration and Naturalization Office
Indentured servants: escape of, 19
Indigo, 12, 14, 19
Industrial Manufacturing Company, 115
Inland Waterways Commission, 147
Intermodalism, 164–65
Interstate Commerce Commission, 148
Interstate Highway, 40, 163
Intracoastal Waterway. *See* Atlantic Intracoastal Waterway
Iron, 33, 60, 66, 135
Ironclads, 75–77

Jacksonville, N. C., 116, 148
Jacobi, Marcus W., 138
Jarman, Harvey, 15
Jefferson, Thomas, 42
Jocelin, Amaziah, 35
John H. Haughton, 60, 61, 70
John Slingsby & Co., 27
Johnston, Gabriel, 7, 19
Jones, Pembroke, 112

Keeler, William F., 98, 99
Kenan, William R., 127
Keystone State, 98
Killick, J. C., 109
Knox, Henry, 40
Kuhn, Joseph E., 141

L'Aimee Marguerite, 40–41
Laird and Gray, 110
Lamb, William, 72, 92, 93, 100, 102
Larkins, William, 112
Laurens, Henry, 20
Lazarus, Aaron, 48
Lee, Lawrence, 9
Lee, Robert E., 81
Lee, Samuel P., 97, 100
Le Havre, 107, 109, 139, 165
Liberty Shipbuilding Corporation, 143–45
Liberty ships, 154, 155, 156
Lifesaving Service. *See* United States, Lifesaving Service

Light House Board. *See* United States, Light House Board
Lighthouses, 37, 129, 137
Lincoln, Abraham: election of, 71; call for troops by, 72
Lisbon, N. C., 120
Little River, S. C., 140, 148, 149
Liverpool, 33, 34, 107, 109, 111, 140
Lobb, Jacob, 26
Lockwoods Folly, 8, 136, 140
Lockwoods Folly River, 122, 149
Lôme, Dupuy de, 127, 128
London, 14, 107
Lord Clyde, 87. *See also Advance*
Lords Proprietors of Carolina, 5
Louisville and Nashville Railroad, 113
Lower Cape Fear, 8, 16, 17, 63, 91, 112, 148; British naval operations in, 28–29; Confederate protection for, 72, 75; importance of naval stores in, 19; improvement of commerce in, 19; inability of to attract backcountry trade, 20; Sons of Liberty in, 26; trade of, 20, 26. *See also* Cape Fear
Lumber mills, 104, 113
Lutterloh Line, 53
Lynch, William F., 77, 82, 95

Mabson, Arthur, 27
McNair & Pearsall (Co.), 110
McRae, Alexander, 51
McRae, Duncan, 63
Madison, James, 42, 43
Maffitt, John N., 102
Mallory, Stephen R., 80, 91
Manufactures, 10, 150
Manufacturing, 10, 14, 81–82, 112–115, 150. *See also* Shipbuilding
Marine hospital, 48, 133
Marine railways, 113, 115
Maritime Commission. *See* United States, Maritime Commission
Marsden, Rufus, 7
Marshall, Frederick William, 31
Martin, James G., 87
Martin, Josiah, 22
Mason, James M., 88
Meares, O. P., 51
Medway, Dr. Alexander R., 87
Merchants 22, 23, 25–26, 27, 30, 103, 110, 111; manner of trade of, 57
Merchants and Farmers Steamboat Company, 119
Merchants Association of Wilmington, 134–35

Merchants Steamboat Company, 52
Merrimac, 84, 88, 96
Metal, scrap, 150, 159
Military Ocean Terminal (MOTSU), 166
Mitchell, J. C., 129
Mitchell and Gerney (Co.), 83
Mobile, 74, 93, 97
Molasses, 10, 34, 66, 149, 151
Monroe, James, 47, 51
Moore, James, 28
Moore, Maurice, 6
Moravians (Unitas Fratrum), 20, 21, 30
Morehead City, 154, 157, 158, 161, 163, 164, 165, 166; rivalry of with Wilmington, 164
Morehead City Port Commission, 156
Morrison, Cameron, 156
Mott, G. F., 157
Mount Airy Railroad Company, 116
Mt. Tizra, 48
Murphey, Archibald, D., 59, 61, 62
Murray, James, 6–7, 14, 17

Napoleon Bonaparte, 41, 43
Nassau, 44, 84, 86, 87, 89, 90, 94, 96, 98, 102
National Company, 151
Naul Shipbuilding Company, 142, 143; shipyard of, 144
Naval stores (tar, pitch, turpentine, resin), 1, 12, 15, 19–20, 32, 33, 47, 50, 56, 57, 60, 61, 64, 66, 67, 68, 69, 82, 93, 95, 96, 104, 106–7, 109, 110, 112, 115, 116, 117, 118, 119, 120, 122, 124, 135, 138, 140
Navassa, 147, 149; bridge at, 146
Navassa Guano Company, 114, 140
Navigation Acts, 9; burden of, 24
Navy. *See* United States, Navy
New Bern, 20, 24, 26, 39, 50, 65, 112, 113, 116, 145; fall of, 74, 75; population of, 30, 46; port of, 28, 44; privateering from, 32
New England, 5; opposition of to War of 1812, 42; ports of, 44; ships of, 69
New Hanover County, 6, 8, 18, 27, 36, 49, 103, 136, 137; court of, 57; Democrats of, 63; militia of, 49; wardens of the poor of, 38
New Hanover County Defense Council, 154
New Hanover Transit Company, 121
New Inlet, 4, 30, 35, 42, 62, 64, 65, 68, 76, 89, 97, 124, 125, 126

New Orleans, 83, 93, 97, 111, 139
Newport News Shipbuilding and Dry Dock Company, 145, 154, 156
New River, 116, 120, 148
New River Canal Company, 120
New York, 12, 16, 33, 54, 56, 66, 72, 93, 106, 109, 112, 122, 128; customs collections of, 45; trade of, 45; ports of, 44
New York and Wilmington Steamship Company, 122. See also Clyde Line
Norfolk, 1, 2, 44, 67, 68, 97, 110, 111, 115, 130, 135, 138, 148, 153, 164, 167
Norfolk, Baltimore & Carolina Line, 152
Norfolk Port Authority, 157
North Carolina, 3, 117
  adverse reputation of in early nineteenth century, 46
  adverse trade patters of, 20–21
  backcountry trade of, 21, 30
  blockade running by, 87–88
  Board of Health of, 132
  Board of Internal Improvements of, 62
  British W. I. market of, 31
  coastal defense of, 41, 42–43, 72
  Confederate protection for, 72, 73
  customs districts of, 10, 39, 104
  customs revenues collected in, 44
  Department of Commerce, 164
  economy of during the Confederation era, 31
  funds of to improve the Cape Fear River, 62
  General Assembly of, 2, 6, 7, 8, 17, 18, 21, 26, 34, 35, 36, 37, 38, 41, 48, 49, 50, 51, 52, 61, 62, 120, 133, 156
  governor of, 136
  highway commission of, 146
  impact of War of 1812 on, 44
  interest of in Cape Fear Navigation Company, 60–61
  interest of in intracoastal canal, 147
  manufacturing in, 16
  militia of, 43
  naval reserves of, 126
  navy of, 29
  neglect of by Confederate States of America, 80
  provincial congresses of, 26, 29, 34
  quarantine station of at Southport, 133
  regulation of commerce of, 34–35
  secession of, 72
  shipbuilding in, 142–43
  State Planning Board of, 157
  shipping of, 11, 12, 19, 27–28, 31, 32, 44–45, 65–68, 104, 164
  tonnage taxes collected in, 39
  U. S. customs districts in, 39
North Carolina (ironclad), 77, 82; construction of, 75–76
North Carolina Cotton Seed Mills, 115
North Carolina Line, 149, 152
North Carolina Ocean Terminals, 158, 161
North Carolina Shipbuilding Company, 154, 156, 157
North Carolina State Docks: containerized cargo at, 161–62; importance of for Wilmington, 158; military traffic at, 161; opening of, 158; shipping facilities of, 162; shipping through, 158
North Carolina State Ports Authority, 156–65 passim; creation of, 156; efforts to improve shipping, 164–65; financing of, 163; members of governing board of, 157; negotiations of with U. S. Maritime Commission, 157; politicization of, 164; problems of, 164; Southport's shipping facility, 164. See also North Carolina Ocean Terminals; North Carolina State Docks
North Carolina State Ports Railroad Commission, 162
Northeast Cape Fear River, 14, 15, 21, 106, 112, 114, 117, 118, 120–21, 143, 144, 146, 149, 166; improvment of navigability of, 17, 121
Northwest Cape Fear River, 4, 21, 22, 57, 59, 112, 118–20, 146, 155; improvement of navigability of, 17, 36, 59, 118–19, 141, 147
Northwind, 137
Nowland, Maurice, 14
Nutt, Henry, 51, 124, 125
Nye, Susan D., 3

Oakes, J. C., 147
Oak Island, 43, 125, 129, 130
Oak Island Lifesaving Station, 130, 137
Ocean Terminals. See North Carolina Ocean Terminals
O'Hanlon, Doyle, 53, 59
Olmsted, Frederick Law, 53, 55, 56
Olustee, 79, 81. See also *Tallahassee*
Onslow County, 21, 49, 56, 68, 116, 120, 125, 148
Orange Court House, 21. See also Hillsborough

Outlaw, David, 63
Overman, Lee, S., 137
Owen Fennell, Jr. (Co.), 110
Paddison, R. P., 119
Page, Rinaldo B., 157
Parsley, Oscar G., 75, 104
Partlow, Capt., 133
Pender County, 120, 121
Pennsylvania, 12, 17, 20
People's Republic of China, 150, 165
Petersburg, Va., 20, 83, 115
Petroleum products, 2, 140, 147, 151, 152, 155, 156, 159, 166
Philadelphia, 12, 27, 33, 37, 66, 106, 112, 122
Philadelphia Convention (1787), 31
Pilotage, 135; regulation of, 17, 25, 58, 131
Pilot Fund, 131
Pilots, 28, 35, 91, 131
Pilot's Association of Southport, 132
Pittsboro, 36, 54
Point Caswell, 119, 120
Pork, 19, 22, 56, 95
Port Albemarle, 104
Port Bath, 10
Port Beaufort, 9, 10, 104
Port Brunswick, 18, 29, 30, 32, 34–35; ships trading to, 16; trade of, 9–15
Port City Cold Storage, Inc., 160
Port Currituck, 9, 10
Port Pamlico, 104
Port physician, 58, 132
Port Roanoke, 9, 10, 32
Port Swansborough, 35
Port wardens, 37, 58, 136
Port Wilmington, 32–33, 34. See also Wilmington
Porter, David D., 73, 98
Potter, Dr. F. W., 132
Potter, Samuel, 55
Potts, Joshua, 30, 43
Powers, Gibbs & Co., 114
Price, Samuel, 56
Privateering, 28–29, 40–41, 43–44, 78–80
Produce Exchange. See Wilmington, Produce Exchange in
Prohibition, 145
Prometheus, 52
Providence, 40
Provincial congress. See North Carolina, provincial congresses of

Public Health Service. See United States, Public Health Service
Quarantine, 18, 87, 88, 95, 132–34
Quejo, Pedro de, 4
Quince, John, 16
Rafts, 15, 18, 56, 61, 68, 118
Railroads, 49–52, 56, 70, 82, 115–17, 120, 148, 153, 159, 162
Raleigh, N.C., 37, 158, 163
Raleigh (ironclad), 76–77, 82
Randall, James, 97
Raymond, Charles, 127
Reid, David, 64
Reilly, James, 102
Restraining (Fisheries) Acts (1775), 27
Retribution, 78. See also *Uncle Ben*
Revenue Act (1764), 24
Revenue cutter. See United States, Coast Guard
Revenue Cutter Service. See United States, Revenue Cutter Service
Rice, 12, 14, 19, 42, 47, 66, 69, 111–12, 122
Richmond, Va., 74, 95, 97
Rivers and Harbors Act: (1881) 126; (1902) 141; (1912) 148; (1927) 148–49
Roads, 20, 21, 22, 49, 117, 146, 160, 163
Roberts, B. M., 121
Robert E. Lee, 88, 90, 93. See also *Giraffe*
The Rocks (dam), 125–26
Roosevelt, Franklin D., 154
Rossevelt, Theodore, 147
Rotterdam, 107, 139
Rum, 10, 29, 34, 66, 145
Russell, Daniel L., 125
Russia, 12; naval stores of, 19
Safety Committee. See Wilmington-New Hanover Safety Committee
Sailors, 18–19, 23; care for, 18, 38, 48; fights of, 38–39; stake of in American Revolution, 25
St. Joseph, 40
Salem, N. C., 21, 22
Salisbury, 22, 54
Sampson, County, 64, 118, 119, 120
Sans Souci Fertilizer Works, 114
Savannah, 1, 2, 67, 74, 107, 111, 134, 135, 164
Savannah District Authority, 157
Sawmills, 47, 106
Scandinavia: naval stores of, 19

Schaw, Alexander, 22
Schaw, Janet, 3, 6
Schuter, John, 40
Scotland, 10, 109
Scott, Kerr, 158
Scott, Robert, 35
Seaboard Air Line, 116, 117, 160, 162
Seaboard Coast Line, 162
Sea-Land Line, 163
Seamen's Friend Society of Wilmington, 48, 133–34
Seawell, Joseph, 52
Secession, 71
Seddon, James A., 80, 87, 96
Seminole, 136, 137, 142, 145
Seymour, Augustus, S., 128
Shallotte, 140
Shallotte River, 122, 149
Shipbuilding, 16–17, 68–69, 75–77, 82, 114–15, 142–45, 154–55
Shipping Board. *See* United States, Shipping Board
Shipping master, 58
Shipyard for Wilmington Committee, 154
Signal Corps. *See* United States, Signal Corps
Sikes, Amos, 53
Skinner, S. W., 119; marine railway of, 115
Slaves, 10, 15, 19; escape of by sea, 58–59, 90
Smallpox, 38, 47, 48
Smallwood, James, 7
Smith, Andrew, 113
Smith, Benjamin, 30, 37
Smith, John, 44
Smith, R. Lawrence, 142
Smith Creek, 166
Smith Island, 64, 89, 125, 129
Smith Island Lighthouse, 146
Smithville, 17, 30, 41, 43, 51, 54, 57, 61–62, 76, 90, 91, 130, 131, 133; advantage of as a port, 61; commerce of with Wilmington, 121. *See also* Southport
Snead, Thomas, 42
Snead's Ferry, 20, 49
Snow's Marsh Channel, 126, 138
Sons of Liberty, 24, 26
South America, 106, 121, 132, 159, 161
South Atlantic Steamship Line, Inc., 152, 159
South Carolina, 14, 17, 20, 21, 29, 67, 71, 106, 110, 112, 114, 116, 117, 147, 160, 164, 167; naval stores of, 12; produce of, 51; secession of, 71; State Ports Authority of, 157; trade of, 44
South Carolina Rail Road, 50, 51
Southeastern Shipping Service, 152
Southern Ore Company, 113
Southport, 121, 126, 127, 128, 132, 133, 134, 136, 140, 149, 164, 166 *See also* Smithville
Southport Boat Harbor, 164
Spaight, Richard Dobbs, 40, 41; proclamation of, 37
Spanish War: Wilmington's role in, 126–29
Speculation, 84–85, 97
Splosna Plavba Line, 159
S. P. McNair (Co.), 110
Sprunt, Alexander, 109, 134. *See also* Alexander Sprunt & Son
Sprunt, James, 101, 109, 134, 139, 140. *See also* Alexander Sprunt & Son
Stamp Act (1765), 23; effect of on Wilmington, 25–26; repeal of, 26
Standard Oil Company, 145, 151
State Bank of North Carolina, 37
State Department. *See* United States, State Department
State Docks. *See* North Carolina State Docks
State Ports Authority. *See* North Carolina State Ports Authority
Steamboats, 46, 52–56, 68, 69, 82–83, 114, 118, 120, 136, 140, 142, 143
Steam Cooperage Manufactory, 113
Stephens, Alexander, 81–82
Stevens, John, 52
Still, William N., Jr., 69
Strachan Southern Shipping Company, 152
Sugar, 10, 29, 34, 66, 94, 95, 149, 151
Sunny Point. *See* Military Ocean Terminal
Superior Court. *See* United States, Superior Court
Sweden, 12, 69, 134
Swift, Alexander J., 56

Taft, William H.: visits Wilmington, 136
Tallahassee, 79, 80. *See also Atalanta; Olustee*
Taylor, Thomas, 85, 91, 93, 95, 97
Telegraph, 130
Tennessee, 114, 135
Texaco Company, 151
Tobacco, 14, 32–33, 46, 66, 70, 93, 150, 152

Todd Shipbuilding Company, 156
Tolar's Landing, 141, 149
Town Creek, 5, 36, 103, 122
Trans-Freight (Co.), 163
Transportation, 48–49, 106. *See also* Bridges; Ferries; Railroads; Roads; Steamboats; Trucking
Treasury Department. *See* United States, Treasury Department
Truck farming, 115, 117
Trucking, 159, 160, 161, 162
Tryon, William, 19, 21, 26
Turpentine distilleries, 113
Tuscarora, 100. *See also* Columbia

Uncle Ben, 77, 78. *See also* Retribution
United Kingdom, 124, 152. *See also* England; Great Britain
United States
 appropriations for internal improvements, 62, 65, 121, 124, 126, 137, 141, 146
 Army Corps of Engineers, 62, 109, 115, 118–19, 120, 121, 125–26, 137, 138, 141, 145, 146, 147, 149, 153, 166, 167
 blockade by. *See* Blockade
 Board of Health, 132
 Coast Guard, 39, 130, 137–38, 145–46, 149
 Coast Survey, 63
 Congress: interest of in an intracoastal waterway, 147. *See also* Rivers and Harbors Act
 Customs Service, 129, 130, 137
 declaration of war against Germany, 142
 Department of Defense, 166
 Department of Justice, 138
 French treaty with, 41
 Hydrographic Office, 130
 Immigration and Naturalization Office, 138
 Lifesaving Service, 130, 137
 Lighthouse Board, 129
 Marine Hospital Service, 133
 Maritime Commission, 154, 155, 156, 157, 158
 merchant marine of, 142
 Navy, 126, 128–29, 155, 156
 operation of marine hospital, 133
 presence of in Lower Cape Fear, 137–38
 protection and promotion of shipping, 129–31
 Public Health Service, 138
 quarantine laws of, 132–33
 regulation of shipping by 39, 123
 Revenue Cutter Service, 40, 129, 130, 134, 136, 137
 shipping of, 40
 Shipping Board, 142, 143, 144, 152
 Signal Corps, 130
 State Department, 127
 Superior Court of, 44
 tariffs of, 39, 111, 112
 Treasury Department, 39, 103
 War Department, 144
Universal Oil and Fertilizer Company, 151
Ursina, M. P., 102

Vance, Zebulon, 78, 79, 80, 88
Vassal, John, 5
Venable, Abraham W., 63
Vermilion, 155
Verrazzano, Giovanni da, 4
Victory ships, 155, 156
Virginia, 5, 11, 12, 16, 21, 22, 29, 50, 52, 67, 72, 114, 115, 117, 135, 147, 164, 167; State Ports Authority of, 157
Virginia, 75, 76
V. P. Loftis Company, 154

Walker, Robert, 7
Warcrete Company, 144. *See also* West Coast Shipbuilding Company
Wardens of the Poor. *See* New Hanover County, wardens of the poor of
War Department. *See* United States, War Department
Warehousing, 135
War of 1812, 30, 36, 42–45; Wilmington's reaction to, 43
Warsaw, N. C., 112, 120
Washington, D. C., 142, 154
Washington, N. C., 32, 39, 65, 112
Washington, George, 14, 39, 40, 41; proclamation of, 40
Waterman Steamship Corporation, 159
Way, Daniel, S., 165
Wayne County, 3, 64
Welles, Gideon, 97, 100
West Coast Shipbuilding Company, 144. *See also* Warcrete Company
Western Railroad Company, 116
West Indies, 4, 10, 11, 14, 33, 34, 38, 42, 54, 66, 106, 115, 121, 122, 128, 145
White, John, 87
Whitehall, N. C., 56

Whiting, William H. C., 74–75, 78, 79, 80, 81, 84, 85, 86, 93, 95, 96, 102
Williams, & Murchison (Co.), 110
Williams Steamship Line, 152
Wilkinson, John, 79, 83, 84, 91, 92, 93
Wilkinson, William, 28
Wilmington, 3, 9, 12, 14, 15, 16, 18, 19, 20, 21, 22, 24, 25, 27, 30, 34, 35, 36, 37, 39, 40, 43, 44, 49, 51, 52, 53, 54, 55, 56, 59, 60, 61, 62, 63, 64, 74, 68, 80, 82, 83, 84, 87, 90, 92, 94, 95, 97, 98, 101, 102, 103, 104, 107, 109, 111, 112, 113, 114, 116–17, 118, 119, 120, 121, 122, 124, 125, 126, 129, 130, 132, 133, 134, 136, 139, 140, 141, 143, 145, 147, 149, 151, 152, 153, 155, 157, 159, 160, 163, 164, 165, 166, 167
  advantages of as a port, 45
  attitude toward Articles of Confederation, 31
  Board of Health in, 47
  Board of Trade in, 70
  bridges at, 146
  businessmen in, 119
  capture of, 77, 103
  Chamber of Commerce, 56, 70, 134, 135, 138, 167
  commerce of, 1–2, 9–15, 22, 25–26, 31–34, 40, 42, 45, 46–47, 50, 56, 57, 63, 65–70, 72, 83–88, 93–97, 100–102, 104–12, 117–24, 138–42, 149–54, 158–67
  commission merchants in, 57
  commissioners of, 8
  Committee of Safety of, 74
  Committee of Thirteen of, 63
  Confederate protection for, 73
  containerized cargo of, 153
  criticism of Confederate Navy in, 78
  customs duties collected in, 45
  danger to, 80, 129
  defense of, 42–43
  dependence of upon cotton, 135
  dependence of upon foreign shipping, 32, 69
  description of, 8, 135
  description of auctions in, 86
  disease in, 38, 47, 48
  economy of following World War II, 156
  emergence of from Revolutionary War, 30–31
  employment of women in during Civil War, 81–82
  enrolled tonnage in, 69
  factors hampering development of, 153–54
  favors secession, 72
  fear of disease in, 37–38
  fertilizer industry in, 114
  fires in, 31, 47
  future of after World War I, 145
  general cargo of, 153
  government of, 7, 19
  Gunboat Committee of, 75
  harbor master of, 138
  high prices of, 84
  hotels in, 47
  impact of World War I on, 142–45
  incorporation of, 7, 104
  industrialization in, 112–15
  intended line of steamers to Cuba, 56
  intended line of steamers to New York, 56
  internal improvements convention in, 64
  internal tributary area of, 153
  location of, 1
  manufacturing in, 81–82, 106, 113–15
  market for rice in, 112
  militia of, 72
  North Carolina State Docks in, 158–67
  occupation by British, 29–30
  occupation by the United States, 103
  origin of, 6–7
  population of, 30, 46, 136
  possible filibustering expeditions from, 128
  possible steamer line to Onslow County, 56
  possible trade with Moravians, 20–21
  preeminent position among North Carolina ports, 45
  privateering in, 28, 43–44, 78
  Produce Exchange in, 134, 135
  pro-French sentiment in, 41
  proposed dry dock facility in, 156
  railroads in 51, 115–17
  reaction to *Chesapeake* Affair, 41
  reaction to secession, 71
  reputation of as naval stores port, 107
  riot in, 18–19
  rivalry with Morehead City, 164
  rumors of attack on, 74–75
  sailors in, 38–39
  Scots and Scots-Irish in, 22
  shipbuilding in, 68–69, 75–77, 114–15, 142–45, 154–55

shipping advantages of, 135
shipping threatened by storms, 134
ships repaired in, 134
shortage of provisions in, 84
support for by Gabriel Johnston, 7
sympathy for Cuban rebels, 127–28
threat of yellow fever in, 87
ties with Dandong, 165
250th anniversary of, 1
urban character of, 70
U. S. government presence, 149
waterfront of, 149
yellow fever epidemic in, 86
See also Port Wilmington
Wilmington (ironclad), 77
Wilmington Ammunition Loading Terminal (WALT). *See* Military Ocean Terminal
Wilmington and Atlantic Steamship Company, 122
Wilmington and Manchester Railroad, 51–52, 55, 70, 82, 115
Wilmington and Masonboro Plank Road Company, 49
Wilmington and Raleigh Railroad, 46. *See also* Wilmington and Weldon Railroad
Wilmington and Smithville Steamboat Company, 56
Wilmington and Topsail Sound Plank Road Company, 49
Wilmington and Walker's Ferry Plank Road Company, 49
Wilmington and Weldon Railroad, 47, 50, 55, 70, 82, 115, 116, 117, 120; steamers of, 50, 54, 55. *See also* Wilmington and Raleigh Railroad
Wilmington and West Indies Navigation Company, 123
Wilmington-Cape Fear Pilot's Association, 137
Wilmington, Charlotte and Rutherford Railroad, 51–52, 106, 115, 116
Wilmington, Columbia, and August Railroad, 106, 115–16, 117
Wilmington Compress and Warehouse Company, 110

Wilmington Cotton Mills, 113
Wilmington Iron Works, 142. *See also* Wilmington Marine Railway
Wilmington Light Infantry, 71, 72
Wilmington Manufacturing Company, 113
Wilmington Marine Hospital Association, 48
Wilmington Marine Railway, 142, 143. *See also* Wilmington Iron Works
Wilmington, New Bern, and Norfolk Railroad, 117
Wilmington-New Hanover Safety Committee, 24, 27–28
Wilmington, Onslow and East Carolina Railroad, 116
Wilmington, Point Caswell and Clinton Railroad and Steamboat Transportation Company, 120
Wilmington Port Commission, 156, 157
Wilmington Produce Exchange, 134, 135
Wilmington Sword Factory, 81
Wilmington Tariff Association, 135
Wilmington Terminal Warehouse Co., 152
Wilmington Wooden Ship Construction Company, 143, 144
Winslow, Warren, 72
Wise, Stephen R., 101
Wood, John Taylor, 79
Wood, Richard E., 101
Woodie & Currie (Co.), 110
Wood products (boards, shingles, staves, plank, scantling, heading, hoops, hogsheads, posts, oars, masts, spars, yards, house frames), 1, 14, 19, 20, 32, 33, 56, 60, 61, 66, 69, 104, 106, 112, 113, 115, 117, 118, 120, 122, 124, 135, 138, 140, 145, 148, 149, 151
World War I, 138; impact on Wilmington, 141–42
World War II, 2, 154, 156
Worth & Worth (Co.), 110
Wright, Dr. S. P., 132
Wright, Thomas, 41
Wright, William A., 75

Yellow fever, 38, 47, 84, 86–87